STUDIES IN HISTORY, ECONOMICS, AND PUBLIC LAW

EDITED BY THE FACULTY OF POLITICAL SCIENCE
OF COLUMBIA UNIVERSITY

Number 304

STATE ADMINISTRATIVE SUPERVISION OVER CITIES
IN THE UNITED STATES

PREFACE

In an age of realism some apology should be made for the publication of a piece of work which in no wise can claim to be an accurate portrayal of the situation it essays to present. Little experience in the field of public administration is necessary, however, to convince the investigator that it is impossible to attain photographic accuracy in an inquiry of this character except through an intensive field investigation. The information contained in the statutes is far from satisfactory for the law and the practice frequently differ quite widely. A statute of Nevada relative to the state board of health illustrates the point very aptly. On paper the department of health of this mountain commonwealth has imposed on it among other things the duty of supervising municipal health activity throughout the state. Owing to the failure of the legislature to make appropriations, however, the state department of health has no field force, no bacteriologist, epidermiologist, or sanitary engineer, and is therefore unable to assist the municipalities as it desires.

Illustrations might easily be multiplied. Despite the fact that on paper the laws of New Mexico and Indiana relative to tax levies are almost identical, two very different situations have developed. In New Mexico the tax commission, according to a letter recently received, " has not attempted to pass upon the wisdom or the necessity of the proposed levies. Their function has been to watch the levies and see that they have not exceeded the limits fixed by law." In Indiana, on the other hand, according to recent information, after the state board had acquired control over the tax levies " so as to prevent, if possible, bankruptcy by large increases in taxes there was such an insistent demand for the public money and such large budgets were proposed that the state board used its powers and trimmed levies in practically every unit in the state." Further illustrations of the variation between the law and procedure seem unnecessary. A study in public administration based primarily upon the statutes quite obviously cannot hope to be an accurate portrayal of the processes of administration.

A somewhat more realistic conception of administrative procedure may sometimes be obtained from reports of state departments and offices. Unfortunately the state reports which set forth the actual processes of administration are few and far between. In this respect the reports of the state departments in the majority of commonwealths are very much inferior to those of the federal government. Consequently, although there is available a limited amount of material elaborating the procedure set forth in the laws, it is, for the most part, exceedingly sketchy.

Certain additional information may be obtained through the process of correspondence. To the state officials who have courteously answered inquiry after inquiry, a great measure of thanks is due. Nevertheless, the investigator, even with the information thus obtained at his disposal, is in no position to maintain that he has the data with which to draw a realistic picture of actual procedure in public administration.

Limitations of both time and facilities, however, have made it necessary to depend exclusively on these sources of information. It has been impossible, moreover, to go into the exceptional position in which certain cities or classes of cities have been placed by special legislation.

Despite this somewhat severe indictment, a certain value does attach to an analysis of this character. In the first place, although not claiming to be much more than a charcoal

sketch of conditions throughout the country, it is, so far as
the writer knows, the only picture of this phase of administration which has thus far been drawn, and it is, the author
hopes, as accurate as the sources of information used make
possible.   In the second place, the material presented here
is quite realistic in the sense that it indicates the extent to
which the philosophy of state administrative supervision has
a legally acknowledged place in our political system.

One word of warning.   In discussing the development of state administrative supervision over cities in the
United States, the author is talking constantly in terms of
mechanisms, processes and devices which he is analyzing
from the point of view of their potentialities as agencies of
state administrative control.   Throughout this general discussion runs the assumption that these agencies will be used
for the benefit of the community.   While such an assumption
may be sound in the vast majority of cases, it is not, needless to say, necessarily true at all times.   Power once placed
in the hands of human beings may be used for good or for
ill.   State officials are no exceptions to this general rule.   An
illustration may drive the point home.   The limited experience of the average architect in designing school buildings has led, in a number of jurisdictions, to the establishment of an architectural division in the state department
of education to which all plans and specifications for new
school buildings must be submitted for approval.   The
architect in charge of this division is usually a specialist in
the field.   It is hoped, therefore, that many of the mistakes
which have characterized the designing of school buildings
in the past may thus be avoided, and that such has been the
case in many states is a frequent claim of the state authorities.   Nevertheless it has been discovered in more than one
commonwealth that the supervising official has used his
position to compel all school boards throughout the state to

adopt certain patented articles in the sale of which he has had a financial interest in the construction of school buildings. The potentiality of such an abuse of power, needless to say, is present in many of the mechanisms we shall analyze. Consequently no discussion of state administrative control would be complete which neglected to call attention to this possibility.

For the errors in this study the author must assume full responsibility. He should, nevertheless, like to express his sincere appreciation for the help which has been given him in connection with the preparation of this manuscript by Professor Howard Lee McBain, Professor Lindsay Rogers, Professor Raymond Moley, and Professor Arthur W. Macmahon.

SCHUYLER C. WALLACE

COLUMBIA UNIVERSITY, NEW YORK CITY, 1928.

TABLE OF CONTENTS

PAGE

PREFACE 5

CHAPTER I

Introduction 11

CHAPTER II

Principles of Administrative Supervision 39

CHAPTER III

Supervision of Public Finance 60

CHAPTER IV

Supervision of Public Health 106

CHAPTER V

Supervision of Public Education 142

CHAPTER VI

Supervision of Dependency and Delinquency 189

CHAPTER VII

Supervision of Municipally-Owned Utilities 212

CHAPTER VIII

Supervision of Other Functions 235

CHAPTER IX

Summary and Conclusion 254

INDEX 275

CHAPTER I

Introduction

THE sociological conditions which produce urban communities quite obviously make those communities logical units of government. Indeed, in many instances they are more easily justified as such than are the states of the Union themselves. Nevertheless, the necessity for these larger areas of administration is apparent; the mere fact that no city lives unto itself alone, but is dependent in large measure upon surrounding rural areas for its very subsistence, would in itself be sufficient justification could no other *raison d'être* be found.

More difficult by far than a justification of the existence of the various units of government is the determination of the proper relation of one to the other. That some relationship will exist may be assumed; that some supervision will be exercised by the larger unit of government may, in the light of historical circumstances, be taken for granted. The degree to which such supervision should be pushed, however, is by no means a settled question. On one side are those who would confine state control to a minimum, who maintain that four thousand years of recorded history substantiate the claim that democracy was born and bred in the smaller communities; who insist that now more than ever it is in the localities that the first lessons in democracy are taught to each oncoming generation and the sense of civic pride so necessary for the maintenance of free institutions is engendered; who believe, furthermore, that individual initiative is thereby fostered, experimentation made possible, and local variations devised to meet local needs;

who contend, moreover, that the influence of state politics is in this manner more easily minimized and responsibility more readily fixed, and that in addition the efficiency of the state government itself is increased, since the burden of supervision, which in many states is exceedingly troublesome, is materially reduced.

On the other side there are those who point out the practical impossibility of separating the welfare of the cities from the welfare of the state. Few indeed, they maintain, are the municipal functions that affect the citizens of the immediate community alone. The administration of the health service of a city is frequently of as much importance to the residents of the surrounding areas as it is to those within the corporate jurisdiction of the municipality itself. Disease germs are no respecters of political boundaries. Similarly, a breakdown in the administration of a municipal sewage system may work havoc in neighboring communities whose water supplies may be affected. Less apparent but equally far-reaching in their consequences, so the proponents of state supervision believe, may be the defects of a faulty educational system. To what extent the presence of several hundred thousand illiterates in an electorate or in an army impairs its efficiency is hard to say. Nor can the result of lax law enforcement or the impairment of justice be any more definitely determined. That the consequences can be confined within a city's limits, however, is difficult to believe. Save in a few of the larger cities, the scope of utility regulation must also be broader than the confines of the city. Consequently, these advocates of state supervision over municipalities are convinced of the fact that in this day of industrial civilization no community can maintain an independent and isolated position.[1]

[1] See *The Journal of Public Administration*, October, 1925 for a discussion of the principles which should determine whether a service re-

Whatever may be the merits of this controversy, it is only one aspect, although an exceedingly important one, of the problem here presented—the proper relationship of American cities to the governments of their respective states. Equally serious, it seems, is the selection of the agency of government best suited to exercise the supervision decided upon. A direct relationship exists, however, between the degree of control to be maintained and the agency of government best fitted for the task. If the control be merely the limitation of municipal officials to the exercise of their legal powers and the prevention of *ultra vires* acts, the judicial branch of the state government is more or less equipped to handle the situation. If, on the contrary, the supervision be extended to the determination of questions of public policy or problems of technique (and needless to say such has been the case), either the state legislature or the administration must be called upon to perform the task. The historic reasons which have caused the legislatures in Anglo-Saxon commonwealths to assume this burden need not detain us here. Suffice it to say that, save in the realm preëmpted by the courts, legislative supervision over cities was begun in the United States at an early date and remains to this day, except in the home rule states, the most important type of control over these subordinate political units.[1] As a consequence, the practice of legislating for cities in exceeding great detail early became part of our legislative tradition, for only in this way did it seem possible to exercise effective control.[2]

quiring local organization is best administered by a central department or by a local authority. The four papers there presented all bear indirectly on the subject we are discussing.

[1] McBain, H. L., *The Law and the Practice of Municipal Home Rule*, New York (1916), pp. 3-4.

[2] *City Manager Year Book*, 1917-1918, p. 67; *National Municipal Review*, vol. i, p. 189; *Nebraska Statutes*, 1915, p. 221.

Two inevitable results have followed. First, with the expansion of municipal activities the burden upon the state legislatures has become heavier and heavier; and second, in part a consequence of the first, the supervision exercised has grown less and less efficient.[1] Indeed, when one remembers that legislatures are often partisan, that frequently they are hardly able to find time to discuss adequately the broad matters of public policy which come before them, that in many states they are predominantly rural and consequently often have little real interest in, and feel little real responsibility for the conduct of municipal affairs, and, finally, that they are always amateurs, one wonders that the system has worked as well as it has.[2] Even the staunchest defender of the *status quo* must admit that to some extent at least the system of legislative supervision has broken down.

There are two possible lines of attack upon the situation which thus presents itself: one is to grant our municipalities a considerable measure of home rule; the other is to seek a supplementary or alternative method of control. These two are not necessarily incompatible, for it is possible both to relax legislative supervision and at the same time to establish a supplementary means of scrutiny. The alternative or supplementary method of control usually suggested is state administrative supervision; that is, supervision by the administrative authorities rather than by the legislative. Its proponents argue that " it is supervision by experts and hence based upon knowledge," that " it is consistent in policy," that " it does not give unnecessary affront to local self-respect," and that " it is effective in what it sets out to do." [3] In substantiation of their claims the experience of

[1] McBain, H. L., *op. cit.*, pp. 8-9, *American City Progress and the Law*, New York (1918), p. 3.

[2] Goodnow, F. J., *Municipal Government*, New York (1909), p. 103 *et seq.*

[3] Munro, W. B., *The Government of American Cities*, New York (1920), p. 76.

Europe is cited.   To Europe consequently an analyst of this type of control must first turn his attention.[1]

In striking contrast to the situation in the United States is that which has developed in Prussia;[2] for, although the Prussian municipality "may claim as falling within its sphere everything that promotes the welfare of the whole community and the material and intellectual advancement of the members" thereof, it is nevertheless subject to close and vigorous supervision.   At the head of the supervising officials stands the Minister of Interior, but between his office and the municipalities two intermediate supervisory bodies, the provinces and the districts, intervene.[3]

In charge of each province is a provincial president, responsible not only for the administration thereof, but also for the supervision of such municipalities as lie therein.   He

[1] The author has made no attempt to do original research in this chapter. It is hoped, however, that from even a birdseye view of the situation as it exists abroad some conclusions may be drawn as to the fields of local activity most commonly supervised and the mechanisms of control most frequently employed. Brief and confessedly second hand though such a survey must be, it may, nevertheless, serve to give perspective to the later, more detailed chapters which analyze the development of the mechanism at home.

[2] The limited material available upon recent changes in Prussian governmental relationships makes it quite possible that some of the statements made thereon are no longer true.   The account here presented does not lose greatly in value because of this, however, for it was under this system that the Prussian city achieved its reputation. The chief sources for the material herein contained are: Dawson, W. H., *Municipal Life and Government in Germany*, New York (1914); Goodnow, F. J., *Comparative Administrative Law*, New York (1909); James, H. G., *Principles of Prussian Administration*, New York (1913); McBain, H. L. and Rogers, Lindsay, *New Constitutions of Europe*, New York (1922); Munro, W. B., *Government of European Cities*, New York (1927), *Municipal Government and Administration*, New York (1923).

[3] Certain aspects of municipal activity, however, are subject to the scrutiny of other Ministers, education for example.

is the court of final appeal in most matters relating to municipal administration. Assisting him in this work is a provincial council, chosen by the various circles within the province. The actions of the provincial authorities, however, are all subject to the direction and supervision of the Minister of Interior.

In more immediate contact with the municipalities are the district officials. At their head is a district president who, like his provincial superior, is appointed and dismissed at the pleasure of the central government; assisting him is a district committee, two of whose members are appointed for life by the authorities in Berlin, four of whom are chosen for six year terms by the the provincial assembly. In the maintenance of the supervision which has been deemed requisite the district president not only participates in the selection of the *magistrat* for all municipalities lying within his district through his power to approve or disapprove all nominations made thereto, but also controls the general tone of municipal administration to a considerable degree through his power to impose penalties for infractions of the rules and ordinances; he may, in fact, take steps leading to the removal of any administrative officer.

The district committee in its turn acts as a court of first instance in disputes arising from changes of boundary, contested elections, and unpaid claims—indeed, in all matters arising out of city administration not specifically cared for elsewhere. Furthermore, all matters falling within the jurisdiction of the administrative courts likewise come to it in the course of an appeal. Moreover, in the event of a deadlock between the two houses of a municipal legislature, this committee may be called upon to cast the deciding vote.

Certain phases of municipal administration have been singled out for even more stringent treatment. For example, the police in the larger towns either retain an independent organization or else occupy the place of a special department within the city administration under the direction of a state official. Within the jurisdiction of the police in Prussia, be it noted, are many functions which in the United States would be designated either as health work or as poor relief. For the effective control of these activities special staffs of auxiliary officers have been attached to the supervising agency. Education is subjected to similar control. Despite the fact that the primary school teachers are selected by the local authorities, they are considered state officers. Principals and head masters are appointed by the supervising officials, while teachers in secondary schools receive their appointments either from the provincial officers or directly from the office of the Interior. Each of the universities, even, has an agent of the government on its staff. A more limited control is exercised over local finance. The consent of the district committee, nevertheless, is necessary not only for the alienation of municipally owned real estate but also for any increase in municipal indebtedness. The duty of scrutinizing all local budgets and compelling the insertion of all obligatory items is, moreover, imposed upon the district president.

These, then, are the supervisory features which have developed in Prussia. That they have not met with unanimous approval, however, is indicated both by the provision in the new Prussian constitution to the effect that "municipalities and groups of municipalities have the right of local autonomy in their affairs under the supervision of the state as may be required by law," [1] and by the further fact that there has already been introduced into the Prussian Landtag a measure designed to modify the system of supervision quite radically.

[1] McBain, H. L. and Rogers, Lindsay, *New Constitutions of Europe,* New York (1922), p. 229.

Equally interesting to the student of state-local relations is the system of administrative control which has developed in France.[1] At the head of the system stands the Minister of the Interior. Under him, subject to his appointment and removal, are the ninety prefects whose duties, at least in part, are concerned with the supervision and direction of the communes. The range of their duties is astonishing, relating as it does to such diverse subjects as elections, agriculture, police, sanitation, public lands, highways, education, communal affairs, etc.[2] Little initiative, however, has been left in their hands. " The minister rules as over a principality with almost despotic sway. He controls the personnel; he renders all final decisions, he is responsible for everything," [3] except insofar as the mass of material pressing for his attention compels him to rely upon his subordinates.

The prefect, consequently, is predominantly an officer of the state. His responsibility to his department is as nothing in comparison with his obligation to the central authorities. (The French department, perhaps it should be stated, is the

[1] The sources of information most generally drawn upon for the account which follows are: Bryce, James, *Modern Democracies*, New York (1921); Buell, R. R., *Contemporary French Politics*, New York (1920); Garner, J. W., "Administrative Reform in France," *American Political Science Review*, 1919, p. 22; Goodnow, F. J., *Comparative Administrative Law*, New York (1909); Lowell, A. L., *Governments and Parties in Continental Europe*, New York (1897); Munro, W. B., *Governments of European Cities*, New York (1927), *Municipal Government and Administration*, New York (1923); Ogg, F. A., *Governments of Europe*, New York (1924); Poincare, R., *How France is Governed*, New York (1919); Sait, E. M., *Government and Politics of France*, New York (1921); Shaw, Albert, *Municipal Government in Continental Europe*, New York (1895); Young, J. T., "Administration and Decentralization in France," *American Academy of Political Science*, vol. ii, Jan., 1898.

[2] Sait, E. M., *Government and Politics of France*, New York (1921), p. 101.

[3] Sait, E. M., *ibid.*, p. 103.

largest subordinate administrative area in France, containing within itself those smaller governmental units, the communes.) We are not, however, interested in the prefect in his relation to departmental affairs, but rather in his relation to the communes. Altogether there are about thirty-eight thousand communes in France, ranging in size from the smallest villages to the largest cities. Although they vary in size and population, one form of organization is common to them all, and one set of powers governs them.[1]

A cursory examination of the powers vested in the municipalities, however, is apt to prove misleading; for, despite the broad declaration of the law to the effect that the local councils shall by their deliberations regulate the affairs of the communes and vote on all subjects of local interest, municipal legislatures are, in fact, distinctly limited in the scope of their jurisdiction. On many matters their action is merely advisory, and on others it is ineffective save with the approval of the higher authorities. Practically complete control over changes in parochial boundaries, the administration of poor relief, the laying-out of main streets and highways, and many matters of education rest with the supervising authorities.[2] True, the advice of the communal council must be sought, but it may be totally disregarded. More important is the limitation imposed upon the council's decisions by the requirement of *tutelle administrative*. " Thus measures affecting the disposition of communal property, those relating to the maintenance of highways, those relating to financial affairs such as the budget, supplementary appropriations and loans, and acts for the establishment of fairs and markets, require the approval of a representative of the central government, usually the prefect, but some-

---

[1] Paris and Lyons alone are exceptions.

[2] Munro, W. B., *Government of European Cities*, New York (1927), p. 51.

times the council-general of the department, the President of the Republic or even Parliament itself." [1] All municipal ordinances, in fact, must receive at least the tacit approval of the departmental authorities, for any municipal ordinance may at any time be suspended by departmental order. Furthermore, should the local executive inadvertently or otherwise neglect or refuse to perform any duty prescribed by law, the prefect may see to it that the obligation is discharged. [2] This general supervision is rendered doubly effective, moreover, by the fact that the prefect, should he deem it necessary, may suspend both the mayor and the communal council. They may be entirely removed, however, only by a decree of the President of the Republic in Council of State.

Four aspects of municipal activity—finance, highways, education, and police — appear to receive particular attention. The taxing power of the local councils is subject to numerous restrictions. In general, they may levy taxes only up to a certain specified amount authorized by law, and all levies thereafter are subject to the approval of the various central authorities; sometimes of the President of the Republic, sometimes of the prefect, sometimes of the council-general. Even the local budget is subject to central supervision. Drawn up by the mayor and passed by the council, it then goes to the prefect, or if it exceeds three million francs, to the Minister of Interior, for his scrutiny. Explanatory data must accompany it. With this information at their disposal, legal and financial experts go over the items and make such recommendations as seem called for; the prefect or the Minister of Interior, however, makes all final decisions. The supervising authority has the right to in-

[1] Garner, James W., "Administrative Reform in France," *American Political Science Review*, 1919, p. 22.

[2] Garner, James W., *ibid.*, p. 23.

crease or reduce any item on the revenue side of the budget, but only to reduce items on the expenditure side. If any of the obligatory items contained in the code have been omitted, however, the prefect may see to it that they are inserted. Closely related to this procedure is the supervision exercised over the city's borrowing power. Within certain narrow limits the municipality may borrow freely, but when sums of any considerable importance are required, the approval of the prefect must be sought. These, in brief, are the financial restrictions.

Equally extensive is the control exercised over streets and highways, involving also, as it does, rights and franchises thereon. All powers relating to the national highways, whether it be construction, repairing, policing, or regulating the traffic, are exercised by the national or departmental authorities. Within this category come in general all the main streets of a city, and whether a street shall be so classified depends upon the decision of the higher officials. This jurisdiction over the main thoroughfares, consequently, gives the central government practically complete control over all utilities desiring to make use of the streets. Indeed, the local authorities may issue franchises on the minor streets only with the approval of the prefect.

The extent of the power of supervision of the departmental authorities over local police matters is indicated in Article 99 of the Municipal Code: " The powers which pertain to the *Maire* . . . . are no hindrance to the right of the prefect to take, for all the communes of his department, or any of them, and in all cases in which they have not been provided by the municipal authorities, all measures relating to the maintenance of public health, safety and tranquility. The right cannot be exercised by the prefect [however] until after a demand in due form to the *Maire* proves of no avail." As a matter of fact practically all action in regard to the municipal police requires the concurrence of the prefect. In the larger towns the commissioner of police must be appointed by presidential decree. In fact, in cities of over 40,000 population the general police organization, salaries, and other details of routine are regulated by presidential promulgation. Furthermore, the municipal council must grant the appropriations asked for by the department. Should any council fail to do so, the prefect may include the omitted items in the revised budget. "In the larger cities the President of the Republic, with the consent of the Council of State, is empowered to increase the budgets of recalcitrant local councils by such sums as are deemed essential to efficient police organization, and these sums can be collected if necessary by an official impost."[1] Parenthetically, it should be pointed out that here, as in Prussia, the police power includes many items which in the United States would be classified as health or charitable activities.

The extent to which the principle of centralized supervision has been developed in the field of education can, perhaps, be realized, when one recalls the incident of the French Minister of Public Instruction who, taking out his watch, remarked that he could tell exactly what every pupil in the French schools was doing as that particular moment. The story is exaggerated; nevertheless it has some point. The national authorities pay the salaries and regulate the standards; the prefects choose the teachers.

Space does not permit a consideration of other departmental-commune relations. A quotation from M. Berthelemy, however, may serve to summarize the situation. "Commissioners of police," says he, "are now appointed by the President or the prefect depending on the importance of the commune. Other collectors are appointed either by the prefect or the sub-prefect. Guards of communal forests

---

[1] Fosdick, Raymond B., *op. cit.*, p. 87.

are appointed by the prefect from lists of candidates presented by the conservators of forests. Teachers, communal inspectors, and agents, public weighers and firemen, although their functions appear to be entirely local in character are appointed by the prefect, and the municipal authorities have no choice whatever in their selection." [1] The control of the national authorities over Paris is even greater, but the special considerations calling forth this added supervision need not concern us here.

What have been the results of the system? How has it worked? Many years ago one observer found in the office of the Minister of the Interior at Paris, "a well equipped bureau of permanent experts, officials trained in every phase of municipal finance, and qualified to exercise intelligent supervision over the budgets of France's towns." [2] His opinion, however, has by no means been universally held. Many French writers have complained and do to-day complain bitterly of a situation in which numerous matters of purely local interest are administered and controlled by a minister at Paris. Two major objections are raised: first, administrative; second, political. "Supervision has been pushed to an extreme," it is said, "which often results in absurd delays and impairs administrative efficiency. According to Noëll, not a franc can be spent, not a chair or a towel purchased without authority from Paris. On one occasion an official had to wait two years to buy a box of pins, the request passing successively through the hands of twenty-five or thirty higher officials." [3] The prefect and the sub-prefects, however, are more than mere administrative agents. They are the mediums through which the Minister of the

[1] M. Berthelemy, quoted in *American Political Science Review*, 1919, p. 19.

[2] Shaw, Albert, *Municipal Government in Continental Europe*, New York (1895), p. 179.

[3] Sait, E. M., *op. cit.*, p. 102.

Interior keeps in touch with the local situation.   In fact, it is frequently said in France that "the first requirement of a good prefect is that he should make a good electioneering agent and that his advancement is dependent largely upon his success in carrying the department for the government candidates. . . . Like the prefect, the sub-prefects are also electioneering agents for the government; and, if one may believe some of the French writers on administration, that is their chief occupation.   They attend political meetings as representatives of the government, exercise a sort of political surveillance over functionaries in their arrondisements, keep the government informed of local political conditions, and use their influence to bring about the election within their districts of deputies in sympathy with the government and of senatorial delegates approved by the government." [1]

So bitter is the feeling against these objectionable features that a strong movement for decentralization exists.   Within it two definite currents are discernible: the one limits itself to the rehabilitation of the present organs of local government through the curtailment of centralized control; the other aims at the suppression of the present units of government and the substitution therefor of great regions based upon natural, economic, and historical boundaries with extensive powers of self-government.   So far, however, the movement has few concrete results to show.   Thus the struggle between centralization and decentralization goes on.

Even more valuable to the American student is the experience of England. [2]   The greater similarity between our

---

[1] Garner, James W., *op. cit.*, p. 40.

[2] The sources of information chiefly relied upon for the following account were: Ashley, Percy, *English Local Government*, London (1905), *Local and Central Government*, London (1906); Attlee, C. K. and

cultures and between our governing traditions gives English development more than passing interest. This is particularly true in the field of state-local relations. The predominance of local legislatures, subject only to the control of a superior policy-determining body, has been as characteristic of England as it has been of the United States. Nevertheless, before the newer demands of an industrial age the older system of control has been slowly changing.

Drastic action was first called forth by the complete collapse of the administration of the poor law. Consequently, here more than elsewhere the traditions of local self-government have given way, and administrative supervision has developed. In one field after another, a similar necessity for change has arisen. With increasing frequency the central government has been impelled to call to its aid permanent staffs of inspectors who have been attached to certain of the central departments. By means of their work it has been possible for the ministry to maintain that supervision which has been deemed requisite.

Robson, W. H., *The Town Councillor*, London (1925); Bannington, B. S., *English Public Health Administration*, London (1915); British Labor Party, *Handbook of English Local Government*, London (1925); Clark, J. J., *The Local Government of the United Kingdom*, London (1925); Fosdick, Raymond, *European Police Systems*, New York (1915); Howe, Frederic C., *The British City*, New York (1907); Lowell, A. Lawrence, *Government of England*, New York (1910); Maltbie, M. R., *English Local Government of Today*, New York (1897); Masterman, C. F. G., *How England is Governed*, London (1921); Morris, Malcolm, *The Story of English Public Health*, London (1919); Munro, W. B., *Government of European Cities*, New York (1927), *Municipal Government and Administration*, New York (1923); Newsholme, Arthur, *The Ministry of Public Health*, London (1925); *The Journal of Public Administration*; Redlich, J. and Hirst, F. W., *Local Governments in England*, London (1903); *Minutes of Evidence taken before the Royal Commission on Local Government*, London (1923); Selby-Bogge, L. A., *The Board of Education*, London (1927); Shaw, Albert, *Municipal Governments in Great Britain*, New York (1895); Troup, Edward, *The Home Office*, London (1925); Webb, Sidney, *Grants-in-aid*, London (1920).

At present the Privy Council, Treasury, Post Office, the Ministries of Labor, Agriculture and Fisheries, Pensions, and the Scottish Boards all have more or less to do with the supervision of municipal enterprises. The bulk of the burden, however, rests upon the Boards of Education and Trade, the Home Office, and the Ministries of Transport and Public Health.[1]

To the Ministry of Public Health have been given practically all the historic powers of the Local Government Board, as well as the powers relative to public health which were scattered through the several departments. Its work for the most part can be divided into four categories: (1) the supervision of the poor law and its administration; (2) a somewhat less extensive control of local health activities; (3) oversight of local housing developments; and (4) a limited control of municipal finance.

The development of administrative supervision in England, as already has been stated, began with the control of the local authorities who were charged with the execution of the poor law. Separate and distinct political bodies exist for this purpose in England. Not only has the ministry extensive powers of inspection and investigation with which to unearth such data as the Parliamentary leaders deem desirable, but in addition it is authorized to enact such rules and regulations in matters relating to poor relief as seem necessary and proper to it. And to such an extent has this latter power been exercised that years ago one observer declared: "It is almost impossible to suggest any subject upon which orders or instructions have not been issued, and oftentimes the minutest details are specified. The time of rising and retiring of workhouse paupers and many other minor matters are stated with great

[1] Clark, John J., *The Local Government of the United Kingdom*, London (1925), p. 28 *et seq.*

precision. The local authorities cannot perform a single duty which is not governed by the Board." [1] Nor has the course of time rendered his statement less apropos.

Three distinct methods of compelling conformity to these regulations and an efficient administration thereof are to be found. The first—an application to the courts for a writ of mandamus or injunction—is judicial, and consequently beyond the scope of these pages. Moreover, so long as a locality goes through the motion of obeying the law a mandamus will not be issued. Thus the plain fact is that the central government cannot hope to obtain anything approaching maximum efficiency in administration by this method. Much more effective is the power given the Ministry of specifying the qualifications requisite in all appointees, determining the conditions of service (salaries, pensions, etc.), and last but by no means least of removing any incumbent who proves unsatisfactory. Quite possibly the new appointee may not be any more satisfactory than the one dismissed, since the local officials have the power of appointment entirely in their hands; nevertheless the continued removal of incapable appointees is very likely to produce the desired results. The third line of pressure is through the supervision which the central authority exercises over finance. Not only does the Ministry control all loans and capital outlays in this connection, but through its audit it supervises all expenditures.

Only a degree less extensive is the control maintained over the local health authorities. By means of the device of provisional orders (a method of sub-legislation subject to the approval of Parliament), the Ministry may alter the territorial divisions of a district, endow it with certain powers, require it to undertake certain services, or even

[1] Maltbie, M. R., *English Local Government of Today*, New York (1897), p. 28.

modify certain details of the health codes that have been placed in various statutes. (Particular emphasis should be given to this device. By means of it Parliament has been able to relieve itself of much tedious detail.) Furthermore, although the local sanitary districts have been authorized to enact by-laws for sanitary purposes, the requirement that all such by-laws must be laid before the Ministry for its approval has enabled the central authority to extend the boundaries of its influence, and to substitute for a heterogeneous conglomeration of local ordinances a series of so-called model by-laws suggested by the Ministry itself.

A system of inspection and inquiry has been developed in this connection also. Inspectors are given comprehensive powers with which to pursue their investigations, and from their work is obtained much of the information which guides both the administration and Parliament. To some extent, public opinion is also educated and directed by it. As a stimulus toward greater efficiency in those phases of the work concerned with venereal disease, tuberculosis, maternity, and child welfare, a system of grants-in-aid has been devised.[1] A grant-in-aid is a contribution by the central

---

[1] Clark, John J., *op. cit.*, p. 115; Newsholme, Arthur, *The Ministry of Public Health*, London (1925), p. 110 *et seq.* "The most drastic control over current expenditure of local authorities and over the manner of its expenditure is in connection with grants-in-aid given to them by the central government. These are 50 per cent of approved local expenditures on maternity and child welfare work and on tuberculosis work; and 75 per cent of approved local expenditures on venereal disease schemes. The total amount of such grants exceeded 74 millions sterling in the financial year 1922-1923. Of this amount:

£1,936,564 was paid to local authorities for tuberculosis service
  882,556 was paid to local authorities in connection with their maternity and child welfare schemes
  407,277 was paid to local authorities for venereal disease services
  389,174 was paid to local authorities for salaries of sanitary officers
   10,323 was paid to local authorities for vaccination
   45,465 was paid to local authorities for port sanitary service
   83,470 was distributed to voluntary agencies and local authorities for work for the blind."

government to a locality to aid in the maintenance of specified services. The aid is given upon certain stipulations. The condition most usually imposed is the maintenance of the service at a given rate of efficiency on penalty of losing the grant. The added burden which threatens the taxpayer of the locality if the grant is lost usually creates a popular sentiment which spurs the officials to maintain the service in a satisfactory condition. The system has the added advantage of attaining its purpose without offending the pride of the locality—such, at any rate, is the contention of its proponents. Fully as effective is the requirement that the nomination of all officers depending wholly or in part upon contributions from the Exchequer must be confirmed by the central agency—a rule which is rendered doubly effective by a further provision enabling the Ministry to remove any local health officer at any time. An additional provision to the effect that a local health officer may be removed by the local authorities only with the consent of the central authorities, is designed primarily to protect efficient local officials from undesirable local pressure. (It is feared, one writer remarks, that the object of the provision has not been wholly accomplished, but insofar as security has been attained, the supervisory authorities should receive full credit.[1]) Should a local board neglect to perform some of its obligatory work and complaint be made, the Minister of Public Health may order it to act; and if the local authority continues remiss in its duty, the central agency may either apply to the courts for a mandamus, or do the work itself and charge the expense thereof to the community.

The judicial function of the Ministry plays but a minor part, although in recent years its importance has increased. Persons aggrieved by decisions of the local authorities may,

[1] Bannington, B. G., *English Public Health Administration*, London (1915).

in certain cases, take an appeal to the Ministry. Moreover, disputes betwen various localities are likewise within its jurisdiction.[1]

Of more recent origin is the central government's control over the housing situation. The Housing Act of 1903 enabled the local authorities to condemn buildings unfit for habitation, but subjected their action to review by the Ministry of Health. Much more drastic was the Housing, Town Planning, etc., Act of 1919. It imposed the duty upon every locality of preparing a scheme dealing with the housing situation according to a schedule of regulations prepared by the Ministry of Health. Where a locality failed to fulfil its obligations under the Act, the Ministry was empowered to transfer its powers to the county council, or else to perform the function itself. Such was the sweep of power thus granted that local by-laws did not apply if they were inconsistent with any plans which had been approved by the Ministry of Health. Furthermore, the Ministry, with the consent of the Treasury, was empowered to pay part of the loss on any scheme of construction with money provided by Parliament. Indeed, practically the entire financing of these projects was placed in the hands of the Ministry of Health, for *local housing bonds* could be issued only with its consent.[2]

The remaining powers of the Ministry of Public Health are concerned with the supervision of local finance. The control exercised by means of the device of grant-in-aid over venereal disease, tuberculosis, maternity, child welfare, and housing activities has already been indicated. The supervision, however, goes much further than this. The Ministry has power, for example, to fix not only the time when many of the accounts must be made up, but also the form in

1 Newsholme, A., *op. cit.*, p. 85.

2 Clark, John J., *op. cit.*, p. 156 *et seq.*

which they must appear. Practically all accounts of the local authorities are subject to its audit except those of the boroughs, which are only partially under its control.[1] The district auditor may examine certain accounts everywhere (such as those connected with distress, education, housing, electric power and police) and the question of extending the Government audit to all borough functions is receiving serious consideration; in at least fifty-nine instances such action has already been taken. Generally, the auditor may disallow items contrary to law and charge them against the persons responsible. From his decision two appeals are possible: one, an application to the King's Bench Division of the High Court for a writ of *certiorari*; the other, an application to the Ministry of Health. More important, perhaps, is the control which is exercised over local bond issues.[2] In most cases the central agency determines the period of the loan, and in some cases the rate of interest as well. Particularly is this true in connection with permanent improvements in the field of health, housing, and charities. Public libraries and institutions for the mentally delinquent also fall under similar control.

At this point, passing mention might be made of certain other departments which exercise more or less control over

[1] Clark, John J., *op. cit.*, p. 128.

[2] "The range of purposes for which loans are sanctioned by the Ministry of Health is wide, including for instance housing, acquisition of land, town halls and offices, hospitals, water supplies, sewerage and sewage disposal works, refuse disposal works, parks and pleasure grounds, public slaughter houses, baths and wash houses, sea defence works. For the year 1925-1926 the Ministry sanctioned loans to the large total of over £90,000,000. In a number of instances loans are subject to the sanction of the Ministry of Health even though the merits of the proposals, other than the financial, are dealt with by other departments, as in the case of schools, roads, police stations, and allotments and small holdings." "The Ministry of Public Health," *The Journal of Public Administration*, 1926, vol. iv, p. 246.

finance. The Ministry of Transport, for example, must approve all loans in connection with electric power plants. The Treasury Department likewise exercises some supervision through the Public Works Loan Board whose function it is to advance money to the municipalities for public works, housing schemes, etc.

Thus it can be seen that the Ministry of Public Health is by no means the only agency through which the central government is maintaining its supervision over municipal activity. In fact, as has already been pointed out, at least four other departments must be considered: the Home Office, the Board of Education, the Board of Trade, and the Ministry of Transport. To a limited extent the constabulary of the country is under the control of the Home Office. The Metropolitan force is immediately under its direction. The same is true of inspectors who enforce the acts relating to mines, factories, workshops, etc. The supervision of local forces, however, is limited. The law requires all counties and boroughs to maintain forces, the direction of which centers in the joint-committee of the county and the watch committee of the borough, both of which are, of course, standing committees of the local legislative bodies they represent. Generally speaking, it has been the policy of the Government to encourage the union of county and borough police in the smaller boroughs. One reason for this, perhaps, is that the supervision of the counties is more extensive than is that of the towns. The approval of the Home Secretary is necessary not only for the appointment of the Chief Constable of the county, but also for many of the by-laws governing the force. Indeed, all police by-laws must receive at least tacit confirmation. The chief stimulus to the maintenance of an efficient local force, however, is the system of grants-in-aid which the central government has established. Upon the certification of the inspectors of the constabulary that the local police are up to the required standards, the Home Office turns over to the local authorities a sum " not exceeding one-half of the total cost of the pay and clothing of the force." The desire to retain this subsidy is strong among the local taxpayers. To check up on the use of the funds thus distributed an audit is, of course, maintained.[1]

The system of grants-in-aid is also the chief cornerstone of the supervision which is exercised over education. All schools accepting money from the Exchequer are subject to inspection by the Board of Education. Furthermore, it is the duty of the local educational authorities to submit plans to the central agency showing the manner in which their obligations are being, or are to be, fulfilled. In addition, the central board maintains a register of recognized teachers who are classified according to rules and regulations drawn up by it. The control which the office at London exercises over the superannuation system also enhances its influence.[2]

Before a local authority may undertake the operation of various municipal utilities, tram-ways, piers, harbor improvements, etc., the sanction of the Ministry of Transport, or in some cases, the Board of Trade is necessary. If the Ministry after an investigation approves the particular project in question, it usually issues a provisional order. If it disapproves, the municipality must seek its permission from Parliament.

This then is the system of central administrative supervision which has developed in England. What have been its results? Here again opinions differ. There are those who see in it and its further development the salvation of the country; there are those who damn it for its extrava-

[1] Fosdick, Raymond, *op. cit.*, p. 49. See also Troup, Edward, *The Home Office*, London (1925).

[2] Selby-Bogge, L. A., *The State Board of Education*, London (1927).

gance and fear it for its bureaucracy.   Maltbie, an American observer who has made a complete study of the system, came to the conclusion that " the England system of central administrative control is theoretically sound, except in a few minor instances; that it has accomplished its purpose, administrative efficiency; and that it is now recognized as a permanent factor in English government." [1]

Not quite so enthusiastic is another distinguished American commentator upon English institutions, President A. Lawrence Lowell.   He concludes, nevertheless, that " the system of central control has done much good, and that mere liability to inspection has no doubt prevented a certain amount of ill-management." [2]   Others commenting on specific phases of British administration have criticised it here and there.   The consensus of opinion, however, seems to be that the central authorities have not made full use of their opportunities; in fact, that the supervision has been exceedingly light.   This in itself, in a measure at least, is an acknowledgment that so far as it has gone central administrative supervision has been beneficial.[3]   There are those, nevertheless, who criticise the existing order and the existing trend.   Quite recently the Geddes Committee denounced the system of grants-in-aid in connection with education as a money-spending device, encouraging only extravagance on the part of local authorities.   G. D. H. Cole, who fears that administrative centralization is pressing hard on the heels of administrative supervision,[4] endeavors to indicate the contrasting possibility of regions of local government large enough to be nearly self-sufficing.

[1] Maltbie, M. R., *op. cit.*, p. 276.

[2] Lowell, A. L., *The Government of England*, New York (1910), vol. ii, p. 294.

[3] Brend, W. H., *Health and the State*, London (1917), p. 309; Fosdick, Raymond, *op. cit.*, p. 51; Bennington, B. R., *op. cit.*, pp. 275-289.

[4] Cole, G. D. H., *The Future of Local Government*, London (1921), p. 6.

Thus it can be seen that even in England two currents of thought are present.

One obvious conclusion can be drawn from this brief survey. The system of legislative supervision over municipalities which exists in the United States is by no means universal, nor is it anywhere else rendered the homage it has been rendered here. On the Continent the traditional system of control has been administrative rather than legislative. The central legislative bodies have laid down in exceedingly broad outline the relation which is to be maintained between the municipalities and the nation, but the detailed working out of that relationship has been left to the administration. To such an extent is this true that legislative supervision of municipalities as we are accustomed to it in the United States is practically unknown. In England where traditionally the legislature has maintained its predominance, legislative supervision is slowly but surely being supplanted. Although originally called upon merely as a supplementary agency of control, the administrative authorities have had shifted to their shoulders greater and greater responsibility in connection with the supervision of the local units of government while Parliament in its turn has tended more and more to restrict the time it is willing to allot to local affairs. It is not putting the matter too strongly, therefore, to say that the consensus of opinion in all of the countries examined is that a certain degree of administrative supervision is imperative. The exact degree of control deemed necessary varies not only from country to country, but also from function to function.

Certain services receive attention everywhere. In each of the countries examined, finance, police, health, destitution, and education are all subject to a more or less detailed scrutiny. In the field of *finance*, municipal borrowing receives attention everywhere, and in France and Prussia local budgets are given approximately equal consideration. *Education,* in its turn, is deemed worthy of official notice to such an extent in each of the aforementioned countries that their educational systems have become almost national in character, and even in England the central office exerts considerable influence in this connection.   No less stringent, on the Continent at least, is the supervision maintained over the *local police.*   And although the oversight in Prussia and France is much greater than that found in England, the prevailing opinion even there seems to be that considerable centralized supervision is necessary.   British opinion, however, is much more emphatic on the question of *health,* and accordingly there has been built up in this field a much more drastic system of control.   The practice of including the supervision of health work among the police activities in both France and Prussia subjects it to still greater central control on the Continent.   And only a shade less severe is the scrutiny exercised over the *care of the dependent.*   Last but by no means least is the control maintained over municipal *utilities.*

In addition, there exists in France and Prussia a certain general oversight, exemplary of which is the power of the district presidents in Prussia to participate in the selection of the *magistrat,* and of the prefect in France to suspend the mayor, or council, or both.

Of what significance is all this for the student of state administrative supervision in the United States?   The mere fact that administrative supervision has made such headway in Europe suggests the possibility at any rate of a similar development on this side of the Atlantic.   Indeed, in the light of the transition from legislative to administrative supervision in England one can hardly escape the impression that such a development is inevitable.   Historically, as previous pages have already indicated, the system of state-local relations in the two countries was very similar. Yet in England as the industrial development of the country has produced problems of local administration exceedingly complicated in character, and exceedingly technical of solution, Parliament has been forced to supplement its supervision by calling to its aid staffs of experts to such an extent that to-day the supervision of these experts frequently supplants rather than supplements that of Parliament. Consequently one cannot help wondering whether such will not be the inevitable course of events in the United States. In the pages which follow it will not be difficult for the reader, if he so desires, to find many indications that such will be the case. Indeed many of the facts there presented are difficult of interpretation in any other way.

But is not such an interpretation at odds with an obvious tendency in American municipal life at the present time— the tendency toward home rule   Such possibly is the case. Nevertheless, the struggle for home rule in the United States has been primarily an effort on the part of the municipalities to free themselves from legislative interference rather than from all supervision. Indeed, one of the talking points in the early days of the home rule fight was the contrast between the tutelage of the American city and the freedom of the Prussian municipality. Be that as it may, it must be acknowledged that state administrative supervision could very easily be pushed to the point where cities would be under even greater restraint than they were in the heyday of legislative control.

A further fact of some significance brought out by the survey is the striking difference in the development. of administrative supervision in England and on the Continent. The emphasis in the English system of control is emphatically on what might be called the persuasive mechanisms of supervision. The devices most commonly used are reports, inspection, advice, and grant-in-aid. Very much less frequently, although more so of recent years, do the words approval, review, orders, ordinances, appointment, or removal appear in the statutes. In France and Prussia on the other hand the situation is entirely reversed. Their chief dependence is placed upon the last named mechanisms. The control on the Continent consequently has inevitably been more stringent than that exercised in Great Britain. Indeed, in many aspects it approximates centralized administration.

There can be little doubt that the course of development in the United States in the setting-up of a system of administrative supervision will resemble that of Great Britain rather than that of the Continent. The same jealousy of their powers exists in the legislatures of the American states as existed in Parliament in England. The same dislike of a bureaucracy is characteristic of public opinion. Insofar as any steps have been taken in the United States toward the establishment of such a system, they have been taken either where local administration has definitely broken down, or where the problems have become so complicated and so technical that it is impossible for anyone not an expert or a technician to solve them—the same causes, be it noted, which were precursors to the establishment of the English system.

Thus the final conclusion to which our survey of administrative supervision over municipalities abroad leads us is: first, the fact that Europe, particularly England, has found it necessary to maintain such a system of control is indicative of the probable development in the United States; second, that it is exceedingly probable that the fields over which this supervision will develop are fairly well marked out by European experience; and third, that the course of the establishment of any such system in the United States will probably follow that of England much more closely than that of either of the Continental countries considered.

CHAPTER II

PRINCIPLES OF ADMINISTRATIVE SUPERVISION

In the foregoing discussion reference has repeatedly been made to certain mechanisms or devices of control. Time and again the words reports, inspection, advice, grant-in-aid, approval, review, orders, ordinances, appointment, and removal have appeared. It might be well, consequently, to examine these devices with the view of discovering the purposes to which they may be put. Any such analysis, however, must of necessity be artificial for no mechanism operates in a vacuum, or singly, but instead in concrete situations in conjunction with various and sundry other mechanisms. Nevertheless, artificial though such an analysis may be, it will, perhaps, contribute to a clearer understanding of the nature and potentialities of these measures of control.

Some idea of their character, of their relation to one another, and to the general problem of administrative supervision, may be obtained by merely placing them in the ascending order of their individual effectiveness. In such a list reports, inspection, advice, and grant-in-aid, the persuasive devices, come first; approval, review, orders, ordinances, removal, appointment and substitute administration follow in order.

REPORTS

So unpretentious is the mechanism of reports that one hesitates to classify it as a means of supervision at all. Nevertheless, but little reflection is necessary to make it quite evident that here is the beginning of control. In many in-

39

stances the mere fact that state officers are known to be accumulating information for future action will in itself have a salutary effect upon any irregularities in local administration. Complete neglect of duty is less likely where reports are required. This negative influence, however, is not the only or indeed the most important potentiality in the requirement. In certain branches of municipal service—in education, health, charities and corrections, for example— it is possible to create an *esprit de corps* and to this end a system of reports can render valuable assistance. By means of judicious publicity, professional pride on the part of the local administrators may be aroused and civic interest on the part of the community developed—both of which, needless to say, make for greater efficiency. In the field of public health and education comparative ratings derived from these reports have been used with considerable effectiveness in certain states and certain communities. The more important rôle played by reports, however, is that enacted behind the scenes. The information thus collected forms a part, possibly the larger part, of the information which determines further administrative action. Strikingly illustrative of this are the morbidity and mortality statistics which are the basis of most quarantines, as well as many other important decisions in the field of public health.

Several variations of the device have developed. Certain information may be specifically required by law, in which case the administrative authorities act as mere automatons in its collection and tabulation. On the other hand, administrative officials may be given wide discretion as to the information to be obtained. In such situations the central authorities, if they are alert and sensitive, may develop the device to its fullest, giving all possible directions to its activities. But what if the administrative officials are not alert? Such a possibility may be provided against through a combination of the variations. The reporting of certain information may be specified in the law, but the administrative authorities may also be given power to collect such other information as they desire. By means of this combination of variations, the collection of a modicum of information is made probable no matter how lacking in initiative and aggressiveness the particular administrative officers may be. In addition, continuity of policy in connection with the character of the information demanded is made certain, and at the same time opportunity is allowed for the play of any executive ability which the administrative officials may have.

INSPECTION

Closely allied to the requirement of reports is the process of inspection, likewise devoted (in one aspect at least) to the collection of information. Consequently, all the comments made above on the potentialities of reports may be repeated here with emphasis, for, theoretically at least, the device of inspection has greater possibilities than the mechanism just discussed. Through it the local authorities are no longer able to misrepresent existing conditions and practices as they have been known to do through the process of doctoring reports. Here too, however, the most important use of the mechanism is as a medium for collecting information on the basis of which future administrative action may be determined. In this particular the device is inextricably bound up with other principles of supervision. To such an extent is this the case that the student of administration must be careful in any attempt to cut the Gordian knot. Does the process of approval, for example, necessarily imply previous use of the mechanism of inspection? Will the system of grants-in-aid, if resolved into its component parts, also reveal its presence? Obviously, in each case information must be amassed—whether through the process of reports or inspection does not appear.

The accumulation of information is not, however, the only purpose to which the device is devoted. In one aspect it appears as a medium for the dissemination of advice, in another as a means for the transmission of orders, in still another it has many of the characteristics of a police activity. Under these latter circumstances the enforcement of the law is its immediate object. The inspectors are but auxiliaries to the prosecuting officials. They obtain evidence of violations of law in the technical fields under their jurisdiction and place it at the disposal of the proper officials who may or may not take action.

At least five variations in procedure have developed in connection with the use of the mechanism. As in the case of supervision through reports the law may specify certain objects of investigation and confine the attention of the inspectors to them. The inevitable consequence results; the state is unable to benefit fully from the experience of the bureau chiefs and department heads.

Opposed to this practice is that which lodges full discretion in the hands of the central authorities. The effectiveness of this proceeding depends, of course, upon the wisdom of those in charge of its administration. It incurs the risk, moreover, if there is much of a turnover among the bureau chiefs, of endangering the value of the device through too frequent changes of the objects of inspection. Obviously, it is possible in this instance, as in the case of the mechanism heretofore discussed, to combine certain features of each method of procedure, and in many cases such a plan has been followed. To insure continuity of inspection, certain objectives have been singled out by law; at the same time, in order that full advantage may be taken of whatsoever executive ability the state may employ, wide discretion has been vested in the department heads empowering them to increase the scope of this activity whenever they see fit.

Two other variations of procedure remain to be considered. In some jurisdictions, state inspection may take place only upon invitation of the localities; in others, the initiative is in the hands of the state. Needless to say, the effectiveness of the device is in large measure impaired by the restrictions imposed in the first instance. Nevertheless, it may be desirable to make use of the mechanism in this form in those services in which the principle of administrative supervison is just being introduced. Whether, apart from this, its use can be justified on grounds of economy is a moot question. The argument in its behalf runs as follows: if the initiative is placed in the hands of the locality but in hands other than those of the local officials—if a few residents of a community, for example, can initiate an inquiry by means of a petition to the state authorities—then it can safely be assumed that should anything improper be suspected, an investigation will be demanded. It must be remembered, however, that much may go on in a municipality without reaching the public.

ADVICE

More positive in its character than either of the devices thus far discussed is the dissemination of advice. It likewise is difficult to resolve into a simple element. Indeed, it seems inextricably bound up with such mechanisms as inspection, approval, grant-in-aid, etc. By means of it state officials, if they have the capacity, can assume that position of natural leadership which should be theirs, and for which there exists a strong demand in many services. The benefits of the mechanism incidentally need not be confined to local officials. The legislature and the public generally may be included within its range. The publicity work of the state administrative boards claims mention in this connection. Particularly effective has been the work done in the field of public health, and to a lesser degree in connection with education, charities and corrections. The advice tendered legislative bodies has, for the most part, been given through the governor's messages, through the general departmental reports, through testimony given before legislative committees or through those informal contacts which inevitably develop between the administration and the legislature. In England, this procedure has gone a step further in the development of the system of provisional orders which, viewed from one angle at least, is nothing but a particular procedure by means of which the administrative authorities furnish advice to Parliament.

The major use made of the device, however, is in connection with local officials. To reach them various methods can be used. The simplest, perhaps, is the maintenance of an extensive system of correspondence, which may consist primarily of circulars and printed matter designed to call attention to particular items of law or procedure of interest to the profession, or may be composed entirely of answers to specific inquiries. It is more than likely that both types of correspondence will be found advantageous. Supplementary to this is the advice which is disseminated through the medium of inspectors. Quite frequently instruction is as much the object of inspection as is the acquisition of information. Individual consideration may thus be given each particular case and all the variations and peculiarities thereof be taken fully into consideration. Excellent as this method appears to be there exist, nevertheless, certain drawbacks, not least of which is the fact that very few states maintain inspectoral staffs capable of making the rounds of the state with sufficient frequency. Consequently, in lieu of inspection, or complementary to it, is the practice (common in certain services) of requiring that all proposed plans or projects be submitted to the supervising officials for criticism and comment. Such a procedure may without question be exceedingly effective. It labors, however, under the handicap of being applicable to very few lines of activity. To subject all municipal action to such a requirement would obviously do more harm than good.

More general in compass is that variation of the mechanism which takes the form of schools of instruction or conferences in which any subject of interest to the profession may be treated. A distinction should possibly be drawn between schools and conferences. At the latter, although the state officials may take the opportunity to impart advice and information, the municipal officials are also expected to take part in the proceedings. At the former, a more formal program is attempted, and the leadership continually resides in the hands of state-appointed officials. Although the conference or school may be superficial or thorough, depending on the ability of the leaders, there is no doubt in either case that the contact on the part of the municipal officials with state officials and with fellow workers is an inspiration and stimulus which no other variation of this mechanism can equal. .Finally, it should be pointed out, the publicity referred to above affects not only the general public but also local government officials.

In connection with the mechanism of advice as in connection with the mechanisms previously discussed three variations in procedure are possible. The state officials may be left free to develop the system as they see fit; or they may be directed to carry out the dissemination of information and advice in a manner specified by law; or they may be directed to take no action except on the specific request of a municipality.

It is impossible to state which one of the numerous channels through which suggestions and recommendations are conveyed to chosen audiences is best; it is even more impossible to maintain that any one of them is sufficiently superior to the others to warrant its exclusive use. By no single method can the most effective results be secured, but rather by a combination of all the variations suggested. Of the three modes of procedure by which the mechanism may be brought into active operation the first two, permitting as they do state initiation, are most likely to produce effective results. The curtailment of initiative in this particular is very likely to create a situation in which the very men who need advice will not receive it, and those who do not need it so much will be the ones who will obtain it. The indifferent and the inefficient will not, for the most part, seek such assistance. Those who will ask for aid will probably be the alert and the aggressive who would have obtained the information desired elsewhere.

SERVICE

Mention should be made at this point of the practice which has developed in a number of jurisdictions of establishing services for the municipalities in various lines of activity. For example, laboratories are frequently maintained in connection with state departments of health to which municipal health officials may send any specimens they desire to have analyzed. At the present moment the New York Crime Commission is recommending the creation of a state bureau of criminal identification which will be used for the most part by the police of the various municipalities. In a sense this activity may be classified as advice in the broadest conception of that term, and throughout the pages which follow it is so treated; nevertheless, such an interpretation of the word is sufficiently unusual to warrant special comment and explanation.

GRANTS-IN-AID

A somewhat stronger pressure than mere appeal to civic or professional pride is present in the device of grant-in-aid. As has already been stated, a grant-in-aid is a contribution from the central government to a locality to aid in the maintenance of certain specified services. The grant is usually made contingent upon the maintenance of the service, and usually upon the existence of a certain degree of efficiency in its administration. In the first instance in which all that is being asked of the municipality is the establishment of the service, the administrative authorities may tend to become mere automatons for the distribution of money. Such is less likely to be the case, however, when the element of efficiency enters into the situation as an objective either in whole or part, for, of necessity, considerable discretion must then be placed in their hands. Under these circumstances the mechanism is frequently much more effective than the mere dissemination of advice. That such should be the case is easily understood since the pocket nerve of the community is touched. Particularly is this so if the object sought is merely increased efficiency within the established services. A sliding scale with a direct correlation between the degree of efficiency maintained and the amount of money granted may be established. The possibility of lightening the tax burden may then be expected to act as a stimulus in the direction desired. It does not of necessity follow, however, that the desideratum will be attained. When the end sought is the inauguration of new services the device has the effect of aiding and abetting whatever sentiment there may be in the community for the establishment of the new service, since the cost thereof is decreased. This factor is frequently the all-important one.

The possible types and variations of the principle are so numerous as to be beyond recording. The requirements set for obtaining the grant-in-aid may be nominal to the degree that the system will become merely a device for the transfer of wealth from the richer communities to the poorer ones. And under certain circumstances such a transfer may be desirable, and in the broadest sense of the phrase *administrative supervision* the most effective supervision possible. On the other hand, the standards set may be of such a character as to compel the utmost efficiency before a cent of the grant is transferred to the local treasuries. Between these extremes every conceivable variation is possible. Again, the grant may be so large that it could not be withdrawn without completely crippling the service; it may be so small as to be of negligible influence; or it may occupy any position between the extremes. It is obvious, however, that the standards established and demanded by the supervising authorities constitute one of the important factors in determining the effectiveness of the device, and the proportion of the cost to be borne by the state constitutes the other. In a limited sense, the greater the grant the greater the stimulus; nevertheless, there is a point at which the device loses its effectiveness. If the municipalities realize that the grant will not be withdrawn under any conditions because of a disastrous effect upon the service, its value as a supervising device has been totally lost.

Special attention, perhaps, ought to be given to one particular combination of elements widely used at one time in educational work in England. It is popularly known as " payment by results." Certain criteria were set up as objectives, and the grants were made to the various communities in proportion to their success in reaching these standards. Through this system it was hoped to stimulate each municipality to put forth a little greater effort each year in order to secure a greater award. In contrast to this arrangement are the multitudinous bases upon which money is distributed in the same field in the United States. In some jurisdictions grants are made on the basis of the school population; in others, on the basis of pupil attendance; in still others, on the basis of the number of teachers employed; and yet in other jurisdictions, according to the ratio the school tax bears to the sum total of local taxation. Grants are being made, moreover, for the development of courses in agriculture, home economics, and industrial training; also for the stimulation of high schools, normal training classes in high schools, and special classes for defectives. The field of education is not, of course, the only field in which the mechanism has been or can be used, but these few concrete examples will give, perhaps, some conception of the variety of purposes to which the device can be turned and the variety of bases upon which the grants may be made.

SUBSIDIES

So closely allied is a system of subsidies to the mechanism of grant-in-aid that one hesitates to make any distinction, whatever. At best the line of demarcation must be exceedingly hazy, for the two devices shade into each other very gradually. The chief difference between the two mechanisms is that a grant-in-aid is always conditional, whereas a subsidy is paid to a locality as a matter of course. As we have already noted, the conditions established in a grant-in-aid may be so simple as to make the grant almost automatic. In such cases the grant-in-aid approaches the status of a subsidy. Nevertheless, the fact is that a condition is always present as a constituent element of the mechanism of grant-in-aid, whereas no such condition is present in a subsidy. An illustration may, perhaps, make the differentiation clearer. A state government grants the municipalities throughout the state a specified sum of money for the introduction and maintenance of courses in home economics, etc. This is clearly a grant-in-aid for the municipalities receive the grant, provided they meet certain conditions—the introduction of these courses. In another state, the state treasurer is directed to divide the state appropriation for education among the various districts in proportion to their relative populations. No conditions whatever are attached. This, consequently, may be classed only as a subsidy which has little or nothing to do with administrative supervision or direction.

APPROVAL

Designed less as a stimulus and more as a deterrent is the requirement of approval, the primary purpose of which is the prevention of actions upon the part of municipalities detrimental to their own interests or to those of the state. Its action is decisive and binding. Not until a move has been made by the local authorities, however, does this mechanism come into play. Through this medium the state authorities merely *visé* proposals which are presented to them. Should the supervising officials refuse to sanction a particular project which has been presented to them, it is possible for the municipality in question to modify the plans slightly and submit them again, or to drop the matter entirely. Obviously, however, the central authorities may impose their will upon localities in all matters necessitated by circumstances or law, for a vigorous use of the mechanism of approval may eliminate every possible alternative.

Four permutations of the process can be discerned; the approval may be of men, or it may be of measures, and it may be either tacit or expressed. The term *express approval* explains itself. The sanction of the supervising official is given to whatsoever plan or project may be under consideration. A positive action is taken. Quite the contrary is true in situations which involve the *tacit approval* of supervising officers. This term denotes the implicit consent which is given to the continuance of an incumbent in office or of an ordinance in operation through the failure of a supervising officer, empowered to remove the unfit or annul the unwise, to act. Such failure on the part of a supervising officer to act need not in a strict sense be construed as approval at all within the usual connotation of that word; nevertheless, for want of a better term, the words *tacit approval* may be employed.

The action of approving the appointment of men to office receives the title confirmation under some circumstances, under others that of licensing. At first blush there seems to be little or no connection between this latter procedure and the mechanism of approval; nevertheless, but slight analysis is necessary to reveal the fact that the issuing of a license, whether to operate a public utility or to teach, is in reality equivalent to giving approval to the individual or the project. It should be noted, perhaps, that the approval of ordinances (measures of a subordinate legislative unit) is sometimes referred to as ratification. Further elaboration of the point seems unnecessary.

Although it has been implied in our previous discussion, specific mention should probably be made of the fact that the use of this mechanism in no way necessitates the making of a decision once and for all; indeed, it may be used as an instrument for continuous control. This is frequently the practice in connection with the operation of water-works and sewage systems where licenses are issued subject to a list of enumerated conditions, the violation of any one of which is stated to be a ground for revocation..

REVIEW

Very closely allied to the device of approval is the mechanism of review. The former, however, is usually called into action before any steps are taken by the municipal authorities. The proposal, not the accomplished fact, is usually passed upon. Such is not the case with the latter, which is most frequently called into play by some action already taken or in the process of being taken. Although there is some overlapping in this respect, there is considerable evidence that such a distinction in the use of the mechanism exists in practice. The scope of the device of approval viewed from this particular angle is consequently somewhat broader than that of review. A further and more important distinction, however, differentiates the two. Whereas the action of state officials in the application of the mechanism of approval is limited in no way whatever, the action of these same officials in the exercise of the principle of review is usually confined to the task of compelling the municipal corporations to conform to the law. This means, in one sense, that the mechanism of review is narrower in its application than that of approval, and in another, much broader, for it may thus be devoted to both negative and positive purposes: negative in preventing illegal actions; positive in compelling municipal officials to take such actions as are prescribed by law.

Two types of review are distinguishable by the manner in which cases are brought before the reviewing body or officer. In one instance, matters go up for consideration only upon the occasion of a controversy, the fact rather than the nature of the controversy calling the machinery of review into action. In the second instance, no such circumstance is necessary. Instead, review takes place automatically in accordance with the dictates of law. Such is almost universally the case in the field of taxation in connection with assessments.

ORDERS

Of a somewhat different nature from the mechanisms of control thus far analyzed is the power of issuing orders. Although all of the devices discussed in the preceding pages have been designed to enable the supervising authorities to influence local officials, nevertheless, final action in all cases, save in those subject to the mechanism of review and under certain circumstances to the device of approval, lies in the hands of the local authorities. Such is not the case in connection with the power to issue orders. By means of this device the supervising agency is enabled to correct any wrong whenever and wherever discovered. The directions issued in this form are mandatory in character. Two distinctions should perhaps be made: first, the distinction between the mechanism of review and the device we are discussing; second, the difference between this device and the power of ordinance-making. The differentiation between the process of review and that of issuing orders may be somewhat artificial, for in final analysis the efficacy of review depends upon the power of the reviewing board to issue orders. From one angle at least, the device of review is only an aspect of the mechanism of issuing orders in which the procedure of investigation has been worked out through a series of rules and regulations. Nevertheless, this very crystalization of the procedure in itself warrants consideration as an independent process. The mechanism of orders in contrast to review, then, is bound by no rules of procedure either in connection with the method of investigation or the subject matter, but may be used as indicated above wherever and whenever deemed necessary.

Less artificial, perhaps, is the line of demarcation between the power to issue specific orders and ordinance-making. An order is applicable only to the instance in hand. No general rule for future conduct is established.

It may be that an order is merely the reiteration, in a form applicable to a particular situation, of principles already written into an ordinance. Such is frequently the case in connection with orders relative to the operation of water-work plants or sewage disposal systems. It may be that the order will contain an injunction nowhere to be found in the ordinances. It must be admitted in the latter case that, although no general rule of wide application is thus established, a tendency to act in a particular way is created through force of precedent.

ORDINANCES

It is the function of the ordinance-making power to establish general rules of conduct for municipal officials to follow. The mechanism is in fact an exercise of legislative power by the supervising authorities. There are, however, ordinances and ordinances. Two classes appear which are so separate and distinct that, save for the usage of the statutes, one would be inclined to coin distinct titles for them. One is a device whereby the action of government officials may be supervised and directed; the other, a means whereby the public may be controlled. The former we may distinguish by somewhat arbitrarily giving it the name—regulations. In this aspect the device is the consummation of the development we have been watching as the mechanisms have been presented. The power inherent in these devices of control has grown step by step as we have analyzed the potentialities of each: first, the power to require reports; then, the right to inspect; next, to advise; fourth, the system of grants-in-aid; fifth, the devices of approval and review; and finally, the mechanisms of orders and ordinance-making. The will of the state supervising officials has been substituted for that of the locality.

Varied, indeed, are the possible applications of the mechanism. The regulations may be "organic acts" establishing the broad outlines of municipal departments; they may be measures governing the establishment of municipal institutions; or they may be mere service orders directing how this or that duty shall be performed. These latter are, of course, the most numerous and vary greatly within themselves. They may fill in only the slightest details of a statute or they may determine the application of a law. Variation is also present in their internal structure. They may regulate matters in great detail "even to the rising of workhouse paupers," or they may be exceedingly vague and indefinite. To undertake a further discussion of the possible types of ordinances is impossible, for they are contrived according to the exigencies of the service.

REMOVAL

Removal or some similar power is obviously necessary to put teeth into these devices. The purpose of the mechanism is apparent. It is, of course, the termination of the services of municipal officials who prove themselves unfitted for the positions they occupy. The definition of unfitness varies from service to service. Incompetency, dishonesty, and immorality are the qualities which most often enter into the definition. Nonfeasance, misfeasance, and malfeasance are other terms quite often found in such descriptions. Two types of action are possible, suspension and permanent removal. Suspension may be used merely as a precaution when charges have been filed against an officer, or as a penalty entailing loss of pay. Permanent removal is, of course, more drastic. The possibility of such action is thought to be, and probably is, a stimulus to efficiency. Should action become necessary the only result achieved, be it noted, is negative. The undesirable official is removed from office, but discretion as to the type of individual who shall fill the office continues to reside with the municipal authorities. Continued use of the power may, of course, lead to positive results, but the principle seems designed to enable the supervising authorities to prevent extreme deterioration in any service rather than to build up a superior personnel.

APPOINTMENT

The building-up of a superior personnel is the function of appointment. The selection of capable officials is its primary object; the retention of capable ones, its secondary; and the mere matter of a convenient method of filling positions may, in some circumstances, constitute a tertiary. In those cases in which the selection of capable officials is the object of the device, the appointments are usually of a permanent character. State officials are frequently given this power in connection with vacancies caused by removal. The theory under such circumstances evidently is that—in the case of elective officials—this is the most convenient way to fill the vacancy, in the case of appointive ones—some check is thus placed upon a repetition of the situation which evoked the removal. The desire to retain capable officials in office has doubtless led to that variation of the device which enables a state supervisory body to reinstate any official who has been removed by the local authorities for insufficient reasons. This variation of the mechanism is used primarily to protect those local office holders who in the performance of their duties inevitably offend powerful local interests—as is frequently the case with the health commissioner or the commissioner of police. It is probably the element of convenience as much as anything else, however, which has brought about the practice of state appointment upon the death or resignation of elected incumbents.

Two characteristics should be noted in respect to these officers who are thus appointed by state authorities. In most instances they must be residents of the locality in which their services are rendered, and in all cases they are supported by municipal funds. It is these two features which give these officers the characteristics of municipal officials and separate them from the state administration. However, if the devices of removal and appointment are combined, it is apparent that little more power would be given the supervising officials if the subordinates concerned were transferred to the ranks of the state administration itself.

SUBSTITUTE ADMINISTRATION

To say that municipal activities are supervised through the administration of those activities by the state itself seems paradoxical. The contradiction in terms, however, is more apparent than real. To empower the state authorities to take over the administration of a municipal service only when the municipal administration thereof has become exceedingly inefficient is obviously nothing more than a mechanism of supervision or control. In some respects it is more drastic than the power of removal, for through it *all* power of discretion is taken from the local authorities and placed in the hands of the state administrative officers. Such is also the case when the initiation of the procedure is conditioned upon the occurrence of an emergency too big for the local unit to handle. Situations of this character occasionally arise in connection with epidemics and floods. The object of supervision under such circumstances is not so much to supplant the local authorities as it is to supplement them.

Whether it is paradoxical or not for the state to supervise municipal activities by permanently administering them is, perhaps, a more debatable question. In the evaluation of the property of common carriers and the apportionment of the value thereof to the different taxing units, something of the sort is accomplished. The state is indirectly influencing and controlling one phase of municipal taxation.

These, then, are the devices of administrative supervision: reports, inspection, advice, grant-in-aid, approval, review, orders, ordinances, removal, appointment, and substitute administration. The three first named grant the state authorities no mandatory power, although enabling them both to amass information and to assume a position of natural leadership. Somewhat greater pressure may be the result of the effective use of grants-in-aid. In the remaining mechanisms, however, the compulsory aspect applies with increasing force in the order in which the mechanisms are named.

Two general purposes seem to permeate the entire process: first, the desire to stimulate the muncipalities to action; second, the desire to prevent unwise action. Sometimes both purposes may be accomplished through the same device. Such is clearly the case with inspection, advice and review. In general, however, it can be said that subsidies, grant-in-aid, appointment, and permanent administration have primarily a positive end in view, whereas the remaining mechanisms (approval, removal, and substitute administration) have essentially a negative one.

These devices, however, as indicated above, do not usually operate singly but in combinations, nor do they operate in a vacuum but in concrete situations for the attainment of concrete objects. The combinations are almost as varied as the objects sought. A number of purposes, nevertheless, are common to the supervision of practically all municipal services. First, perhaps, is the amassing of information; second, a limited control over local personnel; third, some part in shaping plans and developments of an engineering nature; fourth, a share in the determination of certain matters of public policy; and fifth, the oversight of the actual administration of local activities for the purpose of enforcing the requirements of law. To attain these objects, particular combinations of elements are likely to be called into play. In amassing information the mechanisms of reports and inspection are inevitably used, whereas in the control of personnel the devices of reports, inspection, advice, approval, orders, removal, and appointment may all be brought into action, depending more or less upon the degree of control to be maintained. Equally numerous are the possible elements which may enter into the supervision of projected construction work; reports, inspection, advice, grant-in-aid, approval, orders, and ordinances and, under extraordinary circumstances, substitute administration. The participation of the supervising officials in the determination of matters of policy may evoke the mechanisms of reports, advice, grant-in-aid, approval, orders, and ordinances. Needless to say, the last major objective listed above may call forth all the elements or mechanisms discussed. Whether all the devices referred to in these potential combinations will be used depends upon the exigency of the particular situation and the degree of supervision desired. Only a detailed study of the operation of these mechanisms under field conditions will reveal what other combinations can be made to effect other objectives.[1]

[1] For a more extensive discussion of certain aspects of these principles of supervision see John Preston Comer, *Legislative Functions of National Administrative Agencies*, Columbia University Press (1927); John Dickinson, *Administrative Justice and the Supremacy of Law in the United States*, Harvard University Press (1927); and James Hart, *The Ordinance Making Powers of the President of the United States*, Johns Hopkins Press (1925). Although these books draw primarily upon Federal practice and are concerned with the use of certain mechanisms of control, not of municipalities but of the body politic, nevertheless many of the observations contained therein are relevant to the processes of control we have been considering.

CHAPTER III

FINANCE

As early as 1796 Oliver Wolcott observed that, although the valuations made by county commissioners in Virginia were undoubtedly just in respect to the relative value of the different parcels of land within the same county, they were exceedingly unjust when compared with the valuations of other counties. His observation, needless to say, has often been reiterated in later days and in other jurisdictions, frequently with less charity concerning the equity of the local valuations.

An almost innate tendency on the part of individuals and communities to avoid, or at least minimize, taxes has from time immemorial made the maintenance of an equitable tax system difficult if not impossible.[1] It is responsible not only for the complete breakdown in many jurisdictions of the personal property tax, but for the various evasions and undervaluations which have continuously beset the real estate tax.[2] In Kentucky at the present time, for example, more money is actually being raised from dog licenses than from the personal property tax, and in various and sundry jurisdictions the reports of the state commissions contain lists of

[1] Seligman, E. R. A., *Essays in Taxation*, New York (1925), p. 19 *et seq.*; Lutz, Harley L., *Public Finance*, New York (1924), p. 340 *et seq.*

[2] *Florida Tax Commission, Report 1917*, p. 10 *et seq.*; *Louisiana Assessment and Taxation Report 1921*, p. 22; *Michigan Committee of Inquiry into Taxation, Report 1923*, pp. 29-30; *Missouri State Tax Commission, Fourth Biennial Report, 1923-4*, p. 47; *Oregon Committee on Tax Investigation, Report 1923*, p. 127; *State Conference on Taxation in the State of New York, 1921-1924*, pp. 83-4; *Tennessee State Board of Equalization, Report 1919-20*, p. 27 *et seq.*; *State Tax Commissioner of West Virginia, Biennial Report 1920-22*, p. vii.

newly discovered lands (newly discovered so far as the assessment rolls are concerned), painful reminders of successful tax evasion in days past.[1] The frequency with which drastic changes in valuations on corporate property have been made by these same commissions, moreover, indicates something of the extent to which undervaluation has been successful.[2]

A further consequence of this natural attempt to avoid taxation has been the endeavor on the part of localities to escape their due share of state taxes. Since such taxes are apportioned among the communities on the basis of the property valuation therein, the obvious method of evasion is undervaluation. And too frequently assessors, holding their allegiance to their locality higher than their loyalty to the state, have aided and abetted the process with consequent inequalities and injustices.[3]

As a result of this aspect of tax evasion, attempts at equalization were made as early as 1820. Generally speaking, this earlier equalization was more nominal than real; it partook more of the nature of a political struggle than of a scientific process. "In no case was there any pretense at the collection of data on the basis of which an equaliza-

[1] *Alabama State Tax Commission, Report 1914*, p. 23; *The Tax Commission of Wisconsin, Report 1916*, pp. 15-16; *State and Local Taxation, 1910*, p. 362. Indeed, almost any report of a state tax commissioner will reveal similar omissions which have been discovered by the state commission.

[2] *Louisiana Assessment and Taxation Report 1921*, p. 22 et seq.; *State Conference on Taxation in the State of New York*, 1921-24, p. 83 et seq.; *Tennessee State Board of Equalization, Report 1919-1920*, p. 41 et seq.; *The Tax Commission of Wisconsin, Report 1916*, p. 15 et seq. Any report of a state tax commission selected at random will, in all probability, illustrate and substantiate the point.

[3] *Idaho State Board of Equalization, Proceedings 1923*, p. 10 et seq.; *State Tax Commission of Iowa, Report 1923*, pp. 23-29; *Oregon Committee on Tax Investigation, Report 1923*, p. 126 et seq.; *Tennessee State Board of Equalization, Report 1918*, p. 26 et seq.

tion might have been more carefully made, and the information available to any of these [early boards of equalization] was supplied chiefly by the delegations sent in to the state house from the several counties to protest against the valuations established for the several counties."[1] Certainly the members of such bodies were in no position to pass a scientific judgment upon the questions before them.

In 1891 the establishment of a state tax commission in Indiana marked the beginning of a new era. This commission was granted not only the power of adjusting differences in valuation as between the various taxing units (a power formerly granted state boards of equalization), but was also charged with the supervision of the original assessments made by the local assessors. Today similar commissions are to be found in forty states.[2] They have since been given, moreover, the additional function of evaluating the property of common carriers.

State supervision has not stopped here. The stupendous increase in governmental expenditures which marked the first quarter of the twentieth century produced a tremendous popular pressure for economy.[3] That the increase in expenditures was indeed startling becomes apparent from even a cursory examination of the figures; in fact, the more cursory the examination, the more startling do the figures appear.[4] No unit of government escaped. Federal expenditures increased from $520,860,000 in 1900 to $3,244,685,000 in 1923; state expenditures increased from $182,631,000 in 1903 to $1,280,237,000 in

---

[1] Lutz, Harley L., *op. cit.*, p. 344.

[2] Lutz, Harley L., *op. cit.*, p. 345.

[3] National Industrial Conference Board, *Research Report*, # 155, *Taxation and National Income*, New York (1922), # 156, *Cost of Government in the United States*, New York (1926).

[4] Heer, Clarence, *The Post War Expansion of State Expenditures*, New York (1926).

1922; municipal expenditures from \$527,787,000 in 1904 to \$2,115,990,000 in 1923, if only cities over 30,000 are taken into consideration.[1] Nor was the feeling thus produced rendered any less intense by the discovery that the growth in expenditures was more than exceeding the growth in the wealth and income of the country. The fact that the total tax burden of the country consumed but 6.4 per cent of our national income in 1912-13, whereas that of 1920-21 consumed 14.3 per cent, and that of the calendar year 1921 consumed 16.7 per cent seemed to justify the alarm.[2]

As a consequence of the pressure thus engendered, state administrative supervision has been extended over several phases of municipal activity other than the mere evaluation of taxable property. In a number of jurisdictions state supervision of local accounts has been introduced for the purpose of securing greater efficiency and eliminating at least the grosser forms of waste. More radical by far is the con-

---

[1] Lutz, Harley L., *op. cit.*, pp. 56, 63, 65 *et seq.*; *cf.* also National Industrial Conference Board, *Cost of Government in the United States*, p. 86, which makes the comparison both in terms of current dollars and in terms of dollars with the purchasing power of 1913.

(In millions of dollars)

Disbursing Authority	Current Dollars					1913 Dollars		
	1890	1903	1913	1923	1924	1913	1923	1924
Federal*	\$291	\$475	\$692	\$3649	\$3264	\$692	\$2374	\$2180
State	77	182	383	1360	1585	383	855	1059
Local	487	913	1844	5136	5403	1844	3341	3609
Total	855	1570	2919	10145	10252	2919	6570	6848

* The figures on this line include only the net deficits of the postal service, the gross figures being excluded from the totals.

[2] National Industrial Conference Board, *Taxation and National Income*, p. 74.

trol which has developed in a smaller number of states over municipal budgets and budget procedure. In some jurisdictions all increases beyond a statutory limitation are prohibited save with the consent of the supervising officials; in others, *all* items contained in the budget are subject to this same approval.

A similar increase in indebtedness accompanied the vast increases in expenditure. Between 1902 and 1922 the total indebtedness of the municipalities throughout the United States increased from $1,346,843,000 to $4,703,-332,000.[1] Here too, consequently, the states have felt called upon to intervene.

Thus it has come about that at present state administrative supervision of municipal finance is directed into four channels: taxation, accounts, budgets, and indebtedness.

TAXATION

The control over taxation is still the most complete. In its maintenance practically all the mechanisms of supervision heretofore discussed have been brought into play. An extensive system of *reports* has been built up. In some states only certain specified fiscal facts, usually those called for on the assessment blanks, may be demanded by the state officials.[2] In others, all information relative to taxation is

[1] Department of Commerce, Bureau of Census, *Public Debt* (1922), p. 10.

[2] Ala. Gen. Laws 1923, no. 172, §67; Ariz. Rev. Stat. 1913, §4828; Ark. Digest 1921, §9788; Cal. Pol. Code 1923, §§3655, 3692; Colo. Annot. Stat. 1923, §§6306, 6314; Conn. Gen. Stat. 1918, §1319; Ida. Comp. Stat. 1919, §3164; Ill. Gen. Revenue Act, §98; Ind. Annot. Stat. 1926, §14231; Iowa Code 1924, §7139; Kan. Rev. Stat. 1916, chs. 79-1604; Ky. Stat. 1922, §4114-i12; La. Acts 1916, amended 1918, no. 211, §10; Maine Rev. Stat. 1916, ch. 9, §3; Mass. Gen. Laws, ch. 58, §6; Mich. Comp. Laws 1915, §4149; Minn. Gen. Stat. 1923, §2052; Miss. Annot. Code 1917, §7762; Mo. Rev. Stat. 1919, §12847; Mont. Acts 1923, ch. 3, §8; Neb. Comp. Stat. 1922, §5977; Nev. Rev. Laws 1912, §3; N. H. Public Laws 1926, ch. 68, §11;

available.[1] A few concrete cases may help to give a true picture of the place the process occupies in the field and to indicate the various shades of supervision attainable through its operation. In Oklahoma, for example, the local authorities must transmit to the state auditor such information as is specified in the law. In Ohio, all fiscal transactions must be reported in accordance with forms prescribed by the chief inspector and supervisor; the inclusion of certain items in these forms, however, is made mandatory by law. In Maine, the town assessors are at the beck and call of the supervising agency and must furnish the state officials with such information as they may desire at any time. Whether any of these requirements of law will be complied with if no supplementary compulsory provisions accompany them is problematical. Very often, consequently, a clause is inserted in the statute making failure on the part of municipal officials to comply with these provisions a misdemeanor sub-

N. J. Comp. Stat. Supple. 1924, §3474-208-37a; N. M. Laws 1915, ch. 54, §9; N. Y. Cons. Laws 1918, ch. LX, §61; N. C. Cons. Stat. 1919, §7883; Ohio Code 1926, §5612; Okla. Comp. Stat. 1921, §9689; Ore. Laws 1920, §4187; S. C. Code 1922, §365; S. D. Rev. Code 1919, §6587; Tex. Rev. Stat. 1925, §7043; Utah Comp. Laws 1917, §5913; Vt. Gen. Laws 1917, §821; Va. Code 1924, ch. 147, §4; Wash. Comp. Stat. 1922, §11088; W. Va. Code 1923, ch. 29, §5; Wis. Stat. 1925, §68.01; Wyo. Comp. Stat. 1920, §2810.

[1] Ala. Gen. Laws 1925, no. 172, §67; Ariz. Rev. Stat. 1913, §4828; Ark. Digest 1921, §9788; Cal. Pol. Code 1923, §3692; Colo. Annot. Stat. 1923, §6306; Ill. Gen. Revenue Act, §98; Ind. Annot. Stat. 1926, §14217; Ky. Stat. 1922, §4114-i12; La. Acts 1916, amended 1918, no. 211, §10; Maine Rev. Stat. 1916, ch. 9, §3; Md. Code 1924, art. 81, §257; Mich. Comp. Laws 1915, §4149; Minn. Gen. Stat. 1923, §2364; Miss. Annot. Code 1917, §7764; Mo. Rev. Stat. 1919, §12847; Mont. Acts 1923, ch. 3, §8; Nev. Rev. Laws 1912, §3; N. H. Public Laws 1926, ch. 68, §11; N. M. Laws of 1921, ch. 133, §507; N. Y. Cons. Laws 1918, ch. LX, §171; N. C. Cons. Stat. 1919, §7883; Ohio Code 1926, §5624-12; Ore. Laws 1920, §4187; S. C. Code 1922, §365; S. D. Rev. Code 1919, §6587; Utah Comp. Laws 1917, §5913; Va. Code 1924, ch. 147, §4; Wash. Comp. Stat. 1922, §11088; W. Va. Code 1923, ch. 29, §5; Wis. Stat. 1925, §73.03; Wyo. Comp. Stat. 1920, §2810.

ject to fine or imprisonment or both.[1]   In other cases the state authorities are empowered to remove recalcitrant municipal assessors from office.   This point, however, will be elaborated later.

Supplementary to the information thus accumulated is that obtained through the process of *inspection* which is to be found in three fourths of the states.[2]   Typical of the grant of power which has been made in many jurisdictions is that of Kansas which provides:

That it shall be the duty of the commission, and it shall have the power and authority: to investigate the work and methods of local assessors, boards of county commissioners, and county boards of equalization in the assessment, equalization and taxation of all kinds of property, by visiting the counties of the state.   To carefully examine into all cases where evasion or violation of the laws for assessment and taxation of property is

[1] The term "municipal official" in this connection is frequently used to include county officers, for where the municipality is required by law to use the assessment list reviewed and corrected by the state, no attempt has been made to distinguish between those states in which each municipality has its own assessor, board of review, etc., and those jurisdictions in which the original assessment is made subject to county direction.   In either case the final control of the municipal assessment lists rests with the state administrative authorities.

[2] Ala. Gen. Laws 1923, no. 172, §§ 67, 69; Ariz. Rev. Stat. 1913, §§4826, 4829; Ark. Digest 1921, §9789; Cal. Pol. Code 1923, §3692; Colo. Annot. Stat. 1923, §§6306, 6314; Conn. Acts 1925, ch. 109; Ill. Gen. Revenue Act, §3; Ind. Annot. Stat. 1926, §14217; Kan. Rev. Stat. 1923, §79-1401; Ky. Stat. 1922, §4114-i12; La. Acts 1916, amended 1918, no. 211, §10; Maine Rev. Stat. 1916, ch. 9, §10; Md. Code 1924, art. 81, §289; Mass. Gen. Laws, ch. 58, §1; Mich. Comp. Laws 1915, §4147; Minn. Gen. Stat. 1923, §§2364, 2365; Miss. Annot. Code 1917, §7765; Mo. Rev. Stat. 1919, §§12829, 12847; Mont. Acts 1923, ch. 3, §8; Neb. Comp. Stat. 1922, §5830; Nev. Rev. Laws 1912, §3; N. H. Public Laws 1926, ch. 68, §§11, 12; N. J. Comp. Stat. 1910, §5112-37d; N. M. Laws 1915, ch. 54, §9; N. Y. Cons. Laws 1918, ch. LX, §171; N. C. Cons. Stat. 1919, §7883; Ohio Gen. Code 1926, §5624-13; Ore. Laws 1920, §4187; S. C. Code 1922, §365; S. D. Rev. Code 1919, §6587; Utah Comp. Laws 1917, §5983; Va. Acts 1926, ch. 147, §4; Wash. Comp. Stat. 1922, §11088; W. Va. Code 1923, ch. 29, §2; Wis. Stat. 1925, §73.03; Wyo. Comp. Stat. 1920, §2810.

alleged, complained of, or discovered, and to ascertain wherein existing laws are defective, or are improperly or negligently administered, and to prepare and recommend measures best calculated to remedy the defects discovered.

To carry out these provisions of law three principal lines of attack are pursued: first, the accumulation of sales data, etc., on the basis of which a more accurate evaluation of real estate may be made;[1] second, the discovery of property which has been omitted from the assessment lists;[2] and third, the detection of inequitable assessments.[3]

[1] Ala. Gen. Laws 1923, no. 172, §67; Ariz. Rev. Stat. 1913, §4826; Ark. Digest 1921, §9789; Cal. Pol. Code 1923, §3692; Colo. Annot. Stat. 1923, §6306; Conn. Acts 1925, ch. 109; Ill. Laws of 1919, p. 718, §3; Ind. Annot. Stat. 1926, §14217; Kan. Rev. Stat. 1923, §79-1401; Ky. Stat. 1922, §4114-i12; La. Acts 1916, amended 1918, no. 211, §10; Maine Rev. Stat. 1916, ch. 9, §10; Md. Code 1924, art. 81, §289; Mass. Gen. Laws, ch. 58, §1; Mich. Comp. Laws 1915, §4147; Minn. Gen. Stat. 1923, §2364; Miss. Annot. Code 1917, §7765; Mo. Rev. Stat. 1919, §12829; Mont. Acts 1923, ch. 3, §8; Nev. Rev. Laws 1912, §3; N. H. Public Laws 1926, ch. 68, §11; N. J. Comp. Stat. 1910, §5112-37d; N. M. Laws 1915, ch. 54, §9; N. Y. Cons. Laws 1918, ch. LX, §171; N. C. Cons. Stat. 1919, §7883; Ohio Code 1926, §5624-13; Ore. Laws 1920, §4187; S. C. Code 1922, §365; S. D. Rev. Code 1919, §6587; Utah Comp. Laws 1917, §5983; Va. Acts 1926, ch. 147, §4; Wash. Comp. Stat. 1922, §11088; W. Va. Code 1923, ch. 29, §2; Wis. Stat. 1925, §73.03; Wyo. Comp. Stat. 1920, §2810.

[2] Ala. Gen. Laws 1923, no. 172, §69; Ariz. Rev. Stat. 1913, §4829; Ark. Digest 1921, §9788; Cal. Pol. Code 1923, §3692; Colo. Annot. Stat. 1923, §6306; Conn. Acts 1925, ch. 109; Ill. Gen. Revenue Act, §3; Ind. Annot. Stat. 1926, §14217; Kans. Rev. Stat. 1923, §79-1401; Ky. Stat. 1922, §4114-i12; La. Acts of 1916, amended 1918, no. 211, §10; Maine Rev. Stat. 1916, ch. 9, §10; Md. Code 1924, art. 81, §289; Mich. Comp. Laws 1915, §4149; Minn. Gen. Stat. 1923, §§2364, 2365; Miss. Annot. Code 1917, §7058; Mo. Rev. Stat. 1919, §12847; Mont. Acts 1923, ch. 3, §8; Neb. Comp. Stat. 1922, §5830; Nev. Rev. Laws 1912, §3; N. H. Public Laws 1926, ch. 68, §12; N. J. Comp. Stat. 1910, §5111-37c; N. M. Laws 1915, ch. 54, §7; N. Y. Cons. Laws 1918, ch. LX, §171; N. C. Cons. Stat. 1919, §7883; Ohio Gen. Code 1926, §5624-13; Ore. Laws 1920, §4187; S. C. Code 1922, §365; S. D. Rev. Code 1919, §6587; Utah Comp. Laws 1917, §5983; Va. Acts 1926, ch. 147, §4; Wash. Comp. Stat. 1922, §11088; W. Va. Code 1923, ch. 29, §2; Wis. Stat. 1925, §73.03; Wyo. Comp. Stat. 1920, §2810.

[3] Ala. Gen. Laws 1923, no. 172, §69; Ariz. Rev. Stat. 1913, §4829; Ark.

The first line of attack is followed in Missouri where the state tax commission endeavors to accumulate and place before the state board of equalization such data as is necessary to guide the board in arriving at a fair equalization of property valuations between the different taxing units of the state. In 1923 every county in the state was visited by a representative of the commission.

Maps were prepared showing the character of the soil and the valuation placed thereon by informed citizens. In the process frequent consultations were held with farm bureaus and farm club members, local officials, real estate men, abstractors and others. Lists of bona fide real estate transfers were obtained from the offices of recorders of deeds, and loan values from reputable farm loan companies. Agricultural production reports were consulted. Location with reference to marketing centers and many other matters were taken into consideration. Conferences were held with assessing officers and other county officials. Questionaires were sent out to school district clerks, to county agents and farm organizations for information concerning property valuations in their own and also in adjoining counties. Census reports of an agricultural nature were also studied; and the data filed before the commission was analyzed.[1]

Digest 1921, §9789; Cal. Pol. Code 1923, §3692; Colo. Annot. Stat. 1923, §§6306, 6314; Conn. Acts 1925, ch. 109; Ill. Gen. Revenue Act, §3; Ind. Annot. Stat. 1926, §14217; Kan. Rev. Stat. 1923, §79-1401; Ky. Stat. 1922, §4114-i12; La. Acts of 1916, amended 1918, no. 211, §10; Maine Rev. Stat. 1916, ch. 9, §10; Md. Code 1924, art. 81, §289; Mich. Comp. Laws 1915, §4149; Minn. Gen. Stat. 1923, §2364; Miss. Annot. Code 1917, §7765; Mo. Rev. Stat. 1919, §12847; Mont. Acts of 1923, ch. 3, §8; Neb. Comp. Stat. 1922, §5830; Nev. Rev. Laws 1912, §3; N. H. Public Laws 1926, ch. 68, §12; N. J. Comp. Stat. 1910, §5111-37c; N. M. Laws 1915, ch. 54, §7; N. Y. Cons. Laws 1918, ch. LX, §171; N. C. Cons. Stat. 1919, §7883; Ohio Code 1926, §5624-13; Ore. Laws 1920, §4187; S. C. Code 1922, §365; S. D. Rev. Code 1919, §6587; Utah Comp. Laws 1917, §5983; Va. Acts 1926, ch. 147, §4; Wash. Comp. Stat. 1922, §11088; W. Va. Code 1923, ch. 29, §2; Wis. Stat. 1925, §73.03; Wyo. Comp. Stat. 1920, §2810.

[1] *Missouri State Tax Commission, Fourth Biennial Report 1923-24*, pp. 41-2; cf. also *Colorado Tax Commission, Report 1916*, p. 4 et seq.

A similar survey using similar methods was conducted at the same time in all the municipalities of the state. Thus the final recommendations were based upon all the information the commission had been able to collect.

Illustrations of the necessity for the maintenance of a system of state inspection for the discovery of property which has been omitted from the assessment lists could be multiplied almost indefinitely. Louisiana, however, has furnished the most striking example within recent years. For some time preceding 1907 Louisiana had maintained a system of state inspection, which was abandoned in that year and not re-established until 1917. It is possible, consequently, to compare the three periods and thus measure in at least a rough fashion the effect of state administrative supervision of this character upon the evaluation of property. The facts briefly, are these. Between 1907 and 1916 the head of cattle reported on the assessment lists declined from 1,036,528 to 794,445; the value of agricultural land slumped from $54,176,820 to $46,980,607; and other property with some few exceptions fell off accordingly. The sum total value of real estate held a little more than its own, the value thereof in 1907 being $327,987,000 and in 1916 $386,897,-000. Personal property, including public service corporation assets, likewise increased a little, being valued at $175,-317,600 in 1907 and $208,325,000 in 1916. In 1917 some startling changes occurred. Real estate jumped in recorded value from $386,897,000 to $895,537,000; personal property from $208,325,000 to $512,923,000; agricultural land from $46,980,605 to $77,063,018. Some of this increase was due to a revaluation of the property, of course; a goodly amount of it, nevertheless, was due to the addition to the tax rolls of items previously omitted. For example, the total acreage listed for taxation in 1916 was 26,844,770; in 1917 it was 27,912,812 acres. Thus more than one million acres were added to the tax rolls at one stroke. In Caddo Parish alone it was found that more than 15,000 acres of land including 1,600 city lots with a total valuation of more than $1,000,000, had been omitted from the assessment lists. Little more need be said to justify the maintenance of this type of supervision.[1]

Nor is it any more difficult to discover an adequate justification for that supervision which is directed toward the discovery of inequitable valuations. In this connection the work of the State Board of Equalization in Tennessee is particularly interesting. An analysis of the financial abstracts of the state in 1919 by the chief statistician had revealed the fact that a certain very large corporation operating a huge plant in one of the counties of east Tennessee had been assessed only $260,000 on its entire property. An investigation was immediately instituted, expert mechanical engineers were hired, and a revaluation undertaken. As a consequence, the company voluntarily filed a schedule with the office of the chief tax statistician revaluing its property at more than $4,000,000. Under the old assessment this corporation paid the state $1,430; under the new it paid $10,400, an increase to the state alone of $9,000 per annum, to say nothing of the benefits received by the county and municipality in which it is located. Equally astounding was the case of a large mining company with many holdings throughout the state. In 1918 this company was assessed at $43,-000; in 1920 the assessment was $2,650,000. In 1918 this company was paying $236 in state taxes; in 1920 it paid $6,890. It should be kept in mind, furthermore, that these figures refer only to state taxes; local taxes, of course, in-

---

[1] *Louisiana Assessment and Taxation Commission, Report 1921*, p. 22 *et seq.*; *cf.* also *Alabama State Tax Commission, Report 1914*, p. 25; *Montana State Tax Commission, First Biennial Report 1914*, p. 6; *Tennessee State Board of Equalization, Report 1919-20*, p. 52 *et seq.*

creased accordingly.[1] Illustrations might be multiplied quite easily, but a sufficient number have already been used to indicate that a system of state inspection may be quite effective.

Inevitably, in the course of this supervision, the methods and work of the local assessors come under observation, necessitating in many instances further action on the part of the state administrative authorities. In some cases merely direction and advice alone seem to be called for; in others only exceedingly drastic action will remedy the situation.

Four main channels for the dissemination of *advice* seem to have developed: correspondence, pamphlet and newspaper publicity, personal visitations, and conferences.[2] In most states it can be assumed that the state department of finance or other supervising agency has maintained an extensive correspondence with local assessors and taxing officials on points of law and technicalities of procedure. Very frequently, in fact, it is the custom of supervising officials to

---

[1] *Tennessee State Board of Equalization, Report 1919-20*, pp. 63-4.

[2] Ala. Gen. Laws 1923, no. 172, §67; Ariz. Rev. Stat. 1913, §4829; Ark. Digest 1921, §9783; Cal. Pol. Code 1923, §3701; Colo. Annot. Stat. 1923, §6303; Conn. (letter from state official); Ill. Laws 1919, p. 718, §2; Ind. Annot. Stat. 1926, §14217; Kan. Rev. Stat. 1923, §79-1401; Ky. Stat. 1922, §4114-i12; La. Acts 1916, amended 1918, no. 211, §10; Maine Rev. Stat. 1916, ch. 9, §5; Md. Code 1924, art. 81, §254; Mass. Gen. Laws, ch. 58, §1; Mich. Comp. Laws 1915, §4149; Minn. Gen. Stat. 1923, §2364; Miss. Annot. Code, Supple. 1922, §7769e; Mo. Rev. Stat. 1919, §12847; Mont. Acts 1923, ch. 3, §8; Neb. Comp. Stat. 1922, §5963; Nev. Rev. Laws 1912, §3; N. H. Public Laws 1926, ch. 68, §11; N. J. Comp. Stat. 1910, §5112-37d; N. M. Laws 1915, ch. 54, §9, 1921, ch. 133, §507; N. Y. Cons. Laws 1918, ch. LX, §171; N. C. Cons. Stat. 1919, §7883; Ohio Code 1926, §5624-12; Ore. Laws 1920, §4187; S. C. Code 1922, §365; S. D. Rev. Code 1919, §6587; Utah Comp. Laws 1917, §5983; Vt. Gen. Laws 1917, §671; Va. Acts 1926, ch. 147, §4; Wash. Comp. Stat. 1922, §11088; W. Va. Code 1923, ch. 29, §2; Wis. Stat. 1925, §73.03; Wyo. Comp. Stat. 1920, §2810. It is very probable, however, even in those states in which no specific mandate relative to the dissemination of advice is to be found in the law, that the practice has nevertheless to some extent developed.

send out circular letters immediately before the date of assessment, reminding the local officers of their obligations and duties. Numerous pamphlets are also prepared and mailed to interested persons. The exact procedure followed in the use of this avenue for the dissemination of advice varies, of course, from jurisdiction to jurisdiction. The majority of these pamphlets probably deal with matters of law and technicalities of procedure. Their treatment is apt to be more comprehensive and detailed than that of the circular letter.

It is equally impossible to generalize concerning the methods used by the supervising authorities in the course of their visitations. A variation in procedure, however, which may well be copied by other states is recorded in a recent report of the Missouri Tax Commission. In those cases in Missouri where the local assessors have difficulty in placing a fair valuation upon property because of its technical character, the state tax commission through its engineers comes to their aid and assistance by making an appraisal thereof. Among the properties which have been thus appraised are shoe factories, cement plants, pipe-line properties, electric light plants, electric transmission lines, factories of various kinds, local property of railroad companies, telegraph and telephone companies, and large buildings. Thus the commission has been able to render valuable services to local assessing officials.[1]

In a number of states the practice of holding conferences for the dissemination of information and advice is required by law.[2] Here, likewise, several variations exist. In some

[1] *Missouri Tax Commission, Report 1923-4*, p. 46.

[2] Ala. Gen. Laws 1923, no. 172, §67; Ariz. Rev. Stat. 1913, §4826; Ark. Digest 1921, §9788; Colo. Annot. Stat. 1923, §6306; Conn. (letter of state official); Ill. Laws 1919, p. 718, §2; Kan. Rev. Stat. 1923, §79-1401; Ky. Stat. 1922, §4114-i12; La. Acts 1916, amended 1918, no. 211, §10; Maine Rev. Stat. 1916, ch. 9, §5; Minn. Gen. Stat. 1923, §2364; Miss. Rev. Stat.

jurisdictions the conferences are more or less local; in others, state-wide; in still others, a combination of the two modes of procedure is used. Illustrative of the first is the practice in Georgia where twenty-two local conferences were held in 1922. " The minutes of these meetings were digested by the state tax commissioner . . . [who thus] received more reliable information both as to tax values and conditions in the counties of the state . . . than he could have received by personal visits to each of the 160 counties." [1] In Colorado the state conference is favored.

The meetings are held during the winter (in the state capital) before the assessment work for the year is begun, and are excellent practical training schools for the newly elected officials. Committees are appointed to assist in crystallizing the judgment of the assessors on average values and assessment methods, and much information of value to the commission is thus presented. Papers are read by those assessors who have had unusual success in various parts of the work and discussion is freely indulged in. . . . The annual meeting has undoubtedly had a great influence in stimulating the interest of the assessor in the problem of taxation, and every effort should be made to develop its usefulness still further. [2]

A rather unique combination of the two modes of procedure is to be found in Missouri. The conference is state-wide and meets in a central place. Certain sessions are de-

---

1919, §12847; Mont. Acts 1923, ch. 3, §8; N. H. Public Laws 1926, ch. 68, §11; N. Y. Cons. Laws 1918, ch. LX, §171; Ohio Code 1926, §5624-3; S. C. Code 1922, §365; S. D. Rev. Code 1919, §6587; Vt. Gen. Laws 1917, §670; Va. Acts 1926, ch. 147, §4; Wash. Comp. Stat. 1922, §11090; W. Va. Code 1923, ch. 29, §§2, 17; Wis. Stat. 1925, §73.03. In addition to these states in which the holding of such conferences is made more or less mandatory by law, a number of other states make use of the mechanism—often, however, at irregular or infrequent intervals.

[1] *Georgia State Tax Commissioner's Report*, 1922, p. 6.

[2] *Colorado State Tax Commission, Report 1916*, p. 51.

voted to a discussion of matters of general interest, and these are conducted very much on the Colorado plan. Other sessions are devoted to matters of a sectional or local concern. The convention consequently resolves itself into a series of group conferences of assessors from different parts of the state, and in these sectional conferences the problems peculiar to each special locality are threshed out.[1]

The mechanism of *approval* is brought into operation in the field of taxation on a very limited scale. In two states, Colorado and Massachusetts, the bond of the local assessor is subject to the requirement of state approval.[2] In Kansas the removal of an assessor by the local authorities requires similar action.[3] The reason for this provision in all probability is the desire on the part of the legislature to protect local assessors from pernicious political pressure. In Ohio the county auditor may hire expert assistance for assessment purposes, but only with state approval;[4] and in Indiana the appointment of all persons to vacancies in the office of tax assessor is subject to similar supervision.[5] Finally, in Illinois state approval must be obtained by the local assessors for the omission of any and all pieces of property claiming legal exemption from taxation for the first time.[6]

Much more drastic than the dissemination of advice which may or may not be followed and much more extensively used than the mechanism of approval is the process of *review*. In general three modes of procedure are followed. In the first, the state commissions are allowed to review and equalize assessments merely between taxing units;[7] in the second, the

[1] *Missouri Tax Commission, Report 1923-24*, pp. 41-42.

[2] *Colo. Annot. Stat. 1923*, §6227; *Mass. Gen. Laws 1926*, ch. 69, §13.

[3] Kansas Rev. Stat. 1923, §79-1409.

[4] Ohio Gen. Code 1926, §5448.

[5] Ind. Annot. Stat. 1926, §1417.

[6] Ill. Gen. Revenue Act, §148.

[7] Ala. Gen. Laws 1923, no. 172, §70; Ariz. Rev. Stat. 1913, §§4829, 4834;

commissions are granted the further right of making adjustments between different classes of property;[1] and in the third, between individuals.[2] The exact powers thus granted

Ark. Digest 1921, §9790; Cal. Pol. Code 1923, §3693; Colo. Annot. Stat. 1923, §6324; Conn. Gen. Stat. 1918, §1245 (Actually the power here granted is almost nil; the commission can only apply for a mandamus to have the law obeyed); Ga. Annot. Code Supple. 1922, §1116; Idaho Comp. Stat. 1919, §3172; Ill. Laws 1919, p. 718, §2; Ind. Annot. Stat. 1926, §14221 (counties only); Iowa Code 1924, §7141; Kans. Stat. 1923, §79-1409; Ky. Stat. 1922, §4114-i16; Maine Rev. Stat. 1916, ch. 9, §4; Mich. Comp. Laws 1915, §4028; Minn. Gen. Stat. 1923, §2366; Miss. Annot. Code 1917, §7765; Mo. Rev. Stat. 1919, §12855; Mont. Acts 1923, ch. 3, §8; Neb. Comp. Stat. 1922, §5901; Nev. Rev. Laws 1912, §6; N. H. Public Laws 1926, ch. 68, §11; N. J. Comp. Stat., Supple. 1924, §§3478-208-37a; N. M. Laws 1915, ch. 54, §6; N. Y. Cons. Laws 1918, ch. LX, §174; N. C. Cons. Stat. 1919, §7887; Ohio Gen. Code 1926, §5613; Okla. Comp. Stat. 1921, §9689; Ore. Laws 1920, §4209 (While the law confers upon the commission the duty of supervising the system of taxation throughout the state, it does not give the commission the right of reassessment or any other means of exercising the supervisory power. Consequently no attempt is made to control or equalize local valuations by state authority. The state tax commission merely equalizes its own assessments of public service property and makes a hypothetical equalization of county valuations to be used as a basis of apportionment of state taxes to the several counties. Letter from state officials); S. C. Code 1922, §368; S. D. Rev. Code 1919, §6590; Utah Comp. Laws 1917, §5923; Wash. Comp. Stat. 1922, §11222; Wis. Stat. 1925, §70.64; Wyo. Comp. Stat. 1920, §2810.

[1] Ala. Gen. Laws 1923, no. 172, §70; Ariz. Rev. Stat. 1913, §§4829, 4834; Ark. Digest 1921, §9790; Cal. Pol. Code 1923, §3693; Colo. Annot. Stat. 1923, §6324; Ga. Annot. Code, Supple. 1922, §1116; Idaho Comp. Stat. 1919, §3171; Ill. Laws 1919, p. 718, §19; Ind. Annot. Stat. 1926, §14221; Iowa Code 1924, §7141; Kan. Rev. Stat. 1922, §79-1409; Ky. Stat. 1922, §4114-i18; La. Acts 1916, amended 1918, no. 211, §15; Mich. Comp. Laws 1915, §4151; Minn. Gen. Stat. 1923, §2366; Miss. Annot. Code 1917, §7765; Mo. Rev. Stat. 1919, §12855; Mont. Acts 1923, ch. 3, §8; Neb. Comp. Stat. 1922, §5901; Nev. Rev. Laws 1912, §6; N. J. Comp. Stat., Supple. 1924, §3478-208-37a; N. M. Laws 1915, ch. 54, §6; N. C. Cons. Stat. 1919, §7889; Ohio Gen. Code 1926, §5613; Okla. Comp. Stat. 1921, §9689; S. C. Code 1922, §368; S. D. Rev. Code 1919, §6590; Utah Comp. Laws 1917, §5985; Wash. Comp. Stat. 1922, §11222; Wis. Stat. 1925, §70.64; Wyo. Comp. Stat. 1920, §2810.

[2] Ala. Gen. Laws 1923, no. 172, §68; Ariz. Rev. Stat. 1913, §4829; Ark.

may, perhaps, best be seen in the laws themselves. Typical of the statutory grant in the first group of states is the provision in Arkansas to the effect that:

The tax commission shall have the power to raise or lower the values in any county or any subdivision of any county in the state.[1]

In Mississippi the board of supervisors of each county must transmit to the state tax commission by September 1st of each year two copies of the recapitulation of their assessment, on forms prescribe by the tax commission. The action thereon is outlined in the law and is more or less the usual procedure in states falling into the second category:

The state tax commission shall examine such forms and within thirty days after the receipt of the recapitulations from all counties, the chairman of the state tax commission shall send by mail to the board of supervisors instructions in accordance with the provisions of chapter 98 of the laws of 1916 as to what percentage shall be added to or taken from the assessments of the various classes of property on the roll or rolls in order to establish an equitable assessment throughout the state.[2]

The broader scope of power granted the administrative agencies in the third group of states finds full expression in the provision in Kansas which declares that:

The tax commission shall constitute a state board of equaliza-

Digest 1921, §9790; Colo. Annot. Code 1923, §§6306, 6343; Ind. Annot. Stat. 1926, §14229; Kan. Rev. Stat. 1923, §79-1409; Ky. Stat. 1922, §4128-23; La. Acts 1916, amended 1918, no. 211, §16; Mich. Comp. Laws 1915, §4151; Minn. Gen. Stat. 1923, §2366; Mont. Acts 1923, ch. 3, §8; N. J. Comp. Stat., Supple. 1924, §3475-208; N. M. Laws 1915, ch. 54, §5; N. C. Cons. Stat. 1919, §7889; Ohio Code 1926, §5610; S. C. Code 1922, §368; S. D. Rev. Code 1919, §6735; Utah Comp. Laws 1917, §5926; Wash. Comp. Stat. 1922, §11088; Wyo. Comp. Stat. 1920, §2810.

[1] Ark. Digest 1921, §9790.

[2] Miss. Laws 1920, ch. 323, §9.

tion and shall equalize the valuation and assessment of property throughout the state; and shall have power to equalize the assessments of all property in the state between persons, firms or corporations of the same assessment district, between cities and townships of the same county, and between different counties of the state, and the property assessed by the commission in the first instance. Whenever the valuation of any taxing district whether it be county, township, city, school district or otherwise, is changed by the state board of equalization, the officers of such taxing districts who have authority to levy taxes are required to use the valuations so fixed by the state board as a basis for making their levies for all purposes.[1]

The question should be raised at this point, just how much supervision is exercised under the provisions of these various statutes? It must be admitted that, in those states in which the power of review is confined to the equalization of the aggregate valuations of the various counties, the supervision thus maintained is limited. Indeed, it amounts to little more than a check on any attempt on the part of a municipality to evade its just share of state taxes. And even where the state supervising agency may equalize aggregate valuations between units within the various counties, the added power merely enables the state to see to it that no municipality escapes its due share of the county tax. In those states, however, in which the administrative authorities are permitted to make adjustments between the various classes of property, the scope of the control thus exercised is considerably extended, for not only does it become possible for the state officials to see to it that no class or type of property escapes its due portion of state taxation, but, since their action is binding for local assessment purposes as well, it becomes impossible for any class of property to escape its due share of municipal taxation. The jurisdictions which per-

[1] Kans. Rev. Stat. 1923, §11304.

mit the state boards to adjudicate between individual pieces of property grant them all the power of control contained in the mechanism.

The necessity for some such supervision becomes apparent from even a cursory perusal of the tax commission reports. An investigation of property valuations throughout the state of West Virginia, for example, revealed the fact that in some localities property was assessed at approximately 23 per cent of its real value, whereas in others it was assessed as high as 87 per cent.[1] A similar investigation in Indiana disclosed an almost identical situation. In at least three counties the average assessments were 25 per cent or even less of the true value, whereas in three other counties the assessments averaged over 75 per cent. Certain localities in both states, consequently, were paying three times as much of the state tax in proportion to the value of their property as were certain other localities. Similar discrepancies would probably develop in every state in the Union were the local assessing officers subject to no control.

Not only are glaring inequalities between different units of government thus revealed, but equally gross are the discriminations between various classes of property which come to light. The investigation in Indiana referred to above also brought out the fact that in one case property was being assessed at but 14.7 per cent of its true value, whereas in another case the assessments ran as high as 146 per cent of the value of the property; this is but another way of saying that one group of tax payers paid ten times as much taxes in proportion to the value of their property as did another group having its money invested in a different class of property. It was also shown in this same report that the high assessments as a rule were on the smaller properties; in fact,

1 *West Virginia State Tax Commissioner, Report 1920-22*, p. 6; *cf.* also National Institute of Public Administration, 1927, *Organization-Management of the State Government of Virginia.*

there seemed to be an inverse ratio between the value of the property and the rate of valuation thereof.[1]

Glimpses of the mechanism of review in operation may be caught from the tax commissions' reports. So numerous are the variations in the details of procedure, however, that one hesitates to describe the practice in any one state lest the impression be created that the procedure thus described is universal or even general. Nevertheless, only through the medium of specific illustrations is it possible to give a sense of the operating mechanism.[2] The procedure in Kansas, which is outlined rather realistically in a letter of instructions to county clerks, is as nearly typical as it is possible to find and may consequently serve as an example.

On Wednesday, July 13, 1921, at nine o'clock a. m., the members of the tax commission will organize as the state board of equalization in order to equalize for the year 1921 the assessment of all property in the state. . . . All county officers and all citizens of the respective counties who may desire to present to the board requests or petitions concerning the state equalization of 1921 may do so on the days hereinafter assigned for hearing. . . . The counties coming on the respective days will be heard in order of their appearance. As the time of the board will be limited, it is suggested that the county officers and all others having business or other matters to present shall come prepared to make their showing as briefly as possible, and that they come with all facts and figures reduced to writing as near as may be, which they intend to submit in support of their side of any question at issue. Appeals from a county will be as-

[1] *Indiana Tax Commission, Report 1916*, p. vi.

[2] Three distinct variations in the method by which the machinery of review is set in action have been developed. In Michigan the protest of a local unit of government is necessary to call items up for review; in New Jersey the complaint of an individual or corporation is requisite; elsewhere the assessment rolls go up to the state commission for scrutiny and revision automatically.

signed for hearing on one or other of the days named for the hearing of such county. The county clerks are expected to arrange with the appellants from their respective counties for a hearing of appeals on one or other of the days designated for the appearance of the county authorities.[1]

Among the appeals before the commission at this particular hearing was one from J. R. Brown of Mound City protesting the action of the county board of equalization of Cherokee County. The record is interesting.

On March 1, 1920, the applicant was the owner of lots 1, 2 and 3, block 1, Mauns addition to Baxter Springs, Kansas, which property was assessed by the deputy assessor at $450 and equalized by the county and state boards of equalization in session in 1920 at the sum of $445. The applicant also owned lots 12, 13, and 14, block 1, in the same addition to Baxter Springs, which were assessed by the deputy assessor for the lots at $600, and improvements thereon $1,400, in all $2,000. In the equalization of said assessments made by the county and state boards in 1920 the assessment as made was for the lots $660 and for the improvements $1,300, making $1,960 as the equalized assessment of the property for the year 1920. The applicant, considering the property to have been equalized in 1920 at more than it was worth on March 1, 1920, appeared before the county board of equalization in said county at its session for equalizing purposes in 1921, and the county assessor sitting jointly with the board, for the purpose of showing that the property was assessed in 1920 at more than it was worth on March 1, 1920. The said authorities refused to entertain his proposition, and hence the appeal to the state board. At the hearing the appellant did not appear in person, but submitted his proposition upon documentary evidence. The appeal was not opposed by the county authorities. When the appeal was heard other appeals of like character were also heard, and with respect to these appeals there was documentary evidence in the form of affidavits

1 *Kansas Tax Commission, Report 1920-22*, p. 119.

by witnesses shown to have expert knowledge of the value of real estate in Baxter Springs in 1920. After considering all the evidence introduced and other information available, the conclusion is that the appeal should be sustained because it is held that the property was assessed in 1920 at more than it was then worth, and there is a statute that authorizes in such cases a reduction of the assessment as the tax basis for the ensuing tax year to what the property was actually worth on March 1, 1920, when the property was last assessed. It is considered that the assessment for the year 1921 as equalized by this board should be as follows: Lots 1, 2 and 3, block 1, Mauns addition, $445; Lots 12, 13 and 14, block 1, same addition, exclusive of improvements, $660, the improvements $880, thus making the equalized assessment of both properties as above indicated to amount to $1,905 which is held to have been the worth of the two properties on March 1, 1920. As the property was equalized in 1920 at $2,405 and as the same amount appears on the assessment and tax rolls for 1921, the reduction made by this equalization from the equalization made is $500. It is, therefore, by the state board of equalization this 15th day of July, 1921, ordered; that the county clerk of the county of Cherokee be and hereby is directed to change the assessed value of the said two properties for the year 1921 upon the assessment and tax rolls of the county as above set forth.[1]

These illustrations, however, typify merely one mode of procedure. Action relative to the equalization of values between various classes of property may be taken—in fact, frequently is taken—on the basis of the abstracts presented by the county assessors and data collected by the state inspectors rather than upon individual complaint. A careful study of the information thus presented reveals at least the grosser inequalities. Something is obviously wrong, for example, if Ford cars of the same vintage are assessed at $50 in one jurisdiction and $350 in another. Which valua-

[1] *Kansas Tax Commission, Report 1920-22*, p. 131.

tion is correct may be a moot question, but that the value should be roughly the same in both jurisdictions may be taken for granted. Consequently, it is not unusual to see resolutions rectifying these inequities on the pages of reports of proceedings of boards of equalization. In the *Report of the Proceedings of the Board of Equalization of Idaho for 1923,* for example, the following motions appear:

Moved, seconded and carried that the valuation of business lots for the year 1923, as shown by the abstracts of the respective counties, be increased as follows, to wit: Ada county, 2 per cent; Bannock county, 5 per cent; Bear Lake county, 10 per cent; Blaine county, 10 per cent; Fremont county, 5 per cent; Gooding county, 10 per cent; Jefferson county, 5 per cent; Latah county, 5 per cent; Lewis county, 10 per cent; Madison county, 10 per cent; Shoshone county, 5 per cent.

Moved, seconded and unanimously carried that the valuation of business lots in Canyon county, as shown by the abstract for the year 1923, be decreased 5 per cent.

Moved, and seconded, that the valuation of business lots in the other counties in the state, as shown by the abstracts for 1923, be approved as reported. Motion carried.[1]

[1] *Proceedings of the Board of Equalization of Idaho 1923,* p. 10. It is impossible, of course, to fathom the processes of thought which lead the boards of equalization to these decisions. In all probability, in the overwhelming majority of cases the motivating force is the desire for fair play. And yet considerable evidence may be amassed to indicate that such is not always the fact. At a recent conference on taxation in the state of New York, a former tax commissioner frankly stated that very frequently in the case of his commission other forces and influences had been the dominating ones. "During the time that I was a member of the state tax commission, and so *ex officio* a member of the state board of equalization," he said, "I never signed an equalization table; and I am frank, because I made no matter of it at the time—that I did not believe that the equalization table that was finally voted for by the majority of the members of the state board of equalization was a true and accurate table. Some members of the state board of equalization, like members of the boards of supervisors, have a weakness for their friends at home, notwithstanding the fact that we had established a bureau

Closely allied to the control thus established is that maintained through the mechanism of administrative *orders*. These orders should be distinguished from those issued by state boards of equalization sitting as reviewing bodies, for they are subject to no such rigorous rules of procedure as are these latter, nor, indeed, need they be so confined in the scope of their objectives. In fact, in three states the supervising officials are empowered to issue orders to the local assessors on all matters generally related to the duties of their office.[1] " Whenever it appears to the commission," runs the law of Massachusetts, " that the property or any part thereof in any town is not valued for taxation in accordance with law, and that such failure to comply with the law is the result of inadequate methods in keeping the records of valuation or ownership of property, or is due to failure on the part of its assessors or any of them properly to examine the records of registry of deeds and probate court, or to make use of the information required to be furnished to assessors by the commissioner, he shall forthwith direct said assessors to adopt such methods of keeping their records or to make such examination of the records of the registry of deeds and probate courts, or to make use of the information that he has furnished them, as he deems necessary."

For the most part, the use of the mechanism has been

of local assessments and equalization in the state tax department charged with the duty of getting the information that we required in order to act intelligently on state equalization. So somewhat regardless of the information that was brought in, some of the members of the state board given to the weakness, that very human weakness, I admit—of thinking of their friends at home—would suggest rates for their counties for which I individually could see no justification, in the light of the information gathered by the local assessment bureau of the state tax department. For that reason I never signed an equalization table while I was a member of the state board of equalization." *State Conference on Taxation in the State of New York 1921-24*, pp. 83-4.

[1] Colo. Annot. Stat. 1923, §6306; Mass. Gen. Laws, ch. 58, §4; Ohio Gen. Code 1926, §5624-12.

confined to the reassessment of property.[1] But even in this limited form the power of supervision thus given to the state officials is sweeping. Indeed, it enables them to adjust any and all inequalities in valuation between different classes of property and between individual pieces. In some respects the grant of authority thus bestowed is broader than that contained in the mechanism of review, for no limitations whatever are placed upon the time of taking such action or the procedure in connection therewith. In certain cases, as we have already discovered, this is not true of the former mechanism.

Illustrative of the law upon this point and also of the procedure which may be followed is the detailed provision to be found in the code of Kansas.

Whenever upon complaint made to the tax commission by the county assessor or by any deputy assessor, or by the board of county commissioners of any county and a summary hearing in that behalf had, it shall be made to appear satisfactorily to the

[1] Ala. Gen. Laws 1923, no. 172, §71; Ariz. Rev. Stat. 1913, §4829; Ark. Digest 1921, §9790; Ill. Laws 1919, p. 718, §3; Kan. Rev. Stat. 1923, §79-1404; Ky. Stat. 1922, §4128-23; La. Acts of 1916, amended 1918, no. 211, §10; Maine Laws 1917, ch. 25; Md. Code 1924, art. 81, §250; Mich. Comp. Laws 1915, §4151; Minn. Gen. Stat. 1923, §2365; Miss. Annot. Code 1917, §7762; Mo. Rev. Stat. 1919, §12848; Mont. Acts 1923, ch. 3, §10; Neb. Comp. Stat. 1922, §5830; Nev. Rev. Laws 1912, §3; N. H. Public Laws, 1926, ch. 68, §12; N. J. Comp. Stat. Supple. 1924, §3474-208; N. M. Laws 1915, ch. 54, §8; N. Y. Cons. Laws 1918, ch. LX, §173a (1); N. C. Cons. Stat. 1919, §7883; Ohio Gen. Code 1926, §5624-4 (2); S. C. Code 1922, §365; S. D. Rev. Code 1919, §6587; Vt. Gen. Laws 1917, §843; Wash. Session Laws 1925, ch. 18, §5; W. Va. Annot. Code 1923, ch. 29, §12; Wis. Stat. 1923, §70.64.

(1) In New York the state administrative officials are compelled to apply to a court for such order. " In practice this remedy has never been successfully invoked. As related to assessment of individual parcels of real property, the action of the local assessor is finally subject to review by the court on certiorari." (letter from state official).

(2) The tax commission is empowered by this action to revise the lists of exempted property.

commission that the assessment of property in any assessment district in such county is not in substantial compliance with law, and that the interest of the public will be promoted by a re-assessment of such property, said commission shall have author-ity in its discretion, to order a reassessment of all or any part of the taxable property in such district to be made by one or more persons, to be appointed by the commission for that pur-pose, the expense of any such reassessment to be borne by the county in which is situated the district to be reassessed; *Pro-vided,* That the commission may, upon its own motion, order any such reassessment if it shall clearly appear that the public will be benefitted thereby. Due notice of the time and place fixed for a hearing upon any complaint made as aforesaid shall be mailed, at least eight days before the time fixed for the hearing, to the city clerk if the taxing district be a city, and if it be a township then to the township clerk. The person or persons so appointed to make such reassessment shall qualify without delay by severally taking and subscribing an oath or affirmation to support the constitution of the United States and the constitu-tion of the state of Kansas, and to faithfully perform the duties imposed by any such order of reassessment to the best of their ability, and shall file the same with the tax commission. Any person or persons so appointed to reassess any district shall have all the power and authority given by law to deputy assessors, and shall perform all the duties and be subject to all restrictions and penalties imposed by law upon deputy assessors. They shall have access to all public records and files which may be needful or serviceable in the performance of the duty imposed, and while engaged in such duty shall be entitled to have the custody and possession of the assessment roll containing the original assess-ment in such district and all property and other statements and memoranda relative thereto. A blank assessment roll and all property statements and other blank forms needful for the purpose of such reassessment shall be furnished by the county clerk, at the expense of the county. Any such reassessment shall, when completed, be treated exactly as an original assess-ment and be subject to equalization by the county board and to such appeals from the action of any officer having to do with said assessments as are now provided by law in the case of original assessments.[1]

Of a somewhat different character is the supervision maintained in a number of jurisdictions through the power of enacting *ordinances*. In a number of states this grant of authority is confined merely to prescribing the set-up of books, forms of reports and so forth;[2] in others it is all-inclusive.[3] Typical of the statutes enabling the state

[1] *Kansas Rev. Stat. 1923*, §79-1413.

[2] Ala. Gen. Laws 1923, no. 172, §69; Ariz. Rev. Stat. 1913, §4826; Ark. Digest 1921, §9788; Cal. Pol. Code 1923, §3692; Colo. Annot. Stat. 1923, §6306; Conn. Gen. Stat. 1918, §1319; Ill. Gen. Revenue Act, §85; Ind. Annot. Stat. 1926, §14217; Iowa Code 1924, §7119; Kan. Rev. Stat. 1923, §79-1401; Ky. Stat. 1922, §4114-i12; La. Acts 1916, amended 1918, no. 211, §10; Md. Code 1924, art. 81, §249; Mass. Gen. Laws, ch. 58, §1; Mich. Comp. Laws 1915, §4149; Minn. Gen. Stat. 1923, §2364; Miss. Annot. Code 1917, §7769fi; Mo. Rev. Stat. 1919, §12847; Mont. Acts 1923, ch. 3, §8; Neb. Comp. Stat. 1922, §5829; Nev. Rev. Laws 1912, §3; N. H. Public Laws 1926, ch. 68, §11; N. J. Comp. Stat. 1910, §5104-22; N. M. Laws 1915, ch. 54, §9; N. Y. Cons. Laws 1918, ch. LX, §171; N. C. Cons. Stat. 1919, §7883; Ohio Gen. Code 1926, §5623; Ore. Laws 1920, §4187 (1); S. C. Code 1922, §343; S. D. Rev. Code 1919, §6587; Utah Comp. Laws 1917, §§5879, 5909; Vt. Gen. Laws 1917, §676; Va. Acts 1926, ch. 147, §4; Wash. Comp. Stat. 1922, §11088; W. Va. Annot. Code 1923, ch. 29, §2; Wis. Stat. 1925, §70.05.

(1) " The tax commission may also prescribe forms used in assessment and taxation but no power has been delegated to it to compel the adoption of such prescribed forms." (letter from state official).

[3] Ala. Gen. Laws 1923, no. 172, §69; Ariz. Rev. Stat. 1913, §4827; Ark. Digest 1921, §9788; Cal. Pol. Code 1923, §3692; Colo. Annot. Stat. 1923, §6306; Idaho Comp. Stat. 1919, §3167 (1); Ill. Laws 1919, p. 718, §2; Kan. Rev. Stat. 1923, §79-1401; La. Acts 1916, amended 1918, no. 211, §10; Md. Code 1924, art. 81, §249; Mont. Acts 1923, ch. 3, §8; Nev. Rev. Laws 1912, §3; N. H. Public Laws 1926, ch. 68, §11; N. M. Laws 1921, ch. 133, §507; N. Y. Cons. Laws 1918, ch. LX, §171; Ohio Gen. Code 1926, §5624; Ore. Laws 1920, §4187; S. C. Code 1922, §365; Utah Comp. Laws 1917, §5983; Wash. Session Laws 1925, ch. 18, §5.

(1) The rules enacted by the Idaho board must be confined to the process of equalization rather than inclusive of the whole scope of tax activity.

agencies to make use of the mechanism for the control of records and reports is that of Illinois which specifically empowers the state tax commissioner to " prescribe or approve the forms of blanks for schedule returns, reports, complaints, notices and other documents, files and records authorized or required by the provisions of law relating to the assessment of property, or by any rule and regulation of the commission." [1]   A later paragraph in the Illinois code empowers the tax commission " to prescribe rules and regulations for local assessment officers relative to the assessment of property for taxation, which general rules and regulations shall be binding upon all local assessment officers and shall be obeyed by them respectively until reversed, annulled or modified by a court of competent jurisdiction." [2]

It is, of course, difficult to discover the actual procedure followed by the state supervising authorities in the enactment of these ordinances. The method probably varies from state to state and from ordinance to ordinance. The more technical and detailed ordinances are presumably drawn up by the technical men in the employ of the tax commission, and upon their recommendation adopted by the commission or board of equalization. Those of a more general character may possibly be the product of the tax commission's deliberations with or without the aid of specialists.

The control which the state tax commissions exercise over the tax system through the mechanism of *state appointment* is surprisingly small, particularly so in view of the widespread dissatisfaction with our present system of locally elected tax assessors and other local tax officials.[3]   To it, with its short terms and political intrigues, more than to any other

[1] Illinois Laws 1919, p. 719.

[2] *Ibid.*

[3] Del. Rev. Code 1915, §1104; La. Act 231, 1920; Md. Code 1924, art. 81, §250; S. C. Code 1922, §433; W. Va. Code 1923, ch. 29, §95.

single factor, the shortcomings of our tax administration have been justly attributed. The inevitable result of a system of locally elected assessors has been evasion and juggling. The office is not of sufficient importance nor is the pay attached to it sufficiently large to draw men of high caliber. " Not infrequently the place is given to someone simply because he needs it, or because he will do the work for less than anybody else, or because he will be an easy mark for influential tax dodgers. Men of this type soon discover that the surest way to remain long in office is to be easy and accommodating, and above all to keep the assessment of their district down to the lowest possible point." [1]

The number of variations in the degree of control thus exercised almost equals the number of jurisdictions making use of the process. In some states the mechanism is used in connection with assessing officials, in others in connection with boards of review. In South Carolina the valuation and assessment of property for taxation devolves upon township boards of assessors, and special boards of assessors for cities and towns. These are appointed every two years by the governor upon the recommendation of the majority of members of the general assembly from the respective counties. The county auditor who is also the chief supervising assessment official for the counties is appointed in a similar manner. In Maryland a supervisor of taxes for each county is appointed by the tax commission from a list of five names nominated by the county commissioners or, in the case of Baltimore, by the mayor of the city. Should any municipality in Delaware fail to elect a local assessor or should a vacancy occur for any other reason, the governor is empowered to fill the vacant office. In West Virginia the board of public works is empowered to select all local

---

[1] *Report of State Board of Taxation, Iowa 1923*, pp. 28-9; *cf.* also *State Conference on Taxation in the State of New York, 1921-24*, pp. 83-4.

boards of review. The process in Louisiana is somewhat more complicated. The police jury in each parish elects two citizens resident in the parish to the parish board of equalization; the third member, however, is selected by the state tax commission. Should any police jury fail or refuse to select the two members of the board referred to, the governor is then empowered and directed to make the necessary appointments. Thus it appears that the number of variations in procedure actually does equal the number of jurisdictions making use of the mechanism. Needless to say, in those jurisdictions in which the state authorities have been granted the right to order the re-assessment of local property the new appraisers are state-appointed.

The mechanism of state administrative *removal* is employed in only eight jurisdictions in even the slightest degree.[1] The governor of Colorado may, upon charges by the tax commission after a hearing, remove any local assessor from office if convinced that the assessor has wilfully omitted to assess taxable property, or failed to assess it at its true value. Similar powers appear to have been granted to administrative officials in Indiana and Nebraska. In Maryland, this power is confined in its operation to the supervisors of assessors; in South Carolina, to the county auditors; and in Vermont, to boards of appraisers appointed by the commissioners of taxes in appeal cases. No limitation whatever has been placed upon the authority of the governor in Minnesota, who is empowered to suspend or remove from office any official charged with financial duties when it has been made to appear to him that such official is guilty of malfeasance in the performance of his public duties.

Whether the task imposed upon state administrative offi-

[1] Colo. Annot. Stat. 1923, §6346; Ind. Annot. Stat. 1926, §14174; Md. Code 1924, art. 81, §250; Minn. Gen. Stat. 1923, §6954; Neb. Comp. Stat. 1922, §5965; S. C. Code 1922, §434; Vt. Gen. Laws 1917, §843; W. Va. Annot. Code 1923, ch. 29, §95.

cials of evaluating the property of common carriers and other corporations doing business in various portions of a state, and of apportioning the value thereof among the various units of government for local taxation, should be classed as administrative supervision, is perhaps debatable; nevertheless, passing mention of the procedure may at least be made.[1]

Thus it appears that in a number of states the degree of control by the state administrative authorities over the assessment of municipal taxes is practically nil.[2] In others it is confined to the task of making sure that each municipality bears its fair burden of the state and county tax.[3] In still others, state boards of review or similar bodies may actually make adjustments in the municipal assessment lists in that they are empowered to equalize values between different classes of property throughout the state both within and without the municipal taxing units.[4] It is

---

[1] Ala. Gen. Laws 1923, no. 172; Ariz. Rev. Stat. 1913, §4829; Ark. Digest 1921, §9880; Cal. Pol. Code 1923, §3664; Colo. Annot. Stat. 1923, §6339; Ga. Annot. Code 1917, §1023; Idaho Comp. Stat. 1919, §3179; Ill. Laws 1919, p. 718, §2; Ind. Annot. Stat. 1926, §14131; Iowa Code 1924, §§7038, 7085; Kan. Rev. Stat. 1923, §§79-605, 79-709; Ky. Stat. 1922, §4114-i11; La. Acts 1917, no 9; Maine Rev. Stat. 1916, ch. 9, §37; Md. Code 1924, art. 81, §167; Mass. Gen. Laws, ch. 58, §18; Mich. Comp. Laws 1915, §4226; Minn. Gen. Stat. 1923, §2254; Miss. Annot. Code 1917, §7769-o; Mo. Rev. Stat. 1919, §13012; Mont. Acts 1923, ch. 3, §8; Neb. Comp. Stat. 1922, §5847; Nev. Rev. Laws 1912, §5; N. H. Public Laws 1926, ch. 69, §33; N. J. Comp. Stat. Supple. 1924, §3547-208-447d; N. M. Laws 1915, ch. 54, §4; N. Y. Cons. Laws Supple. 1922, ch. 209, §40; N. C. Cons. Stat. 1919, §7925; Ohio Gen. Code 1926, §§5430, 5446; Okla. Comp. Stat. 1921, §9643; Ore. Laws 1920, §4206; S. D. Rev. Code 1919, §6602; Tenn. Code Supple. 1920, §856a-58; Utah Comp. Laws 1917, §5923; Vt. Gen. Laws 1918, §993; Va. Acts 1926, ch. 147, §2208; Wash. Comp. Stat. 1922, §11170; W. Va. Annot. Code 1923, ch. 29, §95; Wis. Stat. 1925, §76.28; Wyo. Comp. Stat. 1920, §2814.

[2] Delaware, Florida, Georgia, Kentucky, Maine, North Dakota, Pennsylvania, Rhode Island, Tennessee and Texas.

[3] Connecticut, Georgia and Oregon.

[4] California, Idaho, Iowa, Oklahoma.

in the remaining states, however, that real supervision is maintained.[1] Not only are the administrative officials empowered to exercise the mechanisms of control used in the states indicated above, but they are also empowered to make such adjustments between individual pieces of property as they see fit, either through the process of equalization or through the right to reassess.

MUNICIPAL ACCOUNTS

Second in the extent of its geographic application in the field of finance is the supervision which is exercised over local accounts. To this end the power of audit or *inspection* is granted the supervising agencies in thirty-five states.[2] Three variations appear in these grants of authority. In some states all municipal accounts are subject to state examination at any time;[3] in others only certain specified

[1] Alabama, Arizona, Arkansas, Colorado, Illinois, Indiana, Kansas, Kentucky, Louisiana, Maine, Maryland, Massachusetts, Michigan, Minnesota, Mississippi, Missouri, Montana, Nebraska, Nevada, New Hampshire, New Jersey, New Mexico, New York, North Carolina, Ohio, South Carolina, South Dakota, Utah, Vermont, Virginia, Washington, West Virginia, Wisconsin, Wyoming.

[2] Ala. Gen. Laws 1923, §736; Ariz. Rev. Stat. 1913, p. 910; Cal. Pol. Code 1923, §689; Conn. Laws 1925, ch. 109; Del. Rev. Code 1915, §2311; Fla. Rev. Stat. 1920, §1956; Ga. Annot. Code 1914, §1565; Idaho Comp. Stat. 1919, §285; Ind. Rev. Stat. 1926, §12642; Iowa Code 1924, §113; Ky. Stat. 1922, §4398a-3; La. Acts 1918, no. 109, §7; Maine Laws 1923, ch. 161, §1; Md. Code 1924, art. 81, §241; Mass. Gen. Laws, ch. 44, §40; Mich. Comp. Laws 1915, §260-2518; Minn. Gen. Stat. 1923, §3279; Miss. Acts 1924, ch. 325, §8; Mo. Rev. Stat. §13302; Mont. Rev. Code 1921, §215; Neb. Comp. Stat. 1922, §4975; Nev. Rev. Laws 1912, §983; N. J. Public Laws 1918, ch. 267, 1921, ch. 105, §3; N. M. Laws 1921, ch. 186, §4; N. Y. Cons. Laws 1918, p. 3266, §33; Ohio Gen. Code 1926, §274; R. I. Laws 1926, ch. 780; S. D. Rev. Code 1919, §6901; Tex. Civil. Stat. 1914, §4510; Utah Code 1917, §4519; Vt. Gen. Laws 1917, §185-21c; Va. Laws 1926, pp. 902-5; Wash. Comp. Stat. 1922, §9958; Wis. Stat. 1919, §1087-39; Wyo. Comp. Stat. 1920, §173.

[3] Cal. Pol. Code 1923, §689; Conn. Laws 1925, ch. 109; Fla. Rev. Stat. 1920, §1956; Idaho Comp. Stat. 1919, §285; (1) Ind. Rev. Stat. 1920,

phases of municipal activity are under such control;[1] in still others state audits may be conducted only upon invitation of a municipality or a group of residents therein.[2] Typical of the statutory authorizations in the first group of states are those of Florida and Indiana. In the former the governor is empowered to authorize and direct the comptroller to examine into the financial affairs of any city in the state. Indeed, should twenty per cent or more of the tax-paying electors of any municipality petition him to do so, such action on his part becomes obligatory. In either event a thorough examination must be made into the financial condition and resources of the municipality indicated, with the view of discovering both the conformity of administrative practice with the law and also the methods

§12642; Iowa Code 1924, §113; La. Acts 1918, no. 109, §7; (2) Md. Code 1924, art. 81, §241; Minn. Gen. Stat. 1923, §3279; Miss. Acts 1924, ch. 325, §8; Mont. Rev. Code 1921, §215; (3) Neb. Comp. Stat. 1922, §4975; Nev. Rev. Laws 1912, §983; (4) N. J. 1918, ch. 267, 1921, ch. 105, §3; N. M. Laws 1921, ch. 186, §4; N. Y. Cons. Laws 1918, p. 3266, §33; Ohio Code 1926, §274; Va. Laws 1926, pp. 902-5; Wash. Comp. Stat. 1922, §9958; Wyo. Comp. Stat. 1920, §173.

(1) The state authorities in Indiana may investigate the actual work to see if it is according to contract, if so petitioned by twenty-five tax payers resident in the city.

(2) This act seems to be applicable only to Baltimore.

(3) This act appears to be applicable to the metropolitan city in each county.

(4) This is not the regular procedure, but it may be made use of if the commissioner believes it necessary. The regular audit is made by accountants who are registered at the bureau of municipal accounts.

[1] Ala. Rev. Stat. 1920, §1956; Ariz. Rev. Stat. 1913, p. 910; Del. School Laws 1921, p. 511; Ga. Annot. Code 1914, §1565; Ky. Stat. 1922, §4398a-3; Tex. Civil Stat. 1914, §4510; Utah Code 1917, §4519; Vt. Gen. Laws 1917, §185-21c.

[2] Maine Laws 1923, ch. 161, §1; Mich. Comp. Laws 1915, §§274, 2518; Minn. Gen. Stat. 1923, §3286; (1) Mo. Rev. Stat. 1919, §13302; R. I. Laws 1926, ch. 780; S. D. Rev. Code 1919, §6901; Wis. Stat. 1919, §1087-39.

(1) This act appears to the applicable only to St. Louis.

and accuracy of the municipality's accounts. The initiative in Indiana likewise rests with the state authorities who may at any time enter any office of a city or town and examine all books therein. If such examination should disclose malfeasance, misfeasance or nonfeasance in office on the part of any officer or employee, the matter, according to the law, must be brought to the immediate attention of the governor, who in turn is expected to direct the attorney general to institute action.

In Alabama and Delaware only that portion of municipal activity which is subsidized by the state is subject to state audit; in Arizona, Georgia, Kentucky, Texas, Utah and Vermont only the work of the local departments of education receives any attention whatever.

South Dakota is more or less typical of those jurisdictions in which state audit may take place only upon local invitation. The state supervising authorities are empowered to examine the books and accounts of a municipality *only* when called upon to do so by the presiding officer thereof or upon the petition of twenty per cent of the resident tax payers.[1]

Some of the results of this inspection have been interesting indeed. Discrepancies in accounts to the detriment of the municipality were found, for example, in twenty out of fifty analyses of municipal accounts made in the state of New York during 1916. In forty-one municipalities included in an analysis of the objects or purposes of expenditure, it was found that approximately $375,000 had been illegally expended.[2] The state officials in Indiana estimate

[1] The frequency with which these audits must be made likewise varies from state to state. In Minnesota an audit must be made every year; in Iowa, every two years; in New York whenever and wherever the supervising authorities deem such an undertaking necessary.

[2] N. Y. Assembly Document, 140th Session, 1917, vol. 26, nos. 61-2. *Special Report on Municipal Accounts by the State Comptroller transmitted to the Legislature April 16, 1917.*

the total savings to the state effected through state audit at approximately $1,000,000. They have not, however, interpreted their function as the mere audit of books, but have attempted to check up on all objects of expenditure to see that full value has been received.[1] Even more impressive have been the results in Ohio.[2]

In addition to the supervision thus maintained, the state agencies exercise a measure of control in a number of jurisdictions through the medium of *aiding* in the installation of accounting systems.[3] Some conception of the potentialities of the process may, perhaps, be obtained from the history of the municipal accounting department in Wisconsin which was established in 1911, and has been rendering auditing and accounting service ever since. "Although the audit and installation service rendered by the tax commission is on a voluntary basis, it now requires a staff of fifteen field accountants to handle the applications which are received. The uniform system of accounts designed by the tax commission has now been installed in fifty-seven of the seventy-one counties and in seventy-two of the one hundred thirty-eight cities. In the case of towns and villages, it is almost impossible to keep accurate account of the number using the system prescribed by this office. In many instances the forms are procured from the manufacturing stationers and installed without formal application to the tax commissioner."[4]

More drastic in its action is the control exercised by the

[1] *Special Report of State Board of Accounts of Indiana*, 1916, p. 6.

[2] See *National Municipal Review, May 1923*, Wylie Kilpatrick, "State Supervision of Municipal Accounts".

[3] Iowa Code 1924, §111; La. Acts 1918, no. 109, §5; Maine Laws 1923, ch. 161, §2; Mass. Gen. Laws, ch. 44. §37; Minn. Gen. Stat. 1923, §3279; Miss. Acts 1924, ch. 325, §3; N. C. Session Laws 1917, ch. 136, sub. ch. 14, §22; N. D. Code 1913, §2088-6.

[4] *Wisconsin Tax Commission, Report 1916*, p. 154.

administrative authorities in twenty states through the process of *ordinance-making*.[1] An example of the statutory provisions conveying this grant of authority to the supervising officials is found in the code of Indiana. It provides that " the state board of accountants shall formulate, prescribe and install a system of accounting and reporting in conformity with the provisions of this act, which shall be uniform for every public officer and every public account of the same class and shall exhibit true accounts and detailed statements of funds collected, received and expended for or on account of the public, for any and every purpose whatever." [2] Another variation, to be found in the Wyoming code, provides that " it shall be the duty of the state examiner to assume and exercise a constant supervision over the books and financial accounts of the several municipal corporations. He shall prescribe and enforce correct methods of keeping the financial accounts of said institutions and shall instruct the proper officers thereof in the due performance of their duties." [3]

[1] Cal. Pol. Code 1923, §687; Colo. Public Acts Spec. Sess. 1918-19, ch. 292; Idaho Comp. Stat. 1919, §285; Ind. Rev. Stat. 1926, §12637; Iowa Code 1924, §111; Kan. Rev. Stat. 1923, §79-1404; (1) Maine Laws 1923, ch. 161, §1; Md. Code 1924, art. 81, §241; (1) Mass. Gen. Laws, ch. 44, §35, ch. 42, §4; (1) Mich. Comp. Laws 1915, §274-2518, Acts 1925, no. 38; Minn. Gen. Stat. 1923, §§3279, 3280; Miss. Acts 1924, ch. 325, §3; (1) (2) Mo. Rev. Stat. 1919, §13302; (3) Neb. Comp. Stat. 1922, §4975; N. H. Public Laws 1926, ch. 68, §22; N. Y. Cons. Laws 1918, p. 3267, §36; Ohio Gen. Code 1926, §277; S. D. Rev. Code 1919, §6897; Wash. Comp. Stat. 1922, §9952; (1) Stat. 1919, §1087-39; Wyo. Comp. Stat. 1920, §176.

(1) This act appears to be applicable only upon invitation of the municipality.

(2) This act appears to be applicable only to St. Louis.

(3) This act appears to be applicable only to the metropolitan city in each county.

[2] Ind. Laws 1911, §7546b.

[3] Wyo. Comp. Stat. 1920, §173.

In a few states this supervision is much more limited in character, in that the full sweep of municipal administration is not included within its scope.[1] Only those municipalities owning or operating a municipal utility in Michigan, for example, are under an obligation to adopt, install and keep a uniform system of accounts, and then it need merely relate to the operation of the utility.

In only one state is the power of *removal* used in this connection. The clause of the Minnesota law indicated above which empowers the governor to suspend or remove from office any official charged with financial duties when it has been made to appear to him that such officer has been delinquent in the performance of his duties naturally includes within its scope all officials having to do with municipal accounts.[2]

MUNICIPAL INDEBTEDNESS

Less widespread geographically, nevertheless exceedingly important, is the control which is exercised over municipal indebtedness.[3] In general two processes of supervision are

[1] Md. Code 1924, art. 81, §241 (all institutions receiving State aid); Mich. Acts 1925, no. 38 (utilities).

[2] Minn. Gen. Stat. 1923, §2210.

[3] Cal. Pol. Code 1923, §678, Stat. 1911, p. 595, 1921, p. 1208; Colo. Annot. Stat. 1923, §6692; Conn. Public Acts 1918-19, §1256; Idaho Session Laws 1921, ch. 171, 1925, ch. 188; Ind. Rev. Stat. 1926, §12639; Iowa Code 1919, §§127, 3662, 4359; Kan. Rev. Stat. 1923, §§10-107, 8, 9, 10, 11, 601; Mass. Gen. Laws, ch. 44, §§24, 28 (town notes); Mich. Public Acts 1925, no. 273, §8; Miss. Laws 1912, ch. 122, §1; Mo. Rev. Stat. 1919, §7762; Neb. Comp. Stat. 1922, §289; N. J. Laws 1917, chs. 154-156, Laws 1919, ch. 266; N. M. Laws 1925, ch. 131; N. C. Laws 1925, ch. 100; N. D. Code 1923, ch. 189; Okla. Comp. Stat. 1921, §4284; R. I. Laws 1926, §780; Tex. Rev. Stat. 1925, §709-716; Wash. Comp. Stat. 1922, §9955 (yearly report); W. Va. Annot. Code 1923, ch. 47a, §16; Wis. Stat. 1925, §67.02. In addition considerable information relative to municipal indebtedness is brought in by the inspectors from their examinations of local accounts. For a further discussion of the material contained in this section see Lane Lancaster, *State Supervision of Municipal Indebtedness*, Philadelphia (1923).

used — *reports* and administrative approval.   Twenty-one states all told maintain some system for the collection of information relative to municipal indebtedness.   The statutes concerned therewith seem to fall into three more or less distinct classes: those concerned merely with the accumulation of information; those in which the receipt of such information is a precursor to later action in connection with the levying of taxes; and finally, those in which reports are the necessary prelude to state approval or disapproval.

The reports required in the states in the first category are of two types, those primarily designed to elicit financial data, and those intended to secure information relative to legal proceedings.   In many cases, however, both purposes permeate the same statute.   Typical of the provisions of law intended to accomplish the first purpose is that of Kansas, which enjoins the municipal officials concerned to transmit to the state auditor a certified statement of the number of bonds, the amount and character thereof, when payable, where payable, and the purpose for which they were issued. Illustrative of the statutes designed to accumulate data relative to the legality of bond issues is that of Nebraska, which makes it mandatory upon the proper officials in all cities throughout the state to send to the auditor of public accounts a transcript of all proceedings involved previous to the issuance of the bonds together with the bonds themselves.

In at least four states, Missouri, Nebraska, New Jersey and North Carolina, the information thus acquired forms the basis on which the state auditor or other supervising official makes the necessary calculations as to the rate of tax levy necessary in the various municipalities to meet the obligations thus incurred.[1]   After being certified to the vari-

---

[1] Mo. Rev. Stat. 1919, §1065; Neb. Rev. Comp. Stat. 1922, §§391-392; N. J. Laws 1917, chs. 154, 155, 156, Laws 1918, ch. 266; N. C. Laws 1925, ch. 100.

ous municipalities, these figures become part of the local tax levy. In the case of New Jersey they constitute mandatory items in every municipal budget. In Missouri they are collected along with the state taxes.

In at least fifteen states these reports, in addition to being a source of information, are a necessary part of the process of approval.[1] For the most part the control thus exercised is confined to the validation of bond issues, that is, checking up on each issue for the purpose of seeing that the bonds have been authorized by and are issued in conformity with the constitution and laws of the state. In the majority of states maintaining this supervision the procedure is entirely administrative. Before any bond issued for a municipal purpose may be negotiated, it must first be presented to the attorney general or state auditor who shall certify on the bond that all the requirements of law have been complied with, if such be the case. Such action is final in the larger number of jurisdictions making use of this method of validation; in a few, however—Mississippi, Missouri, Oklahoma, Texas and West Virginia—an appeal from the decision of the supervising officer to the courts is permitted, providing the action is begun within the time specified by law.

In four states judicial action is immediately involved.[2] Whenever a municipality in Florida, for example, has authorized its governing body through a referendum to proceed

---

[1] Fla. Rev. Stat. 1920, §3296; Ga. Code 1914, §446; Ind. Rev. Stat. 1926, §14240; Iowa Code 1924, §366; Mass. Gen. Laws, ch. 44, §24; Mich. Acts 1925, no. 273, §9; Miss. Laws 1917, extra session, ch. 28; Mo. Rev. Stat. 1919, §1063; Neb. Comp. Stat. 1922, §298; N. Y. Cons. Laws 1918, ch. XXIV, §§22-29; N. C. Session Laws 1925, ch. 100; Okla. Comp. Stat. 1921, §4284; Tex. Rev. Stat. 1925, §§709-716; W. Va. Annot. Code 1923, ch. 47a, §16; Wis. Stat. 1925, §67.02.

[2] Fla. Rev. Stat. 1920, §§3296-3297; Ga. Code 1911, §§445-461, Laws 1920, no. 394; Mo. Rev. Stat. 1919, §§1063-1065 (Missouri has a combination of administrative registration and court action); N. Y. Cons. Laws 1918, ch. XXIV, §§22-29.

with the issuance of bonds, the municipal authorities must
notify the attorney general, who in turn must file a petition
in the circuit court in the name of the state challenging the
city to show cause why the bonds should be issued. Thus
a test case is immediately begun. Any citizen of the state
resident in the city may become a party to it. If the court
is satisfied with the legality of the issue, the bonds are
stamped " validated by court ". If any party to the proceedings is dissatisfied with the decision, an appeal may be
taken to a higher court.

Some differences of procedure exist in the three other
states, but in each case court validation is necessary to legal-
ize the issue.

An interesting combination of the two methods has been
worked out in Mississippi, which is summarized by Professor Lancaster as follows : " The Supreme Court is directed
to appoint a state's bond attorney who shall have the same
qualifications as the attorney general. The proceedings in
local issues are submitted to the bond attorney who then
files his opinion as to the legality of the proposed issue with
the clerk of the Chancery Court in the proper county. A
hearing may be demanded by any person in interest at which
the bond attorney must be present. At the conclusion of
the hearing the judge of the Chancery Court enters an order
in accordance with his findings. This order, if favorable,
validates the issue. Appeal is allowed to the Supreme
Court. The procedure outlined by this law, while not mandatory upon local authorities, seems to be much resorted to
in practice." [1]

Somewhat fuller sweep has been given the mechanism in
Arizona, Indiana, Iowa, Kansas and Nevada.[2] Should

[1] Lane Lancaster, *op. cit.*, p. 59.

[2] Ariz. Laws 1921, ch. 52; Ind. Rev. Stat. 1926, §14240; Iowa Code
1924, §366; Kan. Rev. Stat. 1923, §79-1940; Nev. Acts 1920-1921, ch.
217.

any municipality find it necessary to issue bonds or warrants for an emergency not contemplated in the annual budget or provided against in the annual tax levy, it must first obtain *permission* to do so from the state tax commission, and its decision is final, except in the case of Kansas where it may be overridden by the voters on referendum.   The situation is set forth very clearly in the Nevada statute which provides that " in case of great necessity or emergency, the governing board of any . . . . town or city by resolution reciting the character of such necessity or emergency may authorize a temporary loan, but such resolution shall not take effect until it has been approved by resolution adopted by the state board of revenue, and the resolution of the state board of revenue shall be recorded in the minutes of such city or town."

Even more stringent control is maintained in both Indiana and Iowa, where no municipal corporation may issue any bonds whatever without the consent and *approval* of the state board of tax commissioners if the issuance thereof is protested by ten or more taxpapers in the case of the former, by five or more, in the case of the latter.[1]

MUNICIPAL BUDGETS

Passing mention should be made of the fact that, if any city in Oklahoma or Iowa fails to levy adequate taxes to pay the interest on any bonds or coupons issued by them, or fails to create a sinking fund for the redemption thereof, it becomes the duty of the state administrative officers to meet the emergency.[2]   In Oklahoma the state auditor is directed to ascertain the amount of interest and sinking-fund allotment necessary for the period of the delinquency, and to

[1] Ind. Laws 1919, ch. 59, p. 19 *et seq.*; Iowa Budget Law 1924.

[2] Okla. Comp. Stat. 1921, §4275; Iowa Code 1924, §7181. An interesting development in this connection is the establishment of a state sinking fund in West Virginia which handles all municipal as well as all state money designed for the repayment of the public debt.

certify the same to the treasurer of the county in which the bonds or interest are due. He, in turn, must levy the taxes thus called for. Whenever any municipal corporation in Iowa, charged with the duty of levying a tax to pay any bonds or the interest thereon, fails to do so, the holder of the bonds may " after obtaining final judgment thereon, in addition to any other remedies he may have, file a transcript thereof with the auditor of state, taking his receipt therefor, and the same shall be registered in his office, and the state board of review at its regular annual session shall levy upon the taxable property of the city for which such bonds were issued a sufficient rate of taxation to realize the amount of interest due or becoming due on the bonds so filed, prior to the next levy, and the money arising from such levy shall be known as the bond fund and collected as part of the state tax, paid into the state treasury and placed to the credit of such city for payment of bonds and interest." [1]

In a sense the action of certification referred to heretofore falls into this same category, affecting as it does the contents of the local budgets in all cities with debts outstanding. This is particularly true in Missouri and New Jersey, where the action of the state authorities is final.

Somewhat more extensive is the control over municipal budgets which has been granted the state authorities in some six states. The mainstay of this supervision is the requirement of *approval*. In two jurisdictions its operation is confined to emergency situations, that is situations in which the municipal authorities deem it necessary to exceed the statutory limitation on the rate of levy; [2] in three, it includes all items in the municipal budgets, although in one its action is confined to a particular group of cities; in Iowa, it is confined to certain items in the local budgets.

[1] A similar procedure is followed in California with reference to counties and county securities. Pol. Code 1923, §§4088a, 3715.

[2] Colo. Laws 1913, pp. 560-561; Kan. Rev. Stat. 1923, §79-1942.

The procedure followed in the first two states very closely resembles that followed in obtaining state administrative approval for the issuance of emergency bonds described above. The municipality desirous of exceeding the tax limit must file its request, together with substantiating data relative to the existence of an emergency, with the state tax commission. The decision of the supervising authority in Kansas is final; in Colorado, however, the disapproval of the state board can be overcome by a three-fifths vote of a municipal electorate at a general election.

In Indiana, Iowa, Oregon and New Mexico the control vested in the hands of the state authorities is drastic. Its unusual character justifies detailed consideration.[1] In Indiana all items in all municipal budgets throughout the state may be brought under the jurisdiction of the state authorities through the protest of ten or more taxpayers resident in a municipality. The circumstances which attended the inauguration of this system are worthy of particular note.

In 1919 there was a very large increase in assessments as the result of a strenuous effort to bring assessments to full value. Before undertaking this work the state board asked for power to control levies so as to prevent, if possible, bankruptcy by large increases in taxes. There was such an insistent demand for public money and such large budgets were proposed that the state board used its powers and trimmed levies in practically every unit in the state. The use of this power created an intense feeling, consequently, on the part of the officers who were to spend the money, and at a special session of the legislature in 1920 all control over the levies was taken from the state board.

A modified form of control was provided for by permitting taxpayers to file objections to levies which might be established

[1] Ind. Laws 1919, p. 316; Oregon Budget Facts and Financial Statistics, Multnomah County, Oregon 1925, p. 15 *et seq.*; N. M. Laws 1921, ch. 133, §310-508; *cf.* Wylie Kilpatrick, *State Administrative Review of Local Budget Making*, New York, 1927.

by local officers, and upon the filing of such objections a hearing was to be held by the county councils in each county. In only two counties of the state was this provision taken advantage of. The local officers in many instances went the limit in making their levies, and an average increase of about fifty per cent in the amount of public revenue was collected from the 1920 assessment. In many taxing units, the increase was one hundred per cent or more. This swing of the pendulum so incensed the taxpayers that the 1921 regular session of the legislature again amended the provision by giving the state board jurisdiction of those cases where ten or more taxpayers object to the levies. Although the taxpayers were somewhat bewildered by so many changes and really did not know what to do, there were appeals from about fifty units. In many instances taxpayers appeared before the local tax levying officers, and succeeded in having levies reduced upon threats to take appeals to the state board if their protests were not heeded. In all of the appeals taken, except four, the levies were reduced by the state board.[1]

Somewhat similar, nevertheless much less extensive in its scope is the sweep of authority granted the budget director in Iowa. All contracts entered into by any municipality in the state are made subject to his approval if protested by a certain number of citizens resident in the municipality. The number varies from city to city. Consequently all items of municipal expenditure relative to such contracts are pretty much under state control.[2]

No limitation either in scope or initiative, is imposed upon the authority of a state-appointed commission in Multnomah County, Oregon, the county in which Portland is situated. The levying bodies of all municipalities within the county must submit their budget to a Tax Supervision and Conservation Commission appointed by the governor. After due

[1] Letter of state official.

[2] See Wylie Kilpatrick, *State Administrative Review of Local Budget Making*, New York, 1927.

consideration, this commission may " approve, reject or reduce the same or any item therein, or by unanimous vote of all the members of the commission increase the same . . . . upon the request in writing of the proper tax levying board, if the commission deems an emergency to exist." [1] The system has been in operation eight years, during which time a considerable reduction in the requested tax levies has been effected. In addition to thus putting the brakes on increased governmental expenditures, the supervising agency has been exceedingly active in advocating the budget idea as the basis of economy and efficiency, and in bringing about some measure of financial coördination among the various governing bodies of the county.

The supervision in New Mexico is perhaps the most comprehensive of all. Each political subdivision is required to prepare its budget in accordance with forms prescribed by the tax commission, very frequently with the assistance of the commission's representatives. The proposed budgets are then submitted to the state commission, which scrutinizes and alters them as it sees fit, and places its approval upon a budget only when it has been rendered satisfactory to the members of the commission.

Less important, nevertheless well worth noting, is the fact that the form of the municipal budget may in five states be prescribed by the supervising agency. [2] Sometimes the general outline of the document is set forth in the law, and the commission is given the right merely to prescribe the details. In other cases the administrative officials are empowered to formulate both form and procedure.

---

[1] Budget Facts and Financial Statistics, Multnomah County, Oregon, 1925, p. 15 *et seq.*

[2] Ariz. Laws 1921, §4840; Ind. Stat. 1926, §10216; Iowa Code 1920, §389; Nev. Laws 1920-1921, ch. 717; N. D. Laws 1925, ch. 169. In California and Montana similar regulations exist relative to county budgets.

It thus appears that state administrative supervision of municipal finance has followed four lines of development. The greatest headway has been made in the field of taxation, somewhat less in connection with the audit of municipal accounts, less in connection with municipal indebtendness. State supervision of municipal budgets and tax levies is of rather recent development, and thus far, save in two or three jurisdictions, has made little progress.

CHAPTER IV

HEALTH

THE development of state administrative supervision over municipal health activities resembles in many particulars that already traced in the field of finance. The units of government which originally handled this problem were, of course, the localities,[1] and even today the vast majority of

[1] Some idea of the tremendous size of the problem of public health can, perhaps, be conceived if one remembers that each year in the United States there occur approximately one million five hundred thousand deaths, six hundred thousand of which, it is estimated, could be prevented or at least postponed were the findings of modern medical science properly applied. Analogy with English statistics indicates, furthermore, that at least three million are lying on sick beds throughout the United States every day in the year, half of whom are ill from these very same diseases. (Fisher, Irving, "The Public Health Movement," *Survey*, N. Y., 1912, vol. 29, pp. 376-380.) To attempt to measure illness and death in commercial terms, is, of course, folly. "There is no market value or stock quotation that covers the price of a sob or a tear, the loneliness of an orphan, the life-long darkness of blind eyes or the living death of insanity." The cost is beyond estimation. Even those portions of it which can be translated into commercial terms bring the total to such stupendous figures as to be beyond comprehension. Irving Fisher believes that the losses caused by these diseases amount to at least $1,500,000,000 worth of wealth-producing power per annum. And startling as this may appear, it seems conservative in the light of later estimates. Dr. Hill is inclined to believe that each generation pays at least ten billion dollars for the care and treatment of the sick alone, not to mention that portion of the total loss caused by decreased efficiency and death. (Hill, Hibbert W., *The New Public Health*, New York, 1919, p. 27.) Harry H. Moore of the United States Public Health Service tries to make an estimate of the cost of disease for a single year, and comes to the conclusion that the people of the United States spent approximately $1,400,000,000 for the care and treatment of disease in

the ten thousand public health agents working under governmental auspices are in their employ.[1]   It was not until after the middle of the nineteenth century that the first state board of health was established, and then it was merely a body for the enforcement of quarantine regulations at New Orleans.[2] Since that time state departments have been established in every state in the Union, but the problem is still considered by many primarily a matter of local concern.

How well these local units have performed their task is a disputed question.   There are those who maintain that " full credit ought to be given to local boards of health and health officers for putting the United States on the public health map " and that very little share in that credit is due state or federal officials.[3]   On the other hand, there are those who believe that although " theoretically responsible for the health of the communities they represent, the local boards of health are, generally speaking, the weakest elements in the public health machinery we are so slowly evolving for the physical welfare of the nation.   Aside from certain

1921. (Moore, Harry H., *Public Health in the United States*, New York, 1923.) This estimate likewise fails to take into consideration the cost of decreased efficiency, loss of time, or premature death. Some idea of the size of these items can be obtained from a recent bulletin published by the Bureau of Labor, which estimates that the loss to wage earners alone from preventable disease and premature death amounts to 2,135,400 years per annum. This may be translated into economic terms as the reader sees fit. (*Care of Tuberculous Wage Earners in Germany*, Workman's Insurance and Compensation, Series No. 1, pp. 18 and 19; Bulletin of the United States Bureau of Labor, Whole Number 101—quoted in Gillin, J. L., *Poverty and Dependency*, New York, 1922, p. 398.)

[1] Vincent, George E., *The Rockefeller Foundation* (a review for 1921), p. 15.

[2] Mathews, J. M., *Principles of American State Administration*, New York (1917), p. 375.

[3] McCombs, Carl R., " Relative Functions of State and Local Health Departments," *American Journal of Public Health*, May, 1920, p. 394.

routine matters, such as the enforcement of old-fashioned quarantine, and the placarding of some of the cases of contagious diseases that happen to be reported, and fumigating at the termination of some of them, their energies are too often expended in attempting to abate common nuisances, or settling neighborhood disputes over a chicken pen, or carting away dead animals . . . . functions more fitting for the police departments." [1]

Whatever the facts of the controversy may be, a movement toward centralization in the health service has been going on, explicable in part by the revolution in rapid transportation, in part by the process of urbanization, and in part by the increasing intricacy of scientific knowledge. Where once vast stretches of slightly inhabited country isolated one community from another, bands of steel now lace and interlace the nation binding all parts of the continent into one complex unit. A man may now contract a disease in San Francisco and first become aware of the fact in Chicago, New York or even London. The health problem, consequently, is felt to be no longer local but state-wide or even national in its scope. [2] Along with this development has gone the process of urbanization, carrying with it the complicated problems of city life, many of which are impossible of local solution. One has merely to mention the task of obtaining a pure water supply for the average city in order to drive the point home. Finally, the increasing complexity of scientific knowledge and scientific procedure has necessitated the employment of the skilled expert, and the acquisition of costly equipment, thus placing a burden on many localities which is considerably beyond their means,

[1] *Public Health Administration*, Reprint 390, Public Health Reports, 1917.

[2] Hemenway, H. B., *Legal Principles of Public Health Administration*, Chicago (1914) ; *cf.* also *National Municipal Review*, July, 1914, p. 599.

and compelling them to turn to the state for aid. Inevitably a decided expansion of both state and national health activities has ensued.[1]

The function of the state board of health was at first purely advisory in character. It was confined to making investigations, gathering information, and framing such suggestions for legislative action as seemed desirable.[2] These are still very important functions of these state agencies. No longer, however, do such functions comprise their sole duties. Equally important is their supervision over the activities of local health officials. For the most part health authorities agree that the ideal situation in public health work would be one in which the localities did their work so well that the only function of the state department would be to act as a clearing house for the collection and distribution of information. Nevertheless, a gradual extension of administrative supervision has been thought necessary.[3]

A certain limited control over general sanitary conditions has developed almost everywhere. And in addition, as this and that phase of the local health situation has become acute, the state authorities have been given greater and greater powers of supervision over particular aspects of the problem so that today in many jurisdictions the selection and direction of the local personnel, the promulgation of municipal ordinances, and the construction and operation of municipal water-works plants and municipal sewage systems are all subject to special attention. To a more limited extent this is also true of wading pools, hospitals and places of public assembly.

[1] See Leigh, Robert, *Federal Health Administration in the United States*, New York (1927).

[2] MacNutt, J. S., *Manual for Health Officers*, New York (1915), p. 31.

[3] Overton, Frank and Denno, W. J., *The Health Officer*, Philadelphia (1919), p. 81.

GENERAL SANITARY CONDITIONS

The degree of supervision over general sanitary conditions varies from state to state. The administrative authorities are empowered to *collect certain statistics* prescribed by law practically everywhere, and in at least forty-four jurisdictions they may *collect such additional information* as seems desirable.[1] On the basis of the information thus amassed such action may be taken as either the administrative or legislative authorities deem necessary.

Extensive use is made of the mechanism of *inspection* in approximately the same number of jurisdictions.[2] More

[1] Ala. Pol. Code 1923, §1051; Ark. Digest 1921, §5159; Cal. Pol. Code 1923, §2984; Col. Comp. Laws 1921, §§873, 876; Conn. Gen. Stat. 1918, §2364; Del. Rev. Code 1915, §738; Ga. Annot. Code 1914, §1662; Idaho Comp. Stat. 1919, §1660; Ill. Rev. Stat. 1923, §65-2; Ind. Annot. Stat. 1926, §8186; Iowa Code 1924, §2234; Ky. Stat. 1922, §2055; La. Stat. 1920, p. 779; Maine Rev. Stat. 1916, p. 427; Md. Code 1924, art. 43, §7; Mass. Gen. Laws 1921, ch. iii, §112; Mich. Comp. Laws 1915, §4992; Minn. Gen. Stat. 1923, §5349; Miss. Code 1917, §4836; Mo. Rev. Stat. 1919, §5785; Mont. Rev. Code 1921, §2447; Neb. Comp. Stat. 1922, §8224; N. H. Public Laws 1901, p. 338; N. J. Comp. Stat. Supple. 1911-1924, §89-37; N. M. Session Laws 1919, ch. 85, §10; N. Y. Supple. 1924, p. 464; N. C. Cons. Stat. 1919, §7149; N. D. Comp. Laws 1913, §411; Ohio Code 1926, §1234; Okla. Comp. Stat. 1921, §8677; Ore. Laws 1920, §8370; Penn. Stat. 1920, §4420; R. I. Gen. Laws 1923, §2158; S. C. Code 1922, §2319; S. D. Rev. Code 1919, §7667; Tenn. Code 1919, §3101; Tex. Rev. Civil Stat. 1925, §4430; Utah Comp. Laws 1917, §2723; Vt. Gen. Laws 1917, §5406; Va. Code 1924, §1488; Wash. Comp. Stat. 1922, §6090; W. Va. Code 1923, ch. 150, §2; Wis. Stat. 1925, §143.03; Wyo. Comp. Stat. 1920, §3598.

[2] Ala. Pol. Code 1923, §1051; Ark. Dig. 1921, §5129; Cal. Pol. Code 1923, §2974; Col. Comp. Laws 1921, §871; Conn. Gen. Stat. 1918, §2364; Del. Rev. Code 1915, §738; Fla. Rev. Gen. Stat. 1920, §2007; Ga. Annot. Code 1914, §1662; Idaho Comp. Stat. 1919, §1623; Ill. Rev. Stat. 1923, §65-2; Ind. Annot Stat. 1926, §8122; Iowa Code 1924, §2191; Kan. Rev. Stat. 1923, §65-101; Ky. Stat. 1922, §2049; La. Stat. 1920, p. 776; Maine Rev. Stat. 1916, p. 426; Md. Code 1924, art. 43, §3; Mass. Gen. Laws, 1921, ch. III, §5; Mich. Comp. Laws 1915, §4989; Minn. Gen. Stat. 1923, §5339; Miss. Code 1917, §4821; Mo. Rev. Stat. 1919, §5772; Mont. Rev. Code 1921, §2448; Nev. Rev. Laws 1919, p. 2955; N. H. Public Laws 1926,

or less typical of the grants of statutory authority in this connection is that of Florida by virtue of which agents of the state board of health may visit any and all cities in the state for the purpose of investigating the sanitary conditions therein, and may in the course of such inspection condemn any structures which are potential breeders of disease. If the mayor of the municipality does not immediately remedy matters thus brought to his attention, the state authorities may do whatever they deem necessary to rectify the existing situation—at the municipality's expense. The effectiveness of such a grant of authority depends, of course, upon the number of inspectors provided for in the appropriations and upon the aggressiveness of the state administration.

In some jurisdictions exceedingly vague phrases, such as " the state board of health shall have general control over the enforcement of health laws," or " supervisory power over quarantine and over the care and control of communicable diseases," sometimes cloak a grant of power equally broad and equally effective. Under these circumstances, however, a study of the court decisions would alone reveal the exact scope of the power granted.

Equally widespread is the practice of *disseminating advice* although no mere examination of the statutes would reveal that such is the case. Five variations in procedure are to be found: publicity, correspondence, inspection, the sanitary survey and conferences. Although specific statutory authorization for the use of publicity in

p. 489; N. J. Comp. Stat. Supple. 1911-1924, §89-1g; N. M. Laws 1919, ch. 85, §10; N. Y. Cons. Laws Supple. 1924, p. 464; N. C. Cons. Stat. 1919, §7050; N. D. Comp. Laws 1913, §400; Ohio Code 1926, §1236; Okla. Comp. Stat. 1921, §8668; Ore. Laws 1920, §8360; Penn. Stat. 1920, §8972; R. I. Gen. Laws 1923, §2154; S. C. Code 1922, §2309; S. D. Rev. Code 1919, §7667; Tenn. Code 1919, §3095; Tex. Civ. Stat. 1925, §4419; Utah Comp. Laws 1917, §2707; Vt. Gen. Laws 1917, §6197; Va. Code 1924, §1487; Wash. Comp. Stat. 1922, §5406; W. Va. Code 1923, ch. 150, §2; Wis. Stat. 1925, §143.02; Wyo. Comp. Stat. 1920, §3597.

connection with public health work is to be found in only twenty-three states, it is nevertheless an important method of disseminating advice in practically every state in the Union.[1] Its forms are myriad—pamphlets, healthgrams, newspaper bulletins, lectures, movies, exhibits, etc. In 1915 Dr. Chapin discovered that at least forty-two state boards were carrying on their work by means of health bulletins; thirty-six were conducting lectures; thirty-one furnished lanterns or slides to those who desired to make use of them; and fifteen had instituted the use of health films. It can safely be assumed that the work of the publicity man has been developed and perfected since then. The extent to which this activity influences municipal health authorities is difficult to determine. Nevertheless, a comment by one of the state departments of health is significant: " The awakened interest that is being shown by local health officials in the smaller municipalities may be attributed, in part at least, to a keener realization on the part of the public that the morbidity and mortality rates can and should be substantially lowered by the proper functioning of local health departments. This is indicated by the increasing frequency with which citizens lodge complaints with the state department of health alleging neglect on the part of local officials." [2]

[1] Fla. Rev. Stat. 1920, §1998; Iowa Code 1924, §2191; Ky. Stat. 1922, §2052; La. Stat. 1920, p. 776; Maine Rev. Stat. 1916, p. 427; Md. Code 1924, art. 43, §7; Mass. Gen. Laws 1921, ch. III, §3; Mich. Comp. Laws 1915, §4992; Mont. Rev. Code 1921, §2448; Neb. Comp. Stat. 1922, §8226; Nev. Rev. Laws 1919, p. 2889; N. H. Public Laws 1926, p. 489; N. M. Session Laws 1919, ch. 85, p. 10; N. C. Cons. Stat. 1919, §7050; Ohio Gen. Code 1926, §1236-1; Okla. Comp. Stat. 1921, §8669; R. I. Gen. Laws 1923, §2154; S. C. Code 1922, §2313; S. D. Rev. Code 1919, §7667; Va. Code 1924, §1489; W. Va. Code 1923, ch. 150, §2; Wis. Stat. 1925, §140.05; Wyo. Comp. Stat. 1920, §3598. Although specific statutory authorization is to be found only in these states, similar power has been granted the state authorities in practically every state in the Union by virtue of some " blanket clause " in the health law.

[2] *New Jersey State Department of Health, Report 1921, p. 28.*

Specific reference to inspectors as agents through which this activity may be conducted is found in very few statutes; it is very probable, however, that this medium is used wherever a system of state inspection is maintained.[1] An interesting variation in this procedure is the sanitary survey conducted upon the competitive scoring basis.[2]

Each city is notified a considerable period ahead of time of the coming of the state inspectors who are to undertake the survey so that the local health machinery may be put in a state of highest efficiency. Then the survey is made. During it frequent conferences are held with the local authorities for the purpose of presenting suggestions and recommendations. Generally speaking, these recommendations fall into two distinct classes: " first, those relating to problems of administration which involve little or no increased expense and frequently result in economy of operation; and second, those which involve some expense, which arise from a proper conception of the nature of a modern municipal public health administration and result from the attempt to secure well-rounded departments in which a due proportion of importance is given to all necessary activities." Many of these suggestions are frequently adopted by the municipalities at

[1] In fact specific mention of such procedure is to be found only in the laws of Connecticut, Maryland and Missouri. (Conn. Gen. Stat. 1918, §2374; Md. Code 1924, art. 43, §10; Mo. Laws 1925, p. 253.) Fifteen states indicated in reply to a questionnaire sent to all the state departments of health, however, that this method was generally used in their jurisdictions. (Alabama, Arkansas, California, Florida, Louisiana, Maine, Massachusetts, Michigan, Montana, New Mexico, New York, Ohio, South Dakota, Texas, and Utah.) It is probable, moreover, that the procedure is to be found in all states in which the supervising agency has an adequate staff of inspectors.

[2] Conn. Gen. Stat. 1918, §2364; Md. Code 1924, art. 43, §7; N. H. Public Laws 1926, p. 489; N. J. Comp. Stat. Supple. 1911-1924, §89-le; Okla. Comp. Stat. 1921, §8669; S. C. Code 1922, §2364; W. Va. Code 1923, ch. 150, §2; Wis. Stat. 1925, §140.07.

the instance of the municipal health officer. "At times [however] when the financial officers of a city have objected to a recommendation on the grounds of cost, a conference has been arranged between the fiscal officers, the health officer and the sanitary supervisor engaged in this work which has very frequently resulted in a better understanding of local needs and a greater appreciation of the value of the work of the local department." [1]

A further variation in procedure is the conference or school of instruction. Forty-one states at least make use of the process.[2] In approximately one-third of these warrant for doing so may be found in the statutes. A typical statutory authorization follows: " The state department of health shall make provision for the annual conference of district health commissioners for the consideration of the cause and prevention of dangerous communicable diseases and other measures to protect and improve the public health. Each board of health or other body of persons appointed or acting in place of a board of health shall appoint its health commissioner or health officer a delegate to such annual conference." Elsewhere authority to hold such gatherings is found in some blanket clause in the organic act rendered specific through a by-law of the state department of health.

[1] *New York Department of Health, Report 1920*, p. 61.

[2] Ala. Pol. Code 1923, §1058-12; Ark. Digest 1921, §5145; Ind. Annot. Stat. 1926, §8177; Kan. Rev. Stat. 1923, §65-119; Ky. Stat. 1922, §2054; Md. Code 1924, art. 43, §34; N. J. Comp. Stat. Supple. 1911-24, §8912; N. Y. Cons. Laws Supple. 1918, p. 6544, §7; Ohio Code 1926, §1245; Ore. Laws 1920, §8363; Pa. Stat. 1920, §9012; Tex. Civil Code 1925, §4453; Utah Comp. Laws 1917, §2758; Vt. Gen. Laws 1917, §6209; Wis. Stat. 1925, §140.08. In Arizona, California, Colorado, Connecticut, Delaware, Florida, Louisiana, Maine, Massachusetts, Michigan, Minnesota, Mississippi, Missouri, Montana, Nebraska, New Hampshire, New Mexico, North Carolina, North Dakota, Oklahoma, Rhode Island, South Dakota, Tennessee, Virginia, Washington, and West Virginia a similar procedure is followed by virtue of some "blanket clause" in the state health code which enables the state health authorities to take such action.

More effective, perhaps, than any of these devices is the control exercised through the *ordinance-making* power which has been granted the state health authorities in forty-seven states. In this way the main lines of local health activity may be established and local practice directed. The state board of health may thus in large measure control the duties and functions of all subordinate units. The exercise of the full sweep of this power is prevented in some jurisdictions, however, by the fact that many of the details of public health organization and public health procedure are laid down in the statutes, and by the added fact that in many of the jurisdictions in which the ordinance-making power has been granted, the scope of its activity has been specifically curtailed in this or that particular.

In addition to this supervision over sanitary conditions generally, certain fields of local health activity have been singled out for more intensive control: personnel, local sanitary ordinances, the collection of vital statistics, the construction and operation of water-works and sewage systems, places of public assembly, swimming pools, hospitals, etc.

PERSONNEL

Although the supervision over personnel in the United States is considerably greater than that maintained over sanitary conditions generally, the control has nowhere been extended as far here as on the Continent or even in England. Naturally enough, the *information* collected through the medium of *reports* and *inspection* discussed is used in this connection. Furthermore, much of the *advice* disseminated through the channels already analyzed is intended for the guidance of local officials. Moreover, many of the *ordinances* enacted by the state boards of health, as has already been pointed out, affect the activities of the local personnel directly or indirectly. In some twenty-six states, however, the power of issuing specific *orders* relative to particular conditions or to particular cities has been lodged with the supervising authorities, who consequently have in their possession really drastic powers of supervision if they care to exercise them.[1] This control is still further buttressed in twenty-three jurisdictions by the fact that the state boards of health may *remove* any and every local health officer who fails to perform the duties of his office satisfactorily.[2] Incidentally, similar action may be taken in thirty-three commonwealths in connection with registrars of vital statistics.[3]

[1] Ark. Laws 1916, ch. 16; Del. Rev. Code 1915, §738; Fla. Rev. Gen. Stat. 1920, §2007; Idaho Comp. Stat. 1919, §1657; Iowa Code 1924, §2191; N. J. Comp. Stat. 1910, §2659; Ohio Code 1926, §1237; Pa. Stat. 1920, §8975; S. C. Code 1922, §2313; Va. Code 1924, §1487; Wash. Comp. Stat. 1922, §5406; W. Va. Code 1913, §5339; Wis. Stat. 1918, §1407a-6. The returns from a questionnaire indicate that this power has also been granted under a "blanket authorization" in the state health law in Alabama, Connecticut, Illinois, Indiana, Kansas, Kentucky, Missouri, New Mexico, New York, Oregon, South Dakota, Utah and Wyoming.

[2] Ala. Pol. Code 1923, §1052 (county); Ark. Laws 1916, §623; Conn. Stat. 1918, §2364; Ga. Annot. Code 1914, §1676; Ind. Annot. Stat. 1926, §8122; N. J. Public Laws 1926, p. 492; N. Y. Cons. Laws Supple. 1921-23, p. 1692; N. D. Comp. Laws 1913, §412 (recommended); Ore. Laws 1920, §8369; S. C. Code 1922, §2326; Wash. Comp. Stat. 1922, §6098; W. Va. Code 1923, ch. 150, §3; Wyo. Comp. Stat. 1920, §3644. In a number of states in which no specific warrant for such action seems to appear in the law, the courts have interpreted some of the "blanket clauses" in such a way as to grant the state officials like authority. Such has been the case in Iowa, Kansas, Kentucky, Maine, Missouri (county), Montana, New York, Oklahoma, Tennessee and Utah.

[3] Ala. Pol. Code 1923, §1068; Ark. Laws 1916, §623; Col. Comp. Laws 1921, §973; Del. Rev. Code 1915, §800; Fla. Gen. Stat. 1920, §2071; Ga. Annot. Code 1914, §1676; Idaho Comp. Stat. 1919, §1627; Ind. Annot. Stat. 1926, §8122; Iowa Code 1924, §2392; Ky. Stat. 1922, §2062a-4; La. Stat. 1920, p. 813; Md. Code 1924, art. 43, §18; Minn. Gen. Stat. 1923, §5355; Mo. Rev. Stat. 1919, §5799; Neb. Comp. Stat. 1922, §8231; N. Y. Cons. Laws Supple. 1921-23, §1739; N. C. Stat. 1919, §7090; Okla. Comp. Stat. 1921, §8986; Pa. Stat. 1920, §8988; Tenn. Code 1919, §3118a-8; Va. Code 1924, §1564; Wash. Comp. Stat. 1922, §6098; W. Va. Code 1923, ch. 150, §26; Wyo. Comp. Stat. 1920, §3644. The courts have interpreted certain

Equally effective and much more widely used is the power of *substitute administration* which has been granted the supervising officials in at least forty-two jurisdictions.[1] Upon the failure of a local board to enforce the rules and regulations of a state department or to handle the administration of the local office efficiently, the state department may step in and, through the medium of its own personnel, take over the conduct of all local activities. The procedure is outlined in considerable detail in the law of New Jersey. " The department of health of the state . . . . shall call to the attention of the local authorities any failure on their part to enforce the laws of the state or the sanitary code, and shall issue an order directing them to enforce said laws. If the local authorities fail

"blanket clauses" in the laws of California, Kansas, Maine, Montana, New Jersey, New Mexico, Oklahoma, South Dakota and Utah in such a way as to allow the supervising authorities in these states similar authority.

[1] Ala. Pol. Code 1923, §1051; Ark. Supple. 1911, §5341; Cal. Laws 1918, §2979; Col. Comp. Laws 1921, §883; Conn. Gen. Stat. 1918, §2367; Del. Rev. Code 1915, §739; Fla. Cons. Laws 1914, §1121; Ga. Annot. Code 1914, §1668; Idaho Comp. Stat. 1919, §1659; Ill. Rev. Stat. 1923, §65-2; Ind. Rev. Stat. 1918, §7596b; Iowa Code 1924, §2212; La. Stat. 1920, p. 780; Maine Rev. Stat. 1916, ch. 19, §23; Md. Code 1924, art. 43, §10; Mass. Laws 1902, p. 658; Mich. Comp. Laws Supple. 1922, §§5000-8; Minn. Gen. Stat. 1917, §4646; Miss. Code 1917, §4846; Neb. Comp. Stat. 1922, §8223; N. J. Comp. Stat. Supple. 1911-1924, §89-id; N. Y. Cons. Laws Supple. 1921-23, §6530; N. C. Cons. Stat. 1919, §7051; Ohio Code 1926, §1244; Ore. Laws 1920, §8367; Pa. Stat. 1920, §8983; R. I. Laws 1909, p. 413; S. C. Laws 1912, §1660; Tenn. Code 1919, §3114a-14; Utah Comp. Laws 1917, §2707; Vt. Gen. Laws 1917, §6197; Va. Code 1924, §1496; Wash. Comp. Stat. 1922, §5406; W. Va. Code 1923, ch. 150, §2; Wis. Stat. 1925, §143.03. The procedure also exists by virtue of some "blanket clause" in the laws in Kansas, Missouri, Montana, New Mexico, South Dakota, Texas, and Wyoming.

In Idaho (§1657), furthermore, all disputes as to the abatement of a public nuisance must be referred to the state department of public welfare for adjudication.

to comply with such an order within the time specified or if none is specified within a reasonable time, the department of health shall itself take such action as may be necessary to perform the acts specified in the order. Any contracts which it may make for such purpose shall be binding upon the local municipality, and shall be deemed to have the same force and effect as if duly authorized and made by the local health and municipal authorities. Any money expended by the state and the amount of all obligations incurred by the department of health of the state of New Jersey to comply with such order may be recovered." The exact procedure varies of course from state to state, but in general the broad outlines here set forth are followed in all jurisdictions.

Similar action may likewise be taken in the majority of states in times of epidemic irrespective of the efficiency or inefficiency of health officers.[1]

In a few states neither an epidemic of disease nor the breakdown of the local enforcing machinery seems to be a necessary preliminary for state action. In Vermont, for example, " the state board of health may, in its discretion, exercise all the powers and authority in each village, incorporated town or municipality which is given to the local board of health, and said secretary (of the state board of health) may likewise exercise all the power and authority of a local health officer anywhere in the state."

In a limited number of jurisdictions still greater powers of supervision and direction have been bestowed upon the state health authorities in that the supervising officials are allowed to participate in the selection of the local personnel. In a number of states this participation is

---

[1] The only ground for state interference given in the Montana law is inefficiency. It is very probable, however, that the inability of the local officials to handle an emergency would permit of state interference at such a time in any case.

confined to the requirement that all local appointees be *approved* by the state administrative authorities.[1] New Jersey and Illinois are, perhaps, the most systematic in this supervision. Examinations are held in both states to determine the relative fitness of the candidates for the position of local health officers and only those who pass such examinations will be approved. In New Jersey this policy is extended to include registrars of vital statistics and water supply operators.

The mechanism of *appointment* is somewhat more widely used. In some cases it is essentially of an emergency nature, as, for example, when its operation is confined to filling vacancies caused by removals or to filling places left vacant through the failure of local authorities to act. Nevertheless, the right to make the original appointment of local registrars of vital statistics has been granted the state administrative authorities in at least twenty-five jurisdictions.[2] Characteristic of the statutory grant of authority

[1] The approval of the appointment of all local health officers is required in: Ala. Code 1923, §1052 (county) ; Ark. Digest 1921, §5153; Ga. Code 1914, §1676; Ill. Rev. Stat. 1923, §65-83; Maine Laws 1919, ch. 172, §10; N. J. Comp. Stat. Supple. 1911-1924, §89-56; N. M. Session Laws 1919, §13; New York, Oregon, Pennsylvania; Vt. Gen. Laws 1917, §6209; and W. Va. Code 1923, ch. 150. A similar requirement exists relative to local registrars in Delaware, Maine, New Jersey, New Mexico, New York, and Pennsylvania. Water-works operators are subject to like supervision in Maine, New Mexico, New York, and Ohio. In Massachusetts slaughter-house inspectors are singled out for especial attention.

[2] Ala. Pol. Code 1923, §1068; Ark. Digest 1921, §5149; Col. Comp. Laws 1921, §923; Del. Rev. Code 1915, §800; Fla. Rev. Stat. 1920, §2071; Ga. Annot. Code 1914, §1676; Idaho Comp. Stat. 1919, §1627; Ky. Stat. 1922, §2062a-4; La. Stat. 1920, p. 813; Mo. Rev. Stat. 1919, §5799; Mont. Laws 1907, §1766; Neb. Comp. Stat. 1922, §8230; N. H. Public Laws 1926, p. 491; N. J. Session Laws 1920, ch. 99, §4; Ohio Code 1920, §201; Okla. Comp. Stat. 1921, §8986; Penn. Stat. 1920, §8989; S. C. Code 1922, §2395; Tenn. Code 1919, §3118a-7; W. Va. Code 1923, ch. 150, §26. A "blanket clause" in the health codes of Kansas, South Dakota, Virginia, Washington and Wyoming permits similar action.

in this connection is the provision of law in Nebraska, which states that " in cities of the first class the city physician or clerk, as may be designated by the state registrar of vital statistics . . . . (shall act as local registrar) ; in cities of the second class the state registrar shall appoint as local registrar some member of the board of health, clerk, justice of the peace, or some other proper person." Needless to say, in any jurisdiction in which the supervising authorities have the right to make the original appointment they have also the right to fill any vacancy which may be caused by removal from office.

Somewhat less extensive is the use made of this procedure in connection with regular health officers. Indeed, only eight states make use of the mechanism at all, and in them the extent to which it is used varies from jurisdiction to jurisdiction. The state board of health in Virginia, for example, is empowered to appoint annually the members of the boards of health (save only the mayor who serves ex officio) in all municipalities throughout the state, except those in which the municipal charter specifically provides for another method of selection—which, needless to say, is the case in many Virginia cities.[1] No exception to the general rule of state appointment is made in Vermont.[2] In Michigan, however, the authority granted the state board of health is much more limited, being confined in its operation to the appointment of a milk commission in all cities in which the local board of health does not have at least two physicians in its make-up.[3] Even more restricted is the sweep of power granted state departments of health elsewhere. In New York, for example, the state authorities are empowered to appoint the health officer of the port of New York only; in

---

[1] Va. Code 1924, §1492.
[2] Vt. Gen. Laws 1917, §6217.
[3] Mich. Laws 1915, §5149.

New Jersey the jurisdiction of state officials is confined to Perth Amboy. A compromise scheme exists at Shreveport and Baton Rouge. The governor of the state is empowered to appoint by and with the advice and consent of the senate three members of the municipal board of health in each of these cities respectively; the local council is authorized to appoint the remaining two.[1] A still further limitation upon the system of state appointment exists in South Carolina and West Virginia. In each of these states certain health officers are appointed by the state administration, but only upon the recommendation of the local authority.[2]

Passing mention should perhaps be made of the fact that in at least five jurisdictions state appointment has been resorted to in connection with county boards of health, many of which have jurisdiction over the smaller municipalities.[3]

Elsewhere the mechanism is employed chiefly in emergency conditions or else is clearly substitute in its character, being used for the most part to fill vacancies caused by removal for one reason or another, or else to fill positions left vacant through the neglect or oversight of the local authorities.[4]

[1] La. Stat. 1920, p. 728.

[2] S. C. Code 1912, §1659; W. Va. Code 1923, ch. 150, §6.

[3] Ala. Pol. Code 1923, §1102; Ky. Stat. 1922, §2055; Miss. Code 1917, §4840; S. D. Rev. Code 1919, §7675; Wyo. State Board of Health, p. 15.

[4] Ala. Pol. Code 1923, §1102; Ark. Digest 1921, §5158; Col. Pol. Code 1923, §3073; La. Supple. §856; Maine Rev. Stat. 1916, p. 437; Minn. Gen. Stat. 1923, §5344; Mont. Rev. Code 1921, §2464; N. H. Public Laws 1926, p. 491; N. J. Comp. Laws Supple. 1911-24, §89-12; Ore. Laws 1920, §8369; Tex. Civ. Code 1920, §4426; Wis. Stat. 1925, §140.05. Authority to take similar action is granted the state boards of health in Kansas, New Mexico and Ohio by virtue of a "blanket clause" in the health laws of the respective states.

MUNICIPAL HEALTH ORDINANCES

The enactment of municipal health ordinances has like-wise been singled out for particular attention. In eighteen states certain ordinances at least, must be submitted to the state health authorities for *approval* before they become effective.[1] Sometimes this requirement is sweeping, in-cluding within its compass each and every ordinance of a health character passed by a municipality. At other times it is much more limited, as, for example, in Ohio, where only those rules and regulations of the city health authorities which apply to the operation of municipal sewage systems must secure such approval. Closely allied to this is the con-trol which is maintained over quarantine regulations in some nineteen jurisdictions. In these states no town or city may institute a local quarantine save with the approval of the state board of health.[2]

Supplementary to the control thus maintained is the super-vision exercised through the medium of *review*. In nine states its action is confined to quarantine regulations,[3] but in the remaining jurisdictions it includes within its scope all

[1] Ariz. Rev. Stat. 1911, §5344; Conn. Gen. Code 1918, §2402; Idaho Comp. Stat. 1919, §1655; Ill. Rev. Stat. 1923, §65-84; Mass. Gen. Laws 1911, p. 594; Nev. Laws 1919, ch. 117, p. 226; N. Y. Cons. Laws 1918, p. 468; Ohio Code 1920, §3891; Ore. Laws 1920, §8372; Penn. Stat. 1920, §8977; S. C. Code 1912, §1572; Wash. Comp. Stat. 1922, §6093. Similar supervision may be maintained in Alabama, Arkansas, Florida, Kansas, Maine, and New Jersey by virtue of a "blanket provision" in the laws of the re-spective states.

[2] Ariz. Rev. Stat. 1913, §1214; Ill. Rev. Stat. 1923, §65-84; Ky. Stat. 1922, §2057; La. Stat. 1920, p. 779; Miss. Code 1917, §4845; Mont. Rev. Code 1921, §2467; N. H. Public Laws 1920, p. 504; Ore. Laws 1920, §8372; Tex. Rev. Civil Stat. 1923, §4451; W. Va. Code 1923, ch. 150, §7; Wis. Stat. 1925, §143.05. Similar supervision may be maintained in Alabama, Kansas, Maine, New Jersey, New Mexico, Utah, Virginia, and Washing-ton by virtue of a "blanket provision" in the laws of the respective states.

[3] Connecticut, Illinois, Indiana, Louisiana, Missouri, New Mexico, North Dakota, Ohio, and Utah.

health ordinances of whatever character.[1] In some half dozen states—Arkansas, Michigan, New Jersey, New York, Oregon and Pennsylvania—action is more or less automatic. It differs from the requirement of approval only in that the state authorities may " revoke, modify, supplement or supersede " the ordinances presented which, of course, they cannot do if only the mechanism of approval is at their disposal. In the remaining commonwealths matters are brought up for review only upon the occasion of a controversy. In certain states such adjudication takes place only when a controversy between two or more boards of health arises; in others in the event of a controversy between a local board and individual citizens. An illustration of the statutory grant of authority found in states falling into the first category is that of Idaho, which provides that " all questions arising between local boards of health as to their jurisdiction or their relative duty in the abatement of any particular nuisance shall be referred to the department of public welfare for settlement." More or less typical of the statutory authorizations in those states falling into the second category is that of Iowa, which stipulates that " from any order of the local board of health there lies the right of appeal to the state board of health, which latter board shall have the power to hear and determine such appeal and enforce their orders."[2] Attention should perhaps be called to the fact that in these jurisdictions not only are all ordinances of the local boards of health subject to review, but any specific orders they may have issued are subject to similar supervision.

[1] Idaho Comp. Stat. 1919, §4213; Iowa Code 1924, §2191; N. Y. Cons. Laws 1918, p. 6524; Penn. Stat. 1920, §8977. Similar action may seemingly be taken under a general grant of power given the state department of health in Arkansas, Florida, Kansas, Kentucky, Maine, Massachusetts, Michigan, Montana, Oregon, South Dakota, Virginia, Washington, and Wyoming.

[2] Idaho Comp. Stat. 1919, §1657; Iowa Code 1924, §2191.

That *ordinances* of the state board of health in those fields over which the state board has been given jurisdiction supersede locally enacted ones, is too obvious to require more than passing mention. Nor need much stress be laid upon the equally evident fact that, during those periods when the state health authorities have taken over the local administration because of local inefficiency or the existence of emergency conditions, state ordinances are paramount. Thus it appears that, in case of gross neglect on the part of municipalities in the establishment of local health codes, the state authorities in the vast majority of jurisdictions are empowered, if they deem the situation bad enough, to remedy the defect.

WATER-WORKS SYSTEMS

In forty states the construction and operation of municipal water-works systems have been singled out for special attention. That there is need for such supervision a recent report from the state of Washington strikingly indicates, for in a survey of the water supplies in that state conducted during the years 1920, 1921 and 1922 the fact was revealed that more than 48 per cent of all the water systems in the state were supplying impure and dangerous drinking water.[1]

How effective the mechanism of *reports* is in curing this evil cannot, of course, be accurately measured. It is used in at least a dozen jurisdictions.[2] Much more widespread, and probably much more effective, however, is the supervision

[1] *Washington State Department of Health, Biennial Report 1921-22,* p. 38.

[2] Ala. Pol. Code 1923, §1164; Kan. Rev. Stat. 1923, §65-162; Md. Code 1924, art. 43, §331; Mass. Gen. Laws 1921, ch. iii, §17; Mich. Comp. Laws Supple. 1922, §5029; Mo. Rev. Stat. 1919, §5789; Mont. Rev. Code 1921, §2648; Okla. Comp. Stat. 1921, §8974; Va. Code 1924, §1788. In addition under a "blanket clause" of the health law a similar system of reports is required in Arkansas, New Jersey, and Pennsylvania.

maintained through the process of *inspection*.[1] Characteristic of the statutory grants of power in this connection is that which may be found in the code of
Michigan by which the state board of health is given "supervisory and visitorial power and control over all corporations,
both municipal and private, partnerships and individuals engaged in furnishing water to the public", and is empowered
furthermore " to enter the pumping and filtering stations
. . . . reservoirs, stand pipes, cribs and other property of
such corporations . . . . for the purpose of inspecting the
same." That an efficient force of inspectors operating under
such a grant of power could keep a fairly effective check on
municipal water-supply systems throughout a state and with
the aid of judicious publicity, do much toward forcing municipal officials to eliminate conditions of the character of those
discovered in Washington goes without question.[2]

[1] Ala. Pol. Code 1923, §1161 ; Cal. Pol. Code 1923, §2979 ; Conn. Gen. Stat.
1918, §2385 ; Ga. Code 1911, §1622 ; Ind. Annot. Stat. 1926, §8125 ; Iowa Code
1924, §2191 ; Kan. Rev. Stat. 1923, §65-163 ; Ky. Stat. 1922, §2049 ; Md.
Code 1924, art. 43, §39 ; Mass. Gen. Laws 1902, p. 679, §121 ; Mich. Comp.
Laws Supple. 1922, §5019 ; Minn. Gen. Stat. 1923, §5375 ; Mo. Rev. Stat.
1919, §5787 ; Mont. Rev. Code 1921, §2642 ; N. H. Public Laws 1926, p. 492 ;
N. J. Comp. Stat. 1910, p. 5798 ; N. C. Cons. Stat. 1919, §7117 ; Ohio Code
1926, §1239 ; Okla. Stat. 1921, §8671 ; Ore. Laws 1920, §8460 ; Penn. Stat.
1920, §3625 ; S. C. Code 1922, §2343 ; Tex. Civil Code 1914, §4553a ; Vt.
Gen. Laws 1917, §6313 ; Va. Code 1924, §1787 ; W. Va. Code 1923, ch.
150, §2 ; Wis. Stat. 1925, §144.01 ; Wyo. Comp. Stat. 1920, §3601. In addition under a "blanket clause" in the health laws similar supervision is
being maintained in Colorado, Delaware, Florida, Louisiana, Maine, New
Mexico, New York, North Dakota, South Dakota, Utah, and Washington.

[2] The situation in Ohio is unique in that the statutes make action by the
state board dependent upon local initiative. Only upon the complaint of
the local health administration, or upon a petition of ten per cent of the
electors of any city, may the state authorities take action unless perchance
there has been a complaint by a neighboring community to the effect that
a particular city or town is polluting its water supply. In such a case the
sewage system rather than the water supply of the city complained against
is the proper object of investigation. In either case all action by the state
authorities depends upon local initiative.

Supplementary to the process of inspection is the dissemination of *advice*. Specific directions to this end are to be found in approximately three-fourths of the states in the Union and the practice may be presumed to exist in every state in which any sort of a system of inspection is maintained.[1] That there is need for such action, the merest skimming of the state health reports readily indicates. A recent report from Maryland, for example, describes conditions throughout that state as follows:

The situation at the Takoma Park water filtration plant . . . was typical of practically all the smaller works in the state. They were not equipped with sufficient regulating or controlling devices, nor were they usually operated by men with training in water supply engineering. Nevertheless in a number of instances they were called upon to treat waters of surface streams of unusual fluctuations in physical and sanitary quality. . . . At Takoma Park one of the primary functions of rapid sand filtration was so completely unknown that successful operation could not be expected. The use of alum for coagulating purposes, and for providing a necessary film on the surface of the filter beds was largely ignored except during periods of more than normal turbidity. At times of low water the use of alum was completely omitted, while with excessive rain turbidities alum was frantically poured in without regard to necessity or effi-

1 Ala. Pol. Code 1923, §1161; Col. Comp. Laws 1921, §1013; Ga. Annot. Code 1914, §2005; Ind. Stat. 1926, §8126; Iowa Code 1924, §2191; Kan. Rev. Stat. 1923, §65-163; Md. Code 1924, art. 43, §330; Mass. Gen. Laws 1921, ch. iii, §17; Mich. Comp. Laws Supple. 1922, §5033; Mo. Rev. Stat. 1919, §5789; Mont. Rev. Code 1921, §2648; N. H. Public Laws 1926, p. 525; N. Y. Cons. Laws Supple. 1918, §1419; N. C. Cons. Stat. 1919, §7062; Ohio Code 1926, §1240; Okla. Comp. Stat. 1921, §8975; Ore. Laws 1920, §8460; S. C. Code 1922, §2343; Vt. Gen. Laws 1917, §6197; Va. Code 1924, §1787; Wash. Comp. Stat. 1922, §6006; W. Va. Code 1923, ch. 150, §6a; Wis. Stat. 1925, §144.03. In addition similar supervision may be maintained under a "blanket clause" in the health laws in Connecticut, Delaware, Kentucky, Louisiana, Maine, New Jersey, New Mexico, North Dakota, Pennsylvania, South Dakota, Texas, Utah, and Wyoming.

ciency. Our first duty, therefore, was to explain in detail to the operator, the mode of operation of rapid sand filtration plants, and the importance therein of continuous alum dosage. When this had been done, it was necessary in this plant, as in others, to provide definite data as to the quantity of alum necessary under varying rain conditions, to calibrate various orifices for controlling dosages and to provide in advance a schedule of the necessary quantities of alum to be mixed under all conditions of operation.[1]

Needless to say, Maryland is not unique among the states in this respect.

How limited the effectiveness of this mechanism of control is, and how unsatisfactory may be the results therefrom, however, is so strikingly brought out in a recent Wyoming report that further quotation seems justified. " Early this spring," runs the report, " the water supply of one of our cities was not considered satisfactory from a health standpoint, and the officials of the town were advised. A sporadic effort was made to carry out our advice, but because certain sacrifices were required by certain prominent individuals who were able to bring the usual political pressure to bear upon the municipal authorities, the advice and recommendations were disregarded. In several months a serious infection of gastro-intestinal disease broke out in the city, affecting the health of four hundred people in the community." [2] A later epidemic in this same community resulted in the death of more than a score of its inhabitants.

Consequently, in order to insure against situations of this character, more drastic mechanisms of control have been brought into play in a number of states. In at least thirty-one jurisdictions the *approval* of the state authorities is necessary before the construction of any municipal water

---

[1] *Maryland State Board of Health, Report 1916,* p. 179.

[2] *Wyoming State Board of Health, Report 1921-1922,* p. 5.

supply may begin.[1]   The procedure outlined in the Alabama law is quite characteristic.   " No water-works plant or system may be constructed, nor may any new source of water supply be developed until an application for a permit has been filed with the state board of health.   Furthermore, no municipal corporation may incur any debt, or issue any bonds in aid of a water supply unless a permit has already been obtained." [2]   In this manner the state authorities may make sure that no fundamental errors of construction are made in the erection of any municipal water-works plant, and that the sources of water supply tapped are relatively pure, or at least capable of being rendered pure through the process of filtration.

Not only is the construction of these systems thus subjected to state supervision; in many instances their maintenance and operation are supervised as well.[3]   Only thus has it been thought possible to prevent a repetition of the Wyom-

---

[1] Ala. Pol. Code 1923, §1164; Conn. Gen. Stat. 1918, §2554; Kans. Rev. Stat. 1923, §65-163; Md. Code 1924, art. 43, §335; Mass. Gen. Laws 1902-8, p. 597; Minn. Gen. Stat. 1923, §5344; Mo. Rev. Stat. 1919, §5789; Mont. Code 1907, §1563; N. H. Public Laws 1926, p. 525; N. J. Comp. Stat. Supple. 1911-1924, §5813; N. Y. Cons. Laws Supple. 1918, p. 1340; N. C. Cons. Stat. 1919, §7118; Ohio Code 1926, §1240; Okla. Cons. Stat. 1921, §8975; Ore. Laws 1920, §8461; Penn. Stat. 1920, §8244; Va. Code 1924, §1787; W. Va. Code 1923, ch. 150, §6a; Wis. Stat. 1925, §144.04.   In addition similar supervision may be maintained under a " blanket clause " in the general laws in California, Connecticut, Florida, Iowa, Kentucky, Louisiana, Maine, Michigan, New Mexico, North Dakota, South Dakota, and Washington.

[2] Ala. Pol. Code 1923, §1164.

[3] Ala. Pol. Code 1923, §1164; Ind. Annot. Stat. 1926, §8126; Kans. Rev. Stat. 1923, §65-163; Md. Code 1924, art. 43, §332; Mich. Comp. Laws Supple. 1922, §5033; Minn. Gen. Stat. 1923, §5344; Ohio Code 1926, §1240-2; Okla. Comp. Stat. 1921, §8975; Va. Code 1924, §1790; W. Va. Code 1923, ch. 150, §6a; Wis. Stat. 1925, §144.04.   Similar supervision may be maintained under a " blanket clause " of the general health law in California, Colorado, Connecticut, Missouri, New Jersey, New Mexico, New York, Pennsylvania, South Dakota, Texas and Washington.

ing incident. Three different variations of this type of supervision have developed. In Kansas, for example, the state board of health is authorized to investigate the operation of any water-works plant in the state; and in the event that any supply is not reasonably pure, the supervising authorities may revoke the permit under which the plant operates. One cannot help wondering just how as a practical matter this power could be exercised, for it is obviously impossible to cut off the water supply of an entire city for any considerable period of time whether the matters called to the attention of the municipal authorities are remedied or not. Another variation of this supervision is to be found in Ohio. If a water purification or sewage disposal plant of any city in that state is being operated so inefficiently as to endanger the public health, the state health council must first warn the municipal authorities, but if matters continue unchanged, it may order them to appoint a new manager for the works whose appointment shall be subject to their ratification or approval. New Jersey has merely adopted the emergency provision of Ohio as a customary procedure and requires state approval for all appointments of this character. The state department of health consequently holds, or causes to be held, such examinations as it deems fitting and proper for determining the qualifications of the various aspirants for licenses as superintendents or operators of water purification plants, and issues licenses only to those whom it deems reasonably capable.

Supplementing the supervision thus maintained is the power granted the state officials in at least thirty-three jurisdictions of issuing specific *orders* relative to the management and operation of these systems.[1] That such authority

[1] Ala. Pol. Code 1923, §1169; Col. Pol. Code 1907, §§3062-4; Conn. Gen. Stat. 1918, §2530; Ind. Annot. Stat. 1926, §8125; Iowa Code 1924, §2201; Kans. Rev. Stat. 1923, §65-163; Md. Code 1924, art. 43, §329; Mass. Gen. Laws 1902, p. 697, §118; Mich. Comp. Laws Supple. 1922, §5025; Minn.

is sometimes desirable the Wyoming report quoted above clearly indicates, and additional data leading to the same conclusion could very easily be assembled. Typical of the form which such orders may take is that recorded in an Idaho report some years back, evidently the result of an investigation of a local water supply system which had disclosed conditions fraught with exceedingly great danger to the community.

Now, therefore, be it resolved by the State Board of Health, in special session convened, that the City Council of Idaho Falls be requested to either install a temporary pump in the Snake river near the bridge; which shall be connected with the water mains at that point, from which to furnish the people with a pure water supply, or else syphon Willow Creek where it empties into the city canal, so that it shall no longer endanger the health of that community; that thirty days shall be permitted in which this work shall be commenced, and thereafter completed with all possible dispatch.

Be it further resolved that State Sanitary Inspector James J. Wallis be instructed to see that the order of this Board is carried out, and that he be given discretionary power, so that if the permanent wells, to be sunk by said city from which they intend to get their future water supply can be installed, and thus avoid either the sinking of a temporary pump or the syphoning of Willow Creek, that it be allowed with the understanding, however, that in either event within thirty days bona fide work shall commence on one of the methods indicated in these resolutions.[1]

In a somewhat more limited number of jurisdictions

Gen. Stat. 1923, §5375; N. H. Public Laws 1915, §1618-35; N. Y. Cons. Laws Supple. 1918, p. 6575; Ohio Code 1926, §1251; Okla. Comp. Stat. 1921, §8975; Ore. Laws 1923, §8473; Vt. Gen. Laws 1917, §6314; Va. Code 1924, §1789; Wis. Stat. 1925, §144.03. Similar supervision may be exercised under a "blanket clause" of the general health laws in Arkansas, Connecticut, Florida, Kentucky, Maine, Mississippi, Montana, New Hampshire, New Mexico, North Dakota, Pennsylvania, South Dakota, Texas, Washington and Wyoming.

[1] *Idaho State Board of Health, Report 1912*, p. 8.

the state administrative authorities have been directed to use the *ordinance-making* power to the same end.[1] Thus it is possible for the supervising officials to enact such rules and regulations, relative both to the construction and operation of these enterprises as may seem desirable; certain basic principles may be laid down and certain fundamental errors avoided. If all else fails the state board of health in three or four jurisdictions is empowered to *remove* any water-works operator in the state for inefficiency or such other reason as seems satisfactory.[2]

SEWAGE SYSTEMS

Closely allied to the problem of maintaining a pure water supply is the maintenance of an efficient sewage disposal system. In many states, consequently, state administrative supervision has been extended into this sphere of local activity. In certain of its aspects the supervision already discussed affects both directly and indirectly the operation of many of these plants. Nevertheless, the necessity for dealing specifically with this phase of municipal activity has been recognized in many states. In general, the supervision exercised in this connection very closely resembles that maintained over systems of water supply. The mechanisms of control brought into play are very much the same. In half a dozen states *reports* are called for.[3] These, according to the

[1] Ind. Annot. Stat. 1926, §8122; Iowa Code 1924, §2197; Ky. Stat. 1922, §2054; La. Supple. p. 852; Md. Code 1924, art. 43, §335; Mass. Gen. Laws 1921, ch. iii, §160; Mich. Comp. Laws Supple. 1922, §5025; N. H. Public Laws 1926, p. 525; N. C. Stat. 1919, §7117; Ohio Code 1926, §1240; Ore. Laws 1920, §8460; Vt. Gen. Laws 1917, §6314. In addition similar authority has been granted the health councils under some "blanket clause" of the general health laws in Alabama, Arkansas, Colorado, Missouri, Montana, New Jersey, New Mexico, New York, North Dakota, South Dakota, Texas, Washington, Wisconsin and Wyoming.

[2] Such seems to be the law in Alabama, Arkansas, Colorado and New Jersey.

[3] Kan. Rev. Stat. 1923, §65-166; Md. Code 1924, art. 43, §331; Mich. Comp. Laws Supple. 1922, §5034; N. J. Comp. Laws 1910, p. 819; Ohio Code 1926, §1240; Okla. Comp. Stat. 1921, §8728.

statement of many supervising officials, make it possible to maintain much better control over these plants than would otherwise be the case. " The prescribed tests and reports make it necessary that some intelligent person give some attention to the works. The tests furnish the operator with data valuable in operating a plant in an efficient and intelligent manner. 'Since it is impossible to make monthly inspections of each plant the reports keep the managers in touch with this office so that with a more limited personnel more efficient supervision is possible. (They) also create much more interest and pride in the city disposal plants on the part of city officials than. would otherwise exist." [1]

The backbone of this supervision, however, as in the case of the supervision exercised over water supplies, is the process of *inspection* which is maintained in at least thirty-eight commonwealths.[2] In the vast majority of these, the initiative in this inspection rests with the state authorities. In two, however, Indiana and Wyoming, a complaint on the part of some resident in the community is necessary to set the machinery in action.

Since the mere knowledge of undesirable conditions will not in itself change those conditions, the state agencies in

---

[1] *Report of the Michigan Department of Health 1920*, p. 17.

[2] Conn. Gen. Stat. 1918, §2554; Fla. Rev. Stat. 1920, §2005; Iowa Code 1924, §2191; Kan. Rev. Stat. 1923, §65-164; Md. Code 1924, art. 43, §10; Mass. Gen. Laws 1921, ch. iii, §5; Mich. Comp. Laws Supple. 1922, §5034; Mont. Rev. Code 1921, §2462; N. H. Public Laws 1926, p. 492; N. J. Comp. Laws 1910, p. 819; N. Y. Cons. Laws Supple. 1921-3, p. 1708; Ohio Code 1926, §1240; Okla. Comp. Stat. 1921, §8976; R. I. Gen. Laws 1923, §2336; S. C. Code 1922, §2364; W. Va. Code 1923, ch. 150, §2; Wis. Stat. 1925, §140.05; Wyo. Comp. Stat. 1922, §3601. Similar supervision may be maintained by authority of some "blanket clause" in the general health laws in Alabama, Arkansas, California, Delaware, Georgia, Illinois, Indiana, Kentucky, Louisiana, Maine, Missouri, New Mexico, North Dakota, Oregon, Pennsylvania, South Dakota, Texas, Utah, Virginia and Washington.

a goodly number of jurisdictions have been granted still further powers with which to effect results. In thirty-seven states, for example, the practice of disseminating *advice* has been extensively developed.[1] The provision of law which directs the state authorities to take such action in this connection is very often the one which bestows a similar responsibility upon them in connection with water supplies. The commissioner of health is frequently directed " to consult with, and advise cities which have or are about to have systems of water supply, drainage or sewage, as to the most appropriate source of water supply and the best method of insuring its purity, or as to the best method of disposing of its drainage or sewage with reference to existing or future needs of other cities, towns or persons which may be affected thereby." *All* such plans in a number of states must be submitted to the supervising authorities for their advice before being put into operation.

Moreover, the same reasoning which led to still further grants of supervisory power in connection with water purification plants has led to similar action here. Consequently, in at least thirty-one jurisdictions, the *approval* of the state authorities and not merely their advice is required.[2] Some-

[1] Conn. Gen. Stat. 1918, §2554; Fla. Rev. Stat. 1920, §2005; Iowa Code 1924, §2191; Kan. Rev. Stat. 1923, §65-174; Maine Laws 1917, ch. 98; Md. Code 1924, art. 43, §330; Mass. Gen. Laws 1921, ch. iii, §17; Mich. Comp. Laws Supple. 1922, §5033; Mont. Rev. Code 1921, §2648; N. H. Public Laws 1926, p. 492; N. J. Comp. Laws 1910, p. 819; N. Y. Cons. Laws Supple. 1921-3, p. 1708; Ohio Code 1926, §1240; Okla. Comp. Stat. 1921, §8976; R. I. Gen. Laws 1923, §2336; S. C. Code 1922, §2364; W. Va. Code 1923, ch. 150, §2; Wis. Stat. 1925, §140.05. Similar supervision may be maintained by authority of some "blanket clause" in the general health laws in Alabama, Arkansas, California, Delaware, Illinois, Indiana, Kentucky, Louisiana, Missouri, New Mexico, North Dakota, Oregon, Pennsylvania, South Dakota, Texas, Utah, Virginia, Washington and Wyoming.

[2] Cal. Pol. Code 1915, Act 2830; Conn. Gen. Stat. 1918, §2554; Fla. Rev. Stat. 1920, §2161; Ill. Laws 1912, p. 358, §369; Kan. Rev. Stat. 1923,

times it is the approval of the state board of health that is necessary; at other times, the approval of the state water supply commission. In either case, before any construction work on a drain or sewer may begin, the approval of some state supervising agency is requisite. In general, the procedure followed here very closely resembles that used in con- nection with water supplies. The most frequent form in which such approval is signified is through the issuance of a permit. Typical, in a measure at least, of both the steps that are followed and the form of the final action is a permit issued to School District Number 12, Oyster Bay, August 30, 1920.

Application having been duly made to the state commissioner of health, as provided by section 76 of chapter 49 of the *Laws of 1908,* the Public Health Law, as amended by chapter 553 of the *Laws of 1911* constituting chapter 45 of the *Consolidated Laws,* permission is hereby given to the board of trustees of school district no. 12, Town of Oyster Bay, to discharge sewage effluent from the proposed system of leaching cesspools into the ground waters tributary to the Atlantic ocean within the town of Oyster Bay, Nassau County, New York, in accordance with the plans accompanying the petition, under the following con- ditions: 1. That only sanitary or domestic sewage and no storm water or surface water from streets, roofs, or other areas shall be admitted to the proposed sewage disposal plant. 2. That the sewage disposal plant shown by plans approved this day shall

§65-165; Maine Laws 1917, ch. 198, §6; Md. Code 1924, art. 43, §335; Mass. Gen. Laws 1909, p. 215; Mich. Comp. Laws Supple. 1922, §5033; Minn. Gen. Stat. 1923, §5344; Mont. Rev. Code 1921, §2463; N. H. Public Laws 1913, ch. 205; N. J. Comp. Laws 1910, §5635; N. Y. Cons. Laws Supple. 1921-2, p. 1709; N. C. Laws 1919, §7119; Ohio Code 1926, §1240; Okla. Comp. Stat. 1921, §8976; Ore. Laws 1920, §8460; Penn. Stat. 1920, §18249; W. Va. Code 1923, ch. 120, §6a; Wis. Stat. 1925, §140.05. Similar supervision may be maintained by virtue of some "blanket clause" in the general health laws in Alabama, Iowa, Kentucky, Louisiana, New Mexico, North Dakota, Texas, Virginia, Washington and Wyoming.

be fully constructed in complete conformity with such plans or approved amendments thereof except that the interconnecting pipes be made 5 inches in diameter and the manhole openings be made 24 inches in diameter. 3. That when necessary the sludge shall be removed from the proposed plant in such a manner as to cause no nuisance, and disposed of by burying in some remote place. 4. That wherever required by the state commissioner of health, additional cesspools shall be installed, or detailed plans for some other satisfactory method of disposal of the sewage of the school shall be submitted for approval; and upon the approval of such plans any or all portions of such disposal plant for the complete treatment of sewage shall be constructed and put in operation at such time or times thereafter as said commissioner may designate.[1]

Since the chief aim of the statutes in this connection is the protection of the waters of the state, it is not surprising to discover that in many states in which no general requirement of approval exists, state sanction is nevertheless necessary in so far as all cities that wish to dispose of their waste in lakes, rivers or waterways are concerned.

Not only is the construction of these undertakings subject to state *approval,* but in at least sixteen jurisdictions their operation and maintenance is as well.[2] Moreover, in twenty-six states the supervising officials have been empowered to issue such *orders* relative to the maintenance of these systems as seem desirable.[3] Indeed, in approximately half of the

---

[1] *New York Department of Health, Report 1920,* p. 75.

[2] Conn. Gen. Stat. 1918, §2554; Fla. Gen. Stat. 1920, §2162; Kan. Rev. Stat. 1923, §65-165; Md. Code 1924, art. 43, §332; Mich. Comp. Laws Supple. 1922, §5033; Minn. Gen. Stat. 1923, §5344; Ohio Code 1926, §1240; Okla. Comp. Stat. 1921, §8977; Wis. Stat. 1925, §144.04. Similar supervision may be exercised by virtue of some "blanket clause" in the general health laws in Illinois, Louisiana, New Jersey, New Mexico, New York, Texas and Washington.

[3] Conn. Gen. Stat. 1918, §2554; Fla. Gen. Stat. 1920, §2164; Iowa Code 1924, §2191; Kan. Rev. Stat. 1923, §65-164; Md. Code 1924, art. 43, §329;

states the administrative authorities may guide their operation through the enactment of detailed rules and regulations. With these powers it is hoped the state supervising officials will be able to prevent the contamination of the water supplies of the state from these sources.[1]

VITAL STATISTICS

A fifth field singled out for attention is concerned with the collection of vital statistics. The necessity for accuracy in these reports is apparent. " The state, like an army, cannot protect itself against its enemies unless its executive officers know the location and strength of those enemies. . . . Disease and death are the enemies. Figures show the points of attack; figures also show the effect of measures of control and prevention." [2] By means of these reports the state health authorities are enabled to determine whether adequate control measures have been instituted by the local authorities, and whether or not additional advice and assistance are needed.

Mich. Comp. Laws Supple. 1922, §5034; N. Y. Cons. Laws Supple. 1921-23, p. 1708; Ohio Code 1926, §1240; Okla. Comp. Stat. 1921, §8976; R. I. Gen. Laws 1923, §2336; W. Va. Code 1923, ch. 150, §2; Wis. Stat. 1925, §144.03. Similar supervision may be exercised by virtue of some "blanket clause" in the general health laws in Alabama, Arkansas, California, Indiana, Massachusetts, Missouri, Montana, New Hampshire, New Jersey, New Mexico, North Dakota, South Dakota, Washington and Wyoming.

[1] Ark. Session Laws 1917-19, Act no. 2830; Fla. Gen. Stat. 1920, §2164; Ind. Comp. Laws 1924, §7594; Iowa Code 1924, §2191; La. Supple. 1926, p. 852; Md. Code 1924, art. 43, §335; Mass. Gen. Laws 1921, ch. iii, §160; Mich. Comp. Laws Supple. 1922, §5026; N. J. Comp. Laws 1915, §1619; N. Y. Cons. Laws Supple. 1918, p. 6575; Ohio Code 1926, §1240; S. C. Code 1922, §23131; W. Va. Code 1919, §5342. Similar supervision is exercised by virtue of authority granted under some "blanket clause" of the general health laws in Alabama, California, Kentucky, Montana, New Mexico, North Dakota, Oregon, South Dakota, Texas, Virginia and Wyoming.

[2] *Biennial Report of the Louisiana State Board of Health 1921-22*, p. 18.

To furnish the state health authorities with the material upon the basis of which they may arrive at accurate conclusions, state registrars of vital statistics have been making strenuous efforts to stimulate accuracy in registration. To this end municipalities are used as units of registration in at least forty-five states, and the local registrars are required to send in their reports to the state registrar of vital statistics either directly or through the medium of some regional supervisor.[1] Although in the vast majority of states certain basic facts are called for in the laws, nevertheless, in at least forty-four jurisdictions the supervising authorities may call for such additional *data* as they see fit.[2] In some forty-two states, moreover, the *procedure* to be used in the collection and tabulation of these statistics *may likewise be dictated* by the state authorities.[3] The pressure which

---

[1] Cal. Pol. Code 1923, §3080; Col. Comp. Laws 1921, §970; Conn. Gen. Stat. 1918, §2376; Del. Rev. Code 1915, §797; Fla. Gen. Stat. 1920, §2068; Ga. Code 1914, §1676m; Idaho Comp. Stat. 1919, §1624; Ill. Rev. Stat. 1923, §65-3; Ind. Annot. Stat. 1926, §8123; Iowa Code 1924, §2393; Kans. Rev. Stat. 1923, §65-102; Ky. Stat. 1922, §20620-i; La. Stat. 1920, p. 776; Maine Rev. Stat. 1916, p. 427; Md. Code 1924, art. 43, §16; Mass. Gen. Laws 1921, ch. iii, §29; Mich. Comp. Laws Supple. 1922, §4992; Minn. Gen. Stat. 1923, §5355; Miss. Code 1917, §4871; Mo. Rev. Stat. 1919, §5796; Mont. Rev. Code 1921, §2516; Neb. Comp. Stat. 1922, §8228; N. J. Comp. Laws Supple. 1911-24, p. 2724; N. Y. Cons. Laws Supple. 1921-23, §740; N. C. Cons. Stat. 1919, §7086; N. D. Comp. Laws 1913, §435; Okla. Comp. Stat. 1921, §8667; Ore. Laws 1920, §8487; Penn. Stat. 1920, §8975; R. I. Gen. Laws 1923, §2341; S. C. Code 1922, §2356; Tenn. Code 1919, §3118ac; Va. Code 1924, §1561; Wash. Comp. Stat. 1922, §6011; W. Va. Code 1923, ch. 150, §23; Wyo. Rev. Stat. 1912, §2955. By virtue of by-laws enacted under a general grant of authority a similar procedure exists in Alabama, Arkansas, New Hampshire, New Mexico, Ohio, South Dakota, Texas, Utah and Wisconsin.

[2] New Hampshire seemingly while allowing the state authorities to call for reports does not allow them to prescribe the contents thereof.

[3] Ala. Pol. Code 1923, §1067; Cal. Pol. Code 1923, §3080; Col. Comp. Laws 1921, §970; Conn. Gen. Stat. 1918, §2376; Del. Rev. Code 1915, §797; Fla. Rev. Stat. 1920, §9068; Ga. Annot. Code 1914, §1676m; Idaho

may be put upon the local registrars of vital statistics to carry out these rules and regulations has already been indicated. In at least thirty-three jurisdictions any local registrar who in the judgment of the state board of health " fails or neglects to discharge efficiently the duties of his office . . . . shall forthwith be *removed* from said office by the state board of health." The fact that the local registrars in exactly half the states in the Union owe their positions to state *appointment* may likewise contribute to a certain respect on their part for the rules and regulations of the state authorities.

MISCELLANY

The miscellaneous fields over which state supervision has been exercised include swimming pools, places of public assembly, hospitals, and so forth.

One has but to scan a few paragraphs of a recent Rhode Island report to be convinced that there is something to be said for the practice of state supervision over swimming pools, a practice that is also found in California, Florida and New Mexico.

During the summer of 1920 a number of visits were made

Comp. Stat. 1919, §1624; Ill. Rev. Stat. 1923, §65-3; Ind. Annot. Stat. 1926, §8123; Iowa Code 1924, §2393; Kan. Rev. Stat. 1923, §65-102; Ky. Stat. 1922, §2062a-1; La. Stat. 1920, p. 776; Maine Rev. Stat. 1916, p. 427; Md. Code 1924, art. 43, §16; Minn. Gen. Stat. 1923, §5355; Miss. Code 1917, §4871; Mo. Rev. Stat. 1919, §5796; Mont. Rev. Code 1921, §2516; Neb. Comp. Stat. 1922, §8228; Nev. Rev. Stat. 1919, §2955; N. J. Comp. Laws Supple. 1911-24, p. 2724; N. Y. Cons. Laws Supple. 1921-3, §1740; N. C. Cons. Stat. 1919, §7086; N. D. Comp. Laws 1913, §435; Okla. Comp. Stat. 1921, §§8667, 8983; Ore. Laws 1920, §8486; Penn. Stat. 1920, §§8975, 8985; R. I. Gen. Laws 1923, §2341; S. C. Code 1922, §§2356, 2393; Tenn. Code 1919, §3118a-1; Va. Code 1924, §1561; Wash. Comp. Stat. 1922, §6011; W. Va. Code 1923, ch. 150, §23. Similar supervision is maintained by virtue of some " blanket clause " in the general health law in Arkansas, New Mexico, Ohio, South Dakota, Texas, Utah and Wisconsin.

by state officials in Rhode Island to each of the wading pools in the various playgrounds. Samples of the water were collected for analysis, and *inspection* was made of the prevailing sanitary conditions. So far as possible complete information was obtained as to the care of the pool, the number of persons using it, etc. In all, eight pools were visited.

At practically all of the pools which are fed from the city mains, the volume of water flowing through them was entirely too small to keep the pool clean. . . . Nearly all (of them) are very much overcrowded on hot days and analysis of the water in every one showed evidence of pollution with body wastes. At the Menne Park pool the conditions were particularly bad, owing to the fact that not only is the volume of water flowing very small, but that this water merely flows across one end and does not effect any purification of the main body of water in the pool. Moreover, this pool has a natural earth bottom and is only cleaned in the spring. Frequently as many as 1200 persons use this pool in a day, and at such times the water is extremely dirty and an analysis shows marked evidence of pollution. Although officially designated as " Wading Pools " these pools are really nothing but shallow bathing or swimming pools. Most of the children and adults bring bathing suits, and those who do not, usually go into the water all over in whatever clothes they have on. At some of the pools, tents or houses are provided where patrons may change their clothes and in some instances these houses were also found to be in a filthy condition.[1]

In a few states the mechanism of *grant-in-aid* is called into play in connection with particular types of hospitalization. Such is the case in Washington, Massachusetts and California with respect to hospitals operated by the municipalities for the exclusive treatment of tubercular cases. In commenting upon the results of this supervision the state

[1] *Rhode Island Department of Health, Report 1920*, p. 59.

board of California is emphatic. " Sad comparisons can be made of the excellent care given in hospitals as a result of the subsidy, against the small appropriation and inadequate quarters provided when there is no subsidy or standard to meet." In Alabama, Indiana, Massachusetts, New York and Wisconsin aid is given to venereal disease clinics only. The situation in New York, perhaps, is typical. To aid in the establishment of such clinics, the venereal disease division of the state department of health offered to subsidize any city that undertook the organization of a clinic by supplying it with adequate equipment, providing the city on its part would secure a suitable location and employ a physician to do the work. The division furthermore offered to subsidize the clinic by supplying the required arsphemaminee and by offering to pay, for the first year, one half the salary of the nurse who should be employed to do the follow-up work. At present, the clinics in New York City and forty-two clinics outside the city have taken advantage of the offer and are functioning under these conditions.[1]

Passing mention should perhaps be made of the fact that a similar grant is made in Ohio, Missouri and New Jersey in connection with the extermination of mosquitoes. In Illinois, although no money grant is made, certain professional services are rendered by state officials without cost to the municipalities.

Notice should also be taken of the supervision maintained over places of public assembly. For the most part, however, this is maintained under some clause of a state housing law or else some blanket provision of the health code.[2]

[1] *New York Department of Health, Report 1920*, p. 100.

[2] Conn. Stat. 1918, §2364; Mont. Code 1907, §1482; N. J. Comp. Laws 1910, p. 2657, §6; Vt. Gen. Laws 1917, §6200. Colorado, Delaware, Florida, Illinois, New Hampshire, New Mexico, North Dakota, Oregon, Utah and Virginia likewise maintain such supervision by virtue of some " blanket clause " in the general health laws of the respective states.

It appears consequently that state boards of health have been given considerable power of supervision over local health activity generally, and even greater power over certain particular phases of this activity. In the majority of states these general powers of supervision seem to be designed to allow the state authorities to assume a position of natural leadership. To this end extensive powers for the amassing of information and the dissemination of advice have been lodged in their hands. In addition these supervising agencies have been very frequently permitted to lay down the broad outlines of municipal health activity, and in times of emergency or dire inefficiency on the part of the local authorities to step in and take over the administration of the local health service themselves.

The supervision maintained over those phases of municipal health activity which have been marked for particular consideration—personnel, local sanitary ordinances, the collection of vital statistics, the construction and operation of water-works and sewage system, etc.—is much more intensive and much less a gun behind the door. It is obviously designed to keep these aspects of municipal health activity under constant surveillance by the state authorities.

CHAPTER V

EDUCATION

" To an extent characteristic of no other institution save that of the state itself, the school has power to modify the social order." [1]   Were no other considerations involved, this fact alone would be sufficient justification for raising the question of the proper allocation of this tremendous power.   Needless to say, numerous other factors are present in the situation.   Approximately one fifth of the entire country is enrolled in the public schools, the combined budgets of which total at least a billion and a half dollars a year. The property involved is valued at more than two billions. [2] The task of administering this colossal enterprise, consequently, would also suffice as a reason for raising this question.   And difficult as the burden of administration is, it is completely overshadowed by certain educational problems still awaiting solution.   The presence of approximately 6,000,-000 people in the country over ten years of age who are unable to read or write certainly calls for action.   Equally important is the task of assimilating the alien races who have flocked to our shores, a portion of which, at least, devolves on our public schools.   No less serious is the problem of moral education.   Conservative estimates based upon the 1920 census indicate that an outlaw army more than a million strong is continually preying upon the people of the country. A total of 576,000 jail-birds were actually incarcerated in the

[1] Dewey, John, *Moral Principles in Education,* New York (1909), p. v.

[2] *Statistics of City School Systems 1921-1922,* Bureau of Education Bulletin 1924, No. 34, pp. 4, 6, 221.

142

penal institutions of the country in 1919.[1]   To some degree, at least, this too must be considered an educational problem. The fact is that the industrial revolution has to a considerable extent broken down the training once received in the home, intellectual as well as moral, and this, together with the growing complexity of modern life, is making the task of the schools more and more difficult.

The answer to the question—what agency is best fitted to wield this tremendous power, to carry on this stupendous task of administration, and effectively to solve these educational problems—is, consequently, of considerable importance.   Historically the answer which has been given in the field of education is the same as that which originally was given in the field of health; to wit, the locality.   And there are many who believe this historic answer has been the correct one.   The danger point of centralization, they contend, is, if anywhere, in the realm of education.   In support of this contention they point to Europe.   To the centralized school system of Prussia more than to any other single factor they accredit the ultra-nationalism of the Germans.   Similarly, they believe a centralized school system is in large measure responsible for the chauvinism of the French.   These are by no means the only faults, however, deemed inherent in the system.   The very atmosphere it creates is considered reprehensible.   Even the slight centralization of control which has developed in American has called forth bitter invective.

Says a writer in *School and Society:*

That liberating freedom of thought which Bertrand Russell celebrates as the supreme merit of education, the freeman's inheritance, is as alien to the conception of our reigning schoolmen as intellectual honesty to the traditional diplomat. A bureaucracy by its very nature is primarily and whole-heartedly interested in power, prejudice and prestige. ... The board of educa-

[1] Henderson, G. C., *Keys to Crookdom*, New York (1924), p. 7.

tion, the board of examiners, the board of superintendents—what human bond ties them to the teaching body? Those tight little bureaucracies move and have their beings in smug microcosms of their undisputed own. They are centers of fear and authority, not in any imaginable sense centers of suggestion, inspiration or even enhanced efficiency. . . . System overshadows personality. Conformity ousts originality. Obedience usurps the place of reflection.[1]

This, the believers in decentralization contend, is the inevitable result of centralization.

Their view, nevertheless, is by no means universally accepted. There are those who maintain that a certain degree of centralization is both inevitable and necessary. They contend that " the danger which above all others a democratic nation must avoid is disintegration into units with no immediate concern but self-interest, into individuals to whom social duties and bonds are gradually ceasing to appeal." The most effective preventive of such disintegration is, as they see it, education. And that this great unifying force will be directed toward this end much more effectively if it is vested in the hands of the state authorities than if it lies scattered about in the hands of local boards of education in ten thousand municipalities seems to them obvious.

The great mass of people are comparatively uncultivated, and the uncultivated cannot be competent judges of cultivation. Those who most need cultivation are least capable of finding their way to it by their own lights. By many people education is not desired, and where the end is not desired, the means will not be provided. If the end should be, as it probably would, as in many communities we know it is, erroneously conceived, the means provided would not be suitable. These are the reasons why the state is morally bound to exercise the legal prerogatives of providing public education. *But observe, the same arguments which re-*

[1] Howe, S. C., *School and Society,* 1919, p. 706.

quire the state to provide public education, require it when it delegates powers to a municipality to take all necessary measures to guard against the abuse of these powers.[1]

More forcible, perhaps, than either of these general considerations are certain characteristics which have developed in local educational administration. Take the local school board for example!

Everyone knows the school board. Men get on it who want to get on; the beach-comber who is interested in smuggling into the system his sisters, and his cousins, and his aunts; the solemn man who believes in his kind of education, but is opposed to taxation with or without representation; the safe and sane conservative citizen who gets on to keep the other fellow off, or to keep them from spending too much. Besides these, if there is a college in the community, a college professor crops up in the board at rare intervals to represent the interests of culture in the college faculty ward; or lacking colleges or other legitimate machinery of the higher side of life, the legal profession is usually drawn upon, as the next best traditional contributor to educational experience. . . . This board, of course, knows what education is, not necessarily by having had it, to be sure, any more than a doctor needs to have every disease he treats. It is aware, however, of its own duties which are to levy the school tax, to put up new buildings when it becomes necessary to shine down a rival town; and last, if not least, to hire the teachers.[2]

Even more biting in his denunciation of the existing system is J. P. Munro.

The expenditure of educational funds is in the hands, not of experts but of amateurs . . . of school boards whose members

[1] Maxwell, W. H., *A Quarter Century of Public School Development*, New York (1912), p. 287. Mr. Maxwell, it should be said, changed his point of view before he died. His summing up, however, still stands as a cogent expression of this point of view.

[2] Roberts, H. F., *School and Society*, 1919, p. 370.

know little or nothing concerning this stupendous enterprise over which they have autocratic control; of teachers a majority of whom are untrained and who regard their occupation merely as a make-shift; and in too many cases, of corrupt politicians who look upon the schools as so much added loot in their sacking of the modern Babylon. Think of it! A business capitalized at nearly eight billions of dollars, in which, therefore, every man, woman and child has one hundred dollars at stake; a business, moreover, having branches in every city and town and in almost every hamlet of the United States, is carried on—with notable exceptions which but emphasize the general inadequacy—by boards of directors who know practically nothing about it, and by agents who are largely untrained, underpaid, and temporary. The business, moreover, is so unsafeguarded as to be at the mercy of any unscrupulous men who may desire to use it as a means to their own political fortunes, or as quarry for their "honest graft". . . . Even the best school boards are composed of business men confessedly unacquainted with education since their school days, while the worst are made up of "heelers" with eyes glued upon the funds available for graft or bribery. . . . Is it to be wondered at that school superintendents, even where they exist at all, are most successful when they are most politic, that teachers have little genuine interest in a profession dominated by the untrained or worse. The confessions of experienced school superintendents would make disheartening reading. They would be stories, mainly of dealings with petty despots, ignorant of education, but eager to exercise their absolute authority—stories, therefore, of intrigue, of the flattering of vanities, and catering to personal weakness, of wearing away unreasoning prejudices, of yielding to improper pressures from those having life-and-death power over one's career, of sacrificing the children to save the teachers and to save one's self.[1]

Whether these accounts are exaggerated or not is, per-

[1] Munro, J. P., *New Demands of Education*, New York (1912), p. 8 *et seq.*

haps, a moot question. That there is an element of truth in them is less controversial. At any rate, whether wisely or not, the forces making for centralization have slowly but surely been carrying the day. The first state superintendent of common schools was appointed to office in New York in 1812. By 1844 Illinois, Louisiana, Pennsylvania, Rhode Island, Tennessee, and Vermont had all followed suit. More than half the states had fallen into line by 1850, and by 1861 twelve others had followed their example. Since that date state supervision has come to be a generally accepted fact. The history of the ensuing years is, in reality, merely the history of the gradual strengthening of the supervisory bodies. Today there are few aspects of elementary or secondary education which are not to some extent subject to state administrative supervision. Indeed, in many states practically all local educational activities are subject in a limited degree at least to the guidance of state officials. In certain fields this supervision is much more stringent than in others. Chief among these are the selection of the teaching personnel, the determination of the school curriculum, and the selection of the text books on the basis of which instruction is to be given. In addition, special attention has been paid to the development of courses in agriculture, home economics, and industrial training, as well as special classes for defectives in a great many jurisdictions. School libraries, normal training, high schools, school attendance, the length of school terms and the condition of school buildings have also been singled out as objects worthy of consideration.

GENERAL SUPERVISION

A limited degree of supervision over all educational activity is maintained practically everywhere. In this connection the mechanisms of *reports, inspection* and *advice* are those most widely used. Although in a few states the scope of material which may be called for in the reports is strictly limited to certain data specified in the laws, for the most part the grant of statutory authority in this connection is unusually sweeping.[1]   The provision of the New York code which empowers

1 Annual Reports: Ala. School Code 1924, art. 3, §12; Ariz. Rev. Stat. 1913, §2705; Ark. Stat. 1921, §8797; Cal. Pol. Code 1923, §1532; Col. Comp. Laws 1921, §8273; Conn. Gen. Stat. 1918, §34017; Del. Laws Spec. Sess. 1920, ch. 48, §21; Fla. Rev. Stat. 1920, §464; Ga. Annot. Code 1914, §1466; Idaho Comp. Stat. 1919, §820; Ill. Rev. Stat. 1923, ch. 122, §4; Ind. Stat. 1926, §6520; Iowa Code 1924, §4106; Kan. Rev. Stat. 1923, §72-207; Ky. Stat. 1922, §4399a-9; La. Supple. Stat. 1926, Act 100, §§5, 44; Maine Rev. Stat. 1916, p. 357; Md. Code 1924, art. 79, §19; Mass. Gen. Laws 1921, ch. 72, §3; Mich. Comp. Laws 1915, §5689; Minn. Gen. Stat. 1923, §2977; Miss. Annot. Code Supple. 1917, §7397; Mo. Rev. Stat. 1919, §11185; Mont. Code 1921, §935; Neb. Comp. Stat. 1922, §6478; Nev. Rev. Laws 1919, §3244; N. H. Public Laws 1926, ch. 116, §111; N. J. School Laws, §19; N. M. Session Laws 1923, ch. 148, §105; N. Y. Cons. Laws 1918, p. 2019; N. C. Cons. Stat. 1919, §5442; N. D. Code 1913, §1108; Ohio Code 1926, §7784; Okla. Stat. 1921, §10297; Ore. Laws 1920, §4996; Penn. School Laws 1921, §1002; R. I. Gen. Laws 1923, §976; S. C. Code 1922, §2537; S. D. Rev. Stat. 1919, §7424; Tenn. Code 1917, §1409; Tex. Civil Stat. 1925, §2661; Utah Code 1917, §4518; Vt. Gen. Laws 1917, §1195; Va. Code 1924, §644q; Wash. Stat. 1922, §4523; W. Va. Code 1923, ch. 45, §19; Wis. Stat. 1925, §39.11; Wyo. Comp. Stat. 1920, §2307.

In the majority of states certain specified information may be obtained at the call of the state authorities.   Ala. School Code 1924, art. 3, §12; Ariz. Rev. Stat. 1913, §2705; Ark. Stat. 1921, §8797; Cal. Pol. Code 1923, §1532; Col. Comp. Laws 1921, §8270; Conn. Gen. Stat. 1918, §1017; Del. Laws Spec. Sess. 1920, ch. 48, §21; Fla. Rev. Stat. 1920, §454; Ga. Annot. Code 1914, §1466; Idaho Comp. Stat. 1919, §803; Ill. Rev. Stat. 1923, ch. 122, §4; Ind. Stat. 1926, §6431; Kan. Rev. Stat. 1923, §72-204; La. Supple. Stat. 1926, Act 100, §§5, 44; Maine Rev. Stat. 1916, pp. 357, 362; Md. Code 1924, art. 77, §19; Mass. Gen. Laws 1921, ch. 69, §1; Mich. Comp. Laws 1915, §5691; Minn. Gen. Stat. 1923, §2977; Miss. Annot. Code Supple. 1917, §7397; Mo. Rev. Stat. 1919, §11185; Mont. Code 1921, §935; Neb. Comp. Stat. 1922, §6478; Nev. Rev. Laws 1919, §3244; N. H. Public Laws 1926, ch. 116, §11; N. J. School Laws, §19; N. M. Session Laws 1923, ch. 148, §105; N. Y. Cons. Laws 1918, p. 2019; N. D. Code 1913, §1135; Ohio Code 1926, §7784; Okla. Stat. 1921, §10299; Ore. Laws 1920, §4996; Penn. School Laws 1921, §317; R. I. Gen. Laws 1923, ch. 66, §4; S. C. Code 1922, §2537; S. D. Rev. Stat. 1919, §7424; Tenn. Code 1917, §1409; Tex. Civil Stat. 1925, §2661; Utah Code

the regents to obtain from all schools under their supervision " duly verified reports giving such information and in such form as the regents or the commissioner of education shall from time to time require " is more or less typical of the average statute. It is not uncommon, however, even in connection with as sweeping a grant of power as this, to find enumerated in the law a long list of specific items which must be included in the reports thus demanded. For the most part this information may be obtained whenever the supervising authorities so desire. In a number of the states, however, a definite date is set for an annual report, which may or may not be supplemented by demands for further information as the state authorities see fit.

Augmenting the information thus obtained is that acquired through the process of *inspection*.[1] In many in-

1917, §4518; Vt. Gen. Laws 1917, §1195; Wash. Stat. 1922, §4523; W. Va. Code 1923, ch. 45, §19; Wyo. Comp. Stat. 1920, §142.

Similarly in the majority of jurisdictions the state authorities may request such information as they see fit. Ala. School Code, art. 3, §12; Ariz. Rev. Stat. 1913, §2705; Ark. Stat. 1921, §8797; Cal. Pol. Code 1923, §1532; Col. Comp. Laws 1921, §8273; Conn. Gen. Stat. 1918, §1017; Del. Laws Spec. Sess. 1920, ch. 48, §21; Fla. Rev. Stat. 1920, §554; Ga. Annot. Code 1914, §1466; Idaho Comp. Stat. 1919, §803; Ill. Rev. Stat. 1923, ch. 122, §4; Ind. Stat. 1926, §6431; Iowa Code 1924, §4106; Kan. Rev. Stat. 1923, §72-204; La. Supple. Stat. 1926, Act 100, §§5, 44; Maine Rev. Stat. 1916, p. 357; Md. Code 1924, art. 77, §19; Mass. Gen. Laws 1921, ch. 69, §1; Mich. Comp. Laws 1915, §5691; Minn. Gen. Stat. 1923, §2977; Miss. Annot. Code Supple. 1917, §7397; Mo. Rev. Stat. 1919, §11185; Mont. Code 1921, §935; Neb. Comp. Stat. 1922, §6478; Nev. Rev. Laws 1919, §3244; N. H. Public Laws 1926, ch. 116, §11; N. J. School Laws, §19; N. M. Session Laws 1923, ch. 148, §105; N. Y. Cons. Laws 1918, p. 2019; N. D. Code 1913, §1135; Ohio Code 1926, §7784; Okla. Stat. 1921, §10317; Ore. Laws 1920, §4996; Penn. School Laws 1921, §317; R. I. Gen. Laws 1923, ch. 66, §4; S. C. Code 1922, §2537; S. D. Rev. Stat. 1919, §7424; Tenn. Code 1917, §1409; Tex. Civil Stat. 1925, §2661; Utah Code 1917, §4518; Vt. Gen. Laws 1917, §1195; Wash. Stat. 1922, §4523; W. Va. Code 1923, ch. 45, §19; Wis. Stat. 1925, §39.11; Wyo. Comp. Stat. 1920, §142.

[1] Inspection of elementary schools: Ala. School Code, art. 3, §12; Ariz. Rev. Stat. 1913, §2705; Cal. Pol. Code 1923, §1519; Col. Comp. Laws 1921,

stances in no way other than by personal visitation is it possible to obtain that understanding of a situation so necessary in educational work. And in no other way it might be added is it possible so effectively to disseminate sound advice. In thirty states, consequently, the mechanism has been used for the control of elementary education, and in a somewhat smaller number for the supervision of high schools. The commissioner of education in a number of jurisdictions is personally enjoined to visit every town and city in the state for the purpose of inspecting the schools therein; in others, he is empowered to appoint inspectors for the task. It is very probable that in those states in which a suitable staff is thus placed at the disposal of the state educational authorities, the supervision maintained is superior to that exercised elsewhere. Illustrative of the statutory grants of authority in this connection is the provision in the code of

§8270; Ga. Annot. Code 1914, §1467; Idaho Comp. Stat. 1919, §803; Ind. Rev. Stat. 1921, ch. 197, §1; Iowa Code 1924, §3831; Kan. Rev. Stat. 1915, §8876; Ky. Stat. 1922, §4398a-1; Maine Rev. Stat. 1919, p. 25; Md. Code 1924, art. 77, §35; Mass. Gen. Laws 1921, ch. 69, §1; Mich. Comp. Laws 1922, §2828; Miss. Annot. Code Supple. 1917, §7595; Mo. Rev. Stat. 1919, §11336; Neb. Comp. Stat. 1913, §6901; Nev. Rev. Laws 1919, §3244; N. H. Public Laws 1901, p. 305; N. J. Comp. Stat. Supple. 1911-14, §185-21c; N. Y. Cons. Laws 1918, p. 2019; N. D. Code 1913, §1427; Ohio Code 1920, §7753; Ore. Laws 1920, §4918; R. I. Gen. Laws 1909, p. 207; S. C. Code 1922, §2532; Tenn. Code 1917, §1408; Utah Code 1917, §4518; Vt. Gen. Laws 1917, §1172; Va. Code 1924, §610; W. Va. Code 1923, ch. 45, §19.

Inspection of high schools: Ala. School Code, art. 4, §55; Cal. Pol. Code 1923, §1519; Ga. Annot. Code 1914, §1467; Idaho Comp. Stat. 1919, §803; Ky. Stat. 1922, §4398a-1; Maine Rev. Stat. 1919, p. 25; Md. Code 1924, art. 77, §35; Mass. Gen. Laws 1921, ch. 69, §1; Mich. Comp. Laws 1915, §5641; Miss. Annot. Code Supple. 1917, §7597; Mo. Rev. Stat. 1919, §11336; Nev. Rev. Laws 1919, §3244; N. J. Comp. Stat. Supple. 1911-14, §185-21c; N. Y. Cons. Laws 1918, p. 2019; Ore. Laws 1920, §4918; R. I. Gen. Laws 1923, ch. 81; S. C. Code 1922, §2533; S. D. Rev. Stat. 1919, §7386; Tenn. Code 1917, §1408; Utah Code 1917, §4518; Vt. Gen. Laws 1917, §1172; W. Va. Code 1923, ch. 45, §19.

Indiana setting forth, as it does, the procedure to be followed in that jurisdiction.

The state superintendent of public instruction with the approval of the state board of education shall appoint within thirty days a suitable person to inspect elementary and high schools, if in the judgment of the majority of the state board of education the circumstances and need of the schools warrant the services of more than one inspector.

That such control is highly desirable seems almost axiomatic to officialdom. Over and over again in the reports of the state departments of education is found the contention that such supervision is absolutely essential. Appeal is frequently made to the practice of private business. " On investigation," says a recent report of the superintendent of education in Delaware, " it has been found that one telephone operator in eleven devotes her full time to the remaining ten. The hospitals place one nurse in charge of five to fourteen others. Department stores use one supervisor to twenty-five sales people. Banks have one supervisor over six to fifteen persons. Admitting our school system is a very important business proposition, these figures indicate that the request for supervision and supervisors is not unreasonable." [1]

In this quotation, be it noted, emphasis is placed not upon the acquisition of information by this process, but upon the maintenance of guidance and the *dissemination of advice.* The very substitution of the word supervisor for that of inspector indicates that it is this aspect of the mechanism which is uppermost in the mind of the author of the quotation. "Valuable service is rendered," says another superintendent, not only " in creating a stronger school sentiment, but in making helpful suggestions, encouraging and stimulating

[1] *Report of Delaware State Board of Education 1920,* p. 33.

school officers. Seeing the best in equipment, management and instruction, these officials are in a position to offer officers and teachers the benefit of criticism, timely, restraining and suggestive, in the light of this wise observation. Vested with state authority, they often give progressive superintendents, teachers and school officers needed moral support in communities where a too conservative public opinion prevails. State inspection has been a directing force in the more judicious and economical expenditure of public funds for the construction of school houses, in the employment of trained and competent superintendents and teachers, and in efforts toward the unification of courses of study." [1]

In addition to the *dissemination of advice* in this manner, at least five other channels are used: public addresses, conventions of superintendents, teachers' institutes, the mail, and publicity.

Very frequently no method for the dissemination of advice can be as effective as that of personal visitation, for concrete suggestions after all depend upon first-hand knowledge of conditions, to obtain which in many instances the supervising officer must actually visit the classroom, since there only can the process of teaching be seen. Nevertheless supervision of this character is exceedingly expensive as a single in-

---

[1] *Report on Public Instruction 1905-6*, Minnesota, p. 9. And as a result of this reasoning some twenty-two states specifically direct their educational authorities to make use of this medium for the dissemination of advice: Ark. Stat. 1921, §8949; Cal. Pol. Code 1923, §1532; Del. Laws Spec. Sess. 1920, ch. 48, §7; Fla. Rev. Stat. 1920, §487; Ind. Stat. 1926, §6430; Md. Code 1924, art. 77, §35; Miss. Annot. Code Supple. 1917, §7603; Mo. Rev. Stat. 1919, §11336; Mont. Code 1921, §943; Nev. Rev. Laws 1919, §3244; N. M. Session Laws 1923, ch. 148, §205; N. Y. Cons. Laws 1918, p. 2035; N. C. Cons. Stat. 1919, §5392; N. D. Code Supple. 1925, §1433; Ohio Code 1926, §354; Okla. Stat. 1921, §10306; Ore. Laws 1920, §4918; R. I. Gen. Laws 1923, ch. 65, §1; Tenn. Code 1917, §1408; Utah Code 1917, §4518; Vt. Gen. Laws 1917, §1182; Wyo. Comp. Stat. 1920, §2332. It is probable, however, that such action is common in every state which maintains a system of supervision.

dividual can cover only a limited number of class-rooms in a day. Furthermore many of the points to be made are so general in their character that personal conferences are by no means necessary. Consequently these other avenues of action may very frequently be used with considerable justification.

The effectiveness of disseminating advice through the medium of a group varies, of course, according to the character of the group. Although conceding that some good may be accomplished under all circumstances, one cannot help wondering whether making addresses to the general public is the best use that can be made of a supervisor's time.[1] It seems probable to the casual observer at least that the time spent with specialized groups, city superintendents or teachers, is much more profitably employed. On this theory provision is made in a number of states for holding conventions of county and city superintendents.[2] In some juris-

[1] Cal. Comp. Laws 1921, §8270; Del. Laws Spec. Sess. 1920, ch. 48, §7; Ill. Rev. Stat. 1923, ch. 122, §3; Iowa Code 1924, §3831; La. Stat. Supple. 1926, Act 100, §41; Maine Rev. Stat. 1916, p. 383; Mass. Gen. Laws 1921, ch. 69, §1; Mont. Code 1921, §948; N. M. Session Laws 1923, ch. 148, §205; N. C. Comp. Stat. 1919, §5392; N. D. Code 1913, §1110; Okla. Stat. 1921, §10303; R. I. Gen. Laws 1923, §933; S. C. Code 1922, §2533; Wyo. Comp. Stat. 1920, §2332. It must be conceded that the necessity of educating the general public to the point of accepting or backing an educational policy sometimes justifies extensive use of this avenue for the dissemination of advice.

[2] Ala. School Code, art. 4, §42; Ariz. Rev. Stat. 1913, §2705; Cal. Pol. Code 1923, §1533; Del. Laws Spec. Sess. 1920, ch. 48, §7; Fla. Rev. Stat. 1920, §153; Idaho Comp. Stat. 1919, §803; Iowa Code 1919, §2267; Ky. Stat. 1922, §4512; La. Supple. Stat. 1926, Act 100, §40; Maine Rev. Stat. 1917, p. 183; Md. Code 1924, art. 77, §29; Mass. Gen. Laws 1921, ch. 69, §1; Miss. Annot. Code Supple. 1917, §7603; Mont. Code 1921, §943; N. H. Public Laws 1926, ch. 117, §29; N. J. Comp. Stat. Supple. 1911-14, §185-21c; N. C. Cons. Stat. 1919, §5436; N. D. Code Supple. 1925, §1137; Ohio Code 1926, §354; Ore. Laws 1920, §5011; R. I. Gen. Laws 1923, ch. 74; S. D. Rev. Stat. 1919, §7386; Utah Code 1917, §4524; Vt. Laws 1923, no. 32; Wash. Stat. 1922, §4523; W. Va. Code 1923, ch. 45, §21; Wis. Stat. 1925, §40.695.

dictions this action is mandatory; in others, it seems to be optional. Illustrative of the legislative enactments in this connection are the provisions of law in New Jersey and West Virginia. In New Jersey the law is mandatory. The commissioner of education " shall hold meetings of city and county superintendents at least once in each year for the discussion of school affairs, and ways and means of promoting a thorough and efficient system of education." [1] In West Virginia, on the other hand, the state superintendent of education is merely given " authority to call conferences of county, district and city superintendents . . . . for considering with them any matters relating to the conditions and needs of the schools, and the proper means of improving the schools throughout the state," but no duty to do so is imposed upon him.[2]

Some conception of the manner in which this mechanism operates and the value thereof can be obtained from a comment made by the superintendent of public instruction in Utah some time ago in which he said:

These gatherings are most valuable not only for the excellence of the programs which are furnished almost wholly by the superintendents themselves, but for the opportunities afforded for the informal discussion of the practical daily difficulties of educational administration and supervision as they present themselves in the various city and rural districts throughout the state. The range of subjects presented in the programs, the varied experience of the different superintendents, the keen insight into conditions that exist in the various districts, the frank, constructive criticisms which were in constant evidence and the appreciation the superintendents have for each other are all matters for congratulation. During the convention . . . a number of important matters came up, were discussed and finally made sub-

[1] *Supra.*

[2] *Supra.*

jects for resolutions conveying to the code commission the attitude of the superintendents and indicating certain lines of needed legislation. Among these may be mentioned: the time of taking the school census, violation of contract by teachers, procedure in the formulation of courses of study, the reorganization of the state department, and a number of less important matters.[1]

The value of these meetings obviously depends upon the capacity of those in charge, and for every one that is worth while there undoubtedly are others which are utterly worthless.

Equally effective, or at least of equal potentiality, is the work done through teachers' institutes which are held in the vast majority of states. In some jurisdictions these meetings are held under the aegis of the county or city superintendents by virtue of the authority vested in them by the statutes; in a number of states, however, they have been placed under the control of the state departments of education.[2] One state superintendent describes and evaluates the procedure as follows:

[1] *Utah Superintendent of Public Instruction, Report 1918, p. 37.*

[2] Ala. School Code 1924, art. 4, §43; Ariz. Laws 1921, ch. 134; Ark. Stat. 1921, §8764; Col. Comp. Laws 1921, §8455; Conn. Gen. Stat. 1918, §826; Del. Laws Spec. Sess. 1920, ch. 48, §7; Fla. Rev. Stat. 1920, §153; Ga. Annot. Code 1914, §1474; Idaho Comp. Stat. 1919, §803; Ill. Rev. Stat. 1923, ch. 122, §283; Iowa Code 1924, §4108; Kan. Rev. Stat. 1923, §72-1403; Ky. Stat. 1922, §4509; La. Supple. Stat. 1926, Act 100, §40; Maine Rev. Stat. 1916, p. 383; Md. Code 1924, art. 77, §29; Mass. Gen. Laws 1921, ch. 69, §1; Mich. Comp. Laws 1915, §5641; Minn. Gen. Stat. 1923, §3059; Miss. Annot. Code Supple. 1917, §7776; Mo. Rev. Stat. 1919, §11336; Mont. Code 1921, §836; Neb. Comp. Stat. 1922, §6448; Nev. Rev. Laws 1919, §3244; N. H. Public Laws 1926, ch. 116, §34; N. M. Session Laws 1923, ch. 148, §105; N. Y. Cons. Laws 1918, p. 2259; N. C. Cons. Stat. 1919, §5638; N. D. Code Supple. 1925, §1113; Ohio Code 1926, §7725; Okla. Stat. 1921, §10301; Ore. Laws 1920, §4918; R. I. Gen. Laws 1909, p. 267; S. D. Rev. Stat. 1919, §7388; Tenn. Code 1917, §1409; Utah Code 1917, §4524; Vt. Laws 1923, no. 32; W. Va. Code 1923, ch. 45, §21; Wyo. Comp. Stat. 1920, §2326.

During the past year contact with the larger schools was made for the most part through conferences of teachers at the county teachers' meetings. In several of these a special program on the round table plan was arranged. Topics of general yet immediate interest were outlined, including such matters as the grading of pupils, study habits of pupils, securing supervised study, cooperation of the home, and the teaching of certain subjects such as English. As these meetings brought together the teachers of all classes of schools, the more important activities could be followed and new lines of progress developed. Altogether the round table conference proved a very acceptable and seemingly profitable program.

Equally important as a channel for the dissemination of advice in this field as in all others is the mail. Merely a glance at the mass of material which must be handled by the state departments of education each year is conclusive. An analysis of the correspondence of the department of education in Washington may possibly be of interest. Certainly there is no reason why the correspondence of this department should be heavier than that of departments elsewhere. All told in 1918, the only date for which such an analysis has been made, thirty thousand six hundred and fifty-two communications were received. Of these ten thousand seven hundred and eighty were classified as general. One thousand five hundred and forty-two related to legal problems and approximately the same number, one thousand two hundred and forty-nine, were concerned with the internal operations of the state board itself. Seven hundred and twenty-five dealt with county problems. By far the largest number, however, nine thousand five hundred and sixteen, were concerned with the examination and certification of teachers. High school problems were responsible for four hundred seventy-one inquiries, and educational meetings for six hundred sixty-eight. Vocational education in its turn evoked four hundred sixty-six. Inquiries relative to vouchers and warrant books ran up to four hundred seventy-three, and approximately one hundred and fifteen were received concerning questions of registration and records. Three hundred and ninety-seven pieces of correspondence related to annual reports and apportionment, whereas rural life conferences seemingly necessitated five hundred and twenty, and community centers, four hundred and eighty-nine. In the maintenance of clubs, fairs and extension work over one thousand items of correspondence were involved. The remaining letters were more or less miscellaneous. It is impossible to tell from the data furnished in the report the exact proportion of this correspondence which was maintained with the educational authorities of the various municipalities; nevertheless there can be no question but that they received their due share. What proportion of this correspondence can rightly be classified as advice is also difficult to determine. The bulk of it, however, undoubtedly falls into that category.

The part that publicity plays in this connection likewise, can be measured only roughly. Most state departments of education, however, make extensive use of bulletins and circulars which are sent free to those who are interested.[1]

[1] Ala. School Code 1924, art. 4, §14; Ariz. Rev. Stat. 1913, §2705; Cal. Pol. Code 1923, §1560; Col. Comp. Laws 1921, §8269; Conn. Gen. Stat. 1919, §826; Del. Laws Spec. Sess. 1920, ch. 48, §7; Fla. Rev. Stat. 1920, §153; Ga. Annot. Code 1914, §1466; Idaho Comp. Stat. 1919, §803; Ill. Rev. Stat. 1923, ch. 122, §3; Ind. Stat. 1926, §6442; Iowa Code 1924, §3831; Ky. Stat. 1922, §4395; La. Supple. Stat. 1926, Act 100, §41; Maine Rev. Stat. 1916, p. 383; Md. Code 1924, art. 77, §12; Mass. Gen. Laws Supple. 1921, ch. 69, §1; Miss. Annot. Code 1917, §7603; Mo. Rev. Stat. 1919, §11344; Mont. Code 1921, §938; Neb. Comp. Stat. 1922, §6479; Nev. Rev. Laws 1919, §3244; N. M. Session Laws 1923, ch. 148, §205; N. Y. Cons. Laws 1918, p. 2035; N. C. Cons. Stat. 1919, §5392; N. D. Code 1913, §1110; Ohio Code 1926, §354; Okla. Stat. 1921, §10303; R. I. Gen. Laws 1923, §933; S. C. Code 1922, §2533; Tex. Civil Stat. 1925, §2656; Utah Code 1917,

Amongst the pamphlets most widely distributed in Missouri are: (1) the high school course of study, which contains a detailed outline of the work to be done in the different classes of schools together with the requirements of teachers and school equipment; (2) the elementary courses of study, outlining the work of the eight elementary grades, showing the system of alternation, and giving the requirements for approved rural schools; (3) the school laws, a digest of the laws relating to schools including all opinions and supreme court decisions relative thereto; (4) a syllabus of courses for teacher-training high schools, giving a complete outline of the courses in education and a list of the reference books required; (5) plans for both school buildings and equipment; (6) a high school directory; (7) regulations regarding state and county certificates together with the rules governing the issuance and renewal of such certificates; (8) a circular of high school credits, containing a list of the public high schools, the class to which each belongs and the amount of credit given; (9) the annual report on the condition of the public schools; (10) the premium list of the educational exhibit and state fair, listing all articles for which premiums are offered each year at the state fair; (11) a vocational educational bulletin, giving the plan for the administration of the Smith-Hughes Act together with the requirements for teachers and supervisors; (12) a plant production bulletin outlining a year's work in plant production for the vocational high schools; (13) an animal production bulletin similar to the above; and (14) a bulletin on clothing, food and shelter, outlining courses for two years' work in home economics. While this list can in no wise pretend to be typical, some idea of the uses of publicity in the field of education can, perhaps, be obtained from it.

§4520; Wash. Stat. 1922, §4685; W. Va. Code 1923, ch. 45, §23; Wyo. Comp. Stat. 1920, §2332.

In addition to the supervision thus exercised by the dissemination of advice through these various channels, the mechanism of *grant-in-aid* has been called into play.[1] Two or possibly three purposes have motivated the legislatures in the enactment of this legislation: first, a desire to equalize the revenues available for school purposes among the various communities; second, the maintenance of at least a minimum of efficiency in school management and operation; and third, the development of new services. Very often all three purposes motivate a single grant. Insofar as the purpose of the grant is mainly the equalization of the revenues available for school purposes among the different localities, it falls somewhat afield of the purpose of this study. Insofar as its object is the development of new services it is devoted to a rather specialized pursuit and will be discussed a little later. Insofar as it is devoted to the maintenance of a minimum of efficiency throughout the state in educational activity, it must be considered an agency of control within the scope of this discussion. However, so closely and intricately are the purposes of these grants bound together that some overlapping in any treatment thereof is inevitable.

In some variations of the mechanism it is impossible to discern any supervisory purpose whatever; in others the object is written plainly in the statutes. Just what administrative end is in view when state money is apportioned to the localities upon the basis of property valuation, for example, is difficult to determine. Since the wealthier communities receive the greater amount of state support irrespective of their educational needs or activities, it can hardly be argued that the objective involved is a more effective equalization of the educational opportunities of the state, and certainly no increased efficiency of administration

[1] MacDowell, T. L., *State v. Local Control of Elementary Education*, U. S. Bureau of Education, Bulletin No. 22, 1915.

is attained thereby. Maine and New Jersey, nevertheless, make use of this procedure.[1]

Somewhat more understandable but far from effective from any administrative point of view is the system of apportioning the subsidies upon the basis of school population.[2] Although such a distribution bears a much closer relation to the educational burdens of the various communities than the method of apportionment indicated in the preceding paragraph, nevertheless comparatively little stimulus to the educational authorities results therefrom. The size of the school population in a community is very largely determined by forces over which the school administration has no control. There is no necessary correlation, therefore, between the size of the grant and manner in which the municipality attempts to meet its educational needs. The only effect of the system accordingly may be a lowering of the municipal tax rate. It is assumed, however, and possibly with some justification, that this will not take place, and that a minimum of revenue at any rate is guaranteed the local school board. Such is the method of apportioning certain state funds in thirty-three states.

A somewhat better measure of the relative educational burden of the various school districts is that of pupil-attendance.[3] The cause of expenditure after all is not the potential student, but the pupil in attendance. Thus the locality which is actually facing its problem either through a stricter enforcement of the compulsory attendance law, or through the establishment of high schools, vocational schools, evening schools or other schools can be given aid somewhat in proportion to the effort it is putting forth, whereas the com-

[1] MacDowell, *op. cit.*, p. 17. A transfer of the burden of taxation from one form of wealth to another, is, of course, effected.

[2] *Ibid.*, p. 22.

[3] *Ibid.*, p. 11.

munity which is slack will be docked accordingly. The total effect of this arrangement should be to stimulate to some slight degree, but only to a slight degree, the establishment of continuation schools, and particularly to stimulate the enforcement of the attendance laws, for this method of apportionment penalizes a trifle at least all irregularities in attendance, since both teaching staff and equipment must remain about the same whether the attendance is regular or irregular, and each absence means so much less than the possible total the community might receive from the state school fund. This variation of the mechanism is used in connection with certain school funds in eleven states.

Another basis of distribution found in three jurisdictions is in inverse ratio to the value of property.[1] Its prime object, of course, is an equalization of educational opportunities and is based upon the general theory that given equal or nearly equal educational appropriations something like equal educational systems will develop.

A somewhat different objective is sought in those statutes which apportion the subsidies upon the basis of the ratio of the local school levy to the sum-total of taxation for local purposes.[2] An attempt is obviously being made here to stimulate local taxation for educational purposes.

Of similar design although with a somewhat different purpose is that apportionment which is based upon the number of teachers employed.[3] It furnishes some slight incentive to the employment of an adequate number of teachers, or perhaps it might be more accurate to say that such a grant destroys part of the barrier that is responsible for whatever under-staffing may exist, namely, lack of funds.

Thus it appears that the mechanism of grant-in-aid may

[1] MacDowell, *op. cit.*, p. 11.

[2] *Ibid.*, p. 11.

[3] *Ibid.*, p. 11.

be used merely as a method for the redistribution of wealth or as a means of raising the general standards of education. Even when it accomplishes merely a transfer of wealth, it is probably conducive to the development of higher standards of educational administration in the backward regions of the state. Elsewhere, as in the last two variations of the mechanism described, although no great power is concentrated in the hands of state officials, the system does nevertheless create a situation in which the municipality must act, if the full benefits of state aid are to be obtained.[1]

The prevailing conception of education as a state function, however, has called for more drastic means of control than is possible through any of the mechanisms thus far discussed. For the most part this more stringent supervision has been confined to particular phases of educational activity, personnel, curriculum, textbooks, etc. In a number of jurisdictions, nevertheless, the mechanisms of *review* and *ordinance making* have been called into full play.

More than half the states permit their state educational authorities full discretion in prescribing the blanks for reports, records, etc.[2] And surprisingly large number seem to have granted these authorities the full sweep of the ordinance-making power, within the limits, of course, set up by the state constitution and the statutes.[3] In Louisiana, to

---

[1] MacDowell, *op. cit.*, p. 11.

[2] Ala. School Code 1924, art. 4, §56; Ark. Stat. 1921, §8797; Cal. Pol. Code 1923, §1519; Col. Comp. Laws 1921, §8269; Conn. Gen. Stat. 1918, §826; Fla. Rev. Stat. 1920, §483; Ga. Annot. Code 1914, §1466; Idaho Comp. Stat. 1919, §803; Ind. Stat. §1926, §6441; Iowa Code 1924, §3831; Ky. Stat. 1922, §4392; Maine Rev. Stat. 1916, p. 384; Mass. Gen. Laws 1921, ch. 69, §4; Neb. Comp. Stat. 1922, §6474; N. H. Public Laws 1926, ch. 116, §11; N. J. Comp. Stat. Supple. 1911-14, §185-16; Ore. Laws 1926, §4918; Penn. School Laws 1921, §1013; R. I. Gen. Laws 1923, §935; S. C. Code 1922, §2533; S. D. Rev. Stat. 1919, §7386; Tenn. Code Supple. 1920, §1420; Tex. Civil Stat. 1925, §2656; Utah Code 1917, §4519; Vt. Laws 1923, no. 32; Wash. Stat. 1922, §727; W. Va. Code 1923, ch. 45, §19.

[3] Ariz. Rev. Stat. 1913, §2697; Cal. Pol. Code 1923, §1519; Col. Comp.

become specific, the state board of education is instructed to prepare rules and regulations for the direction of the schools of the state which shall have the force of law, and which must be enforced by the parish superintendents and local school boards.[1] The superintendent of schools in Mississippi is given general supervision over the free public schools and " may prescribe such rules and regulations for the efficient organization and conduct of the same as he may deem necessary." [2] In New York the regents " shall exercise legislative functions concerning the educational system of the state, determine its educational policies . . . . and establish rules for carrying into effect the laws and policies of the state relating to education, and the powers, duties, and trusts conferred or charged upon the university." [3] Fuller powers of policy determination can scarcely be imagined.

In a somewhat smaller number of jurisdictions, all controversies arising under the school laws of the states are subject to the *adjudication* of the state educational authorities.[4] "Any person considering himself aggrieved [by any

Laws 1921, §8256; Del. Laws Spec. Sess. 1920, ch. 48, §7; Ill. Rev. Stat. 1923, ch. 122, §3; Ind. Stat. 1926, §6446; Ky. Stat. 1922, §4382; La. Supple. Stat. 1926, Act 100, §4; Md. Code 1924, art. 77, §11; Miss. Annot. Code Supple. 1917, §7595; N. H. Public Laws 1926, ch. 116, §5; N. M. Session Laws 1923, ch. 73, §101; N. Y. Cons. Laws 1918, p. 2016; Ohio Code 1926, §357; Ore. Laws 1926, §4963; S. C. Code 1922, §2549; Va. Code 1924, §609; W. Va. Code 1923, ch. 45, §14.

[1] *Supra.*

[2] *Supra.*

[3] *Supra.*

[4] Ala. School Code 1924, art. 4, §42; Fla. Rev. Stat. 1920, §153; Ill. Rev. Stat. 1923, ch. 122, §3; Ind. Stat. 1926, §6792; Iowa Code 1924, §4302; Ky. Stat. 1922, §4396; Md. Code 1924, art. 77, §11; Miss. Annot. Code Supple. 1917, §7580; Mont. Code 1921, §943; N. J. Comp. Stat. Supple. 1911-1924, §185-21c; N. M. Session Laws 1923, ch. 73, §101; Ohio Code 1926, §361; Ore. Laws 1926, §4918; R. I. Gen. Laws 1923, §1017; S. C. Code 1922, §2562; Tex. Civil Stat. 1925, §2656; Vt. Gen. Laws 1917, §1273 (Disputes over transportation only); Wash. Stat. 1922, §5065.

action of a local school board in New York, for example], may appeal or petition to the commissioner of education who is hereby authorized and required to examine and decide the same and his decision shall be final." [1]   Almost as sweeping are the powers granted in this connection in Rhode Island. " Any person aggrieved by any decision or doings of any school committee may appeal to the commissioner of schools who shall examine and decide the same without cost to the parties." [2]   Nothing contained in this section is to be construed, however, so as to deprive the aggrieved party of any legal remedy.

PERSONNEL

In addition to the control thus exercised over educational activities generally, certain phases of local administration have been deemed worthy of special consideration.   Of these, the matter of teaching personnel, is, perhaps, the most outstanding.   Not only has the recruiting of the force been subjected to extensive regulation, but conduct in office has likewise been made a matter of state administrative concern. The part played in this connection by the mechanisms of *reports, inspection* and *advice* needs no further elaboration.

Passing notice should be given, however, to that variation of the system of *grants-in-aid* which has been devised to bear directly upon this problem.   By arranging the state grant in such a way that it is less profitable for a community to pay a salary below a certain minimum and thereby lose the grant than it is to pay the higher salary and obtain the subsidy, the mechanism has been used to raise teaching salaries, and incidentally to attract into the profession a higher type of individual than would otherwise be willing to

[1] *Supra.*
[2] *Supra.*

make teaching a life work.[1] The exact arrangement necessary to accomplish this object must, of course, be worked out in connection with each specific situation. Similarly the mechanism has been used to raise the general level of educational attainments of the teaching profession,[2] and also to secure an adequate staff to carry the teaching load.[3] In a number of jurisdictions an attempt has been made through this medium to develop a system of local supervision. Certain qualifications deemed imperative in a local superintendent have been specified and the grant conditioned on the appointment to office of a man possessing the required attainments.[4]

Much more drastic and direct, however, is the control exercised in at least forty-four jurisdictions through the process of *examination and certification*.[5] In this procedure the

[1] Mass. Gen. Laws 1921, ch. 70, §2; Mo. Rev. Stat. 1919, §11265; Ohio Code 1926, §1210; Penn. School Laws 1921, §§1150, 2304; Utah Gen. Laws 1917, §4567.

[2] Ill. Rev. Stat. 1923, ch. 122, §335; Kan. Rev. Stat. 1923, §72-5002; Mass. Gen. Laws 1921, ch. 70, §2; Minn. Gen. Stat. 1923, §3030; N. D. Code Supple. 1925, §1441; Penn. School Laws 1921, §1150; Utah Code 1917, §4567.

[3] Cal. Pol. Code 1923, §1532; Idaho Comp. Stat. 1919, §907; Ill. Rev. Stat. 1923, ch. 122, §335; Mass. Gen. Laws 1921, ch. 70, §2; Mo. Rev. Stat. 1919, §11179; Mont. Code 1921, §1211; Nev. Rev. Laws 1919, §3390; N. Y. Cons. Laws 1918, p. 2201; N. C. Cons. Stat. 1919, §5481; Ohio Code 1926, §7600; Penn. School Laws 1921, §2304.

[4] Ark. Stat. 1921, §89; Conn. Gen. Stat. 1918, §895; Md. Code 1924, art. 77, §23; N. Y. Cons. Laws 1918, p. 2200; N. C. Cons. Stat. 1919, §5481; Ohio Code 1924, §§4744-1, 4744-4; Tenn. Code Supple. 1920, §1400a-1; Vt. Laws 1923, no. 32.

[5] Approval or certification of high school teachers: Ala. School Code 1924, art. 3, §17; Ariz. Rev. Stat. 1913, §2701; Ark. Stat. 1921, §9017; Col. Comp. Laws 1921, §1519a; Del. Laws Spec. Sess. 1920, ch. 48, §14; Fla. Rev. Stat. 1920, §493; Ga. Annot. Code 1914, §1498; Idaho Comp. Stat. 1919, §951; Ill. Rev. Stat. 1923, ch. 122, §3; Ind. Stat. 1926, §6447; Iowa Code 1924, §3869; Kan. Rev. Stat. 1923, §72-102; Ky. Stat. 1922, §4386; La. Supple. Stat. 1926, Act 100, §8; Maine Rev. Stat. 1916, p. 385; Md. Code

mechanisms of *approval and ordinance-making* are for the most part inseparably intertwined. Technically speaking, the act of certification is the act of approval; the setting-up of examinations, the process of ordinance-making.

The purpose of the examination is, of course, to furnish the supervisory authorities with adequate information upon which to base their judgment before indicating their approval through the issuance of a certificate. Some idea of the

1924, art. 77, §31; Mass. Gen. Laws 1921, ch. 69, §5; Mich. Comp. Laws 1922, §5814; Minn. Gen. Stat. 1923, §2907; Miss. Code 1917, §7794; Mo. Rev. Stat. 1919, §11334; Mont. Code 1921, §836; Neb. Comp. Stat. 1922, §6426; Nev. Rev. Laws 1919, §3255; N. H. Public Laws 1926, ch. 116, §24; N. J. Comp. Stat. Supple. 1911-24, §185-29; N. M. Session Laws 1923, ch. 148, §105; N. Y. Cons. Laws 1918, p. 2211; N. C. Cons. Stat. 1919, §5643; N. D. Code Supple. 1925, §1109; Ohio Code 1926, §7726; Okla. Stat. 1921, §10292; Ore. Laws 1926, §4956; Penn. School Laws 1921, §1113; R. I. Gen. Laws 1923, §1000; S. D. Rev. Stat. 1919, §7387; Tenn. Code Supple. 1920, §1449a-5; Tex. Civil Stat. 1925, §2890; Utah Code 1917, §4506; Vt. Gen. Laws 1917, §1202; Va. Code 1924, §688; Wash. Stat. 1922, §4529; W. Va. Code 1923, ch. 45, §97; Wis. Stat. 1925, §4057; Wyo. Comp. Stat. 1920, §2356.

Approval or certification of elementary school teachers: Ala. School Code 1924, art. 3, §17; Ariz. Rev. Stat. 1913, §2701; Ark. Stat. 1921, §9017; Cal. Pol. Code 1923, §1519a; Conn. Gen. Stat. 1921, ch. 238, §3230; Del. Laws Spec. Sess. 1920, ch. 48, §14; Fla. Rev. Stat. 1920, §493; Ga. Annot. Code 1914, §1498; Idaho Comp. Stat. 1919, §951; Ill. Rev. Stat. 1923, ch. 122, §3; Ind. Stat. 1926, §6447; Iowa Code 1924, §3869; Kan. Rev. Stat. 1923, §72-102; Ky. Stat. 1922, §4386; La. Supple. Stat. 1926, Act 100, §8; Maine Rev. Stat. 1921, p. 181; Md. Code 1924, art. 77, §31; Mich. Comp. Laws 1922, §5814; Minn. Gen. Stat. 1923, §2907; Miss. Code 1917, §7794; Mo. Rev. Stat. 1919, §11334; Mont. Code 1921, §836; Neb. Comp. Stat. 1922, §6426; Nev. Rev. Laws 1919, §3255; N. H. Public Laws 1926, ch. 116, §24; N. J. Comp. Stat. Supple. 1911-24, §185-29; N. M. Session Laws 1923, ch. 148, §105; N. Y. Cons. Laws 1918, p. 2211; N. C. Cons. Stat. 1919, p. 5643; N. D. Code Supple. 1925, §1109; Ohio Code 1926, §§8707-3, 7726; Okla. Stat. 1921, §10292; Ore. Laws 1926, §4956; Penn. School Laws 1921, §1016; R. I. Gen. Laws 1923, §1000; S. D. Rev. Stat. 1919, §7387; Tenn. Code Supple. 1920, §1449a-5; Tex. Civil Stat. 1925, §2890; Utah Code 1917, §4506; Vt. Gen. Laws 1917, §1202; Va. Code 1924, §688; Wash. Stat. 1922, §4529; W. Va. Code 1923, ch. 45, §97; Wis. Stat. 1925, §3922; Wyo. Comp. Stat. 1920, §2356.

necessity for this supervision may be obtained from only a brief perusal of the state reports. A letter cited below recently received by Superintendent Blair of Illinois may possibly serve to illustrate how great this necessity really is, for although the letter comes from an applicant for a position in a rural school, similar situations without doubt arise in connection with the administration of municipal educational systems.[1] Local sentiment was responsible for the fact that a woman, who to judge from her letter was hardly literate, had been placed in charge of the local school. Sympathy had superseded reason. And as a consequence the children of the district were compelled to go through life with the handicap of her inefficient teaching.

The requirement of state *approval* eliminates in some measure pressures of this kind as well as many others, for the mere fact that state officials live at a distant point makes them more difficult of access, and the fact that they are more likely to be men with a professional point of view means, of course, that they are less likely to get the functions of charity and education mixed. It has the advantage, moreover, of eliminating to some degree the " necessity " of yielding to the exigencies of local politics.

[1] "Dear Mr. Blair,

I have written on the teacher's examinations twice but failed. My memory is not so good as I wish it were. I have had a great deal of trouble but love teaching. Everyone is well pleased with me and I could get this school again or a third or fourth grade in town, both have been mentioned to me by the director, but I have only an emergency certificate. The county superintendent issued me an emergency certificate through sympathy and because the directors of this school and many others urged it. Now Mr. Blair won't you please let me have a certificate without emergency written on it for I just can't pass those awful examinations. I taught two terms when I was seventeen and eighteen years old. Now I am forty-six."

Yours truly,

School and Society, 1924, p. 76.

The procedure followed in the maintenance of this supervision varies, needless to say, from state to state. So excellent, however, is the description of the administrative machinery used in this connection in Alabama, found in one of the reports of the state superintendent, that the temptation to quote at length is irresistible. Although it cannot be claimed that this procedure is in any way typical, nevertheless, some idea of the general nature of the process can perhaps be obtained from this analysis.

To guard the gateway to the teaching profession of Alabama the law provides for a state board of examiners, and no person is eligible to teach in any public school who does not hold a state certificate. . . . The grand total of applicants for 1917-18 was 10,160 as compared with 12,263 the previous year. Of the 10,160 applicants 7,825 were white and 2,335 colored. By reference to the consolidated report of the board of examiners for 1917-18, it will be seen that certificates were issued as follows: life, 90; first, 803; second 1679; third, 3226; making a total of 5,798 who received certificates as against 4,976 the year before. The total number rejected was 4,362. Thus 52 percent of those actually writing the examination received certificates. . . . All the examination papers are graded by the two members of the board of examiners with the assistance of certain other well qualified persons who are retained as regular graders for each examination. Some of these graders have served for a decade and are thoroughly familiar with the work. Each applicant, therefore, may be fully assured that his or her papers will receive the most careful consideration possible. The papers are kept on file subject to inspection by the applicant for six months subsequent to the examination, after which they are destroyed. I am pleased to report that the work of the graders, as a rule, has proved highly satisfactory. I regret, however, to say that there are still a few applicants who endeavor to use unfair means in procuring a certificate by examination. The board is exercising every available precaution to detect and eliminate this type of applicant. A list of the names and addresses of all who are rejected for cheating is mailed to every county superintendent in the state.[1]

In many jurisdictions the county or city superintendents act as agents of the state department of education in the physical conduct of the examinations. The questions, however, are usually prepared by the state authorities and the answer papers are returned to them. In a number of jurisdictions also these local superintendents may issue temporary licenses entitling the holder to teach within their respective jurisdictions for a limited period of time, at the end of which they must usually obtain a state certificate. There are exceptions, of course, and many of the larger cities are free from state control entirely. The supposition in these instances is that the educational authorities in these jurisdictions, far from employing a teaching personnel below the standards imposed by the state, will actually require standards considerably higher than it is practical for the state departments to impose throughout the state at the present time.

The standards which are required of the teaching personnel are sometimes fixed by law. More often, however, they are left to the discretion of the state educational authorities. " The state board of education," runs the law in Vermont, " shall provide for the examination and certification of teachers, appoint times and places of examination, designate the examiners, *fix the standards required for certification,* classify the grades of certificates to be granted, prepare and procure the printing of questions for such examinations and blanks for teachers' certificates, and make all necessary regulations for such examinations and certification and for the revocation of certificates, and all expenses

[1] *Alabama State Department of Education, Report 1918,* p. 73.

connected with such examination and certification shall be
paid by the state." [1]   Equally sweeping is the grant of
authority in North Carolina, which provides that " the board
of examiners and institute conductors shall have entire control of examining, accrediting without examination and
certificating all applicants for the position of teacher, principal, supervisor, superintendent and assistant superintendent in all public elementary and secondary schools of North
Carolina urban and rural.   The board shall *prescribe rules
and regulations for examining, accrediting without examina-*

[1] Ordinances prescribing the qualifications of teachers: Ala. School Code
1924, art. 3, §17; Ariz. Rev. Stat. 1913, §2701; Cal. Pol. Code 1923,
§1519a; Del. Laws Spec. Sess. 1920, ch. 48, §14; Idaho Comp. Stat. 1919,
§803; Ind. Stat. 1926, §6946; Iowa Code 1924, §3861; Kan. Rev. Stat. 1923,
§72-1301; Ky. Stat. 1922, §4386; Maine Rev. Stat. 1916, p. 385; Md. Code
1924, art. 77, §16; N. H. Public Laws 1926, ch. 116, §8; N. J. Comp. Stat.
Supple. 1911-24, §185-29; N. M. Session Laws 1923, ch. 118, §105; N. Y.
Cons. Laws 1918, p. 2211; N. C. Cons. Stat. 1919, §5642; Ohio Code 1926,
§§7807-1, 2, 7822, 7833; Okla. Stat. 1921, §10292; S. C. Code 1922, §2549;
Utah Acts 1919, ch. 84; Vt. Gen. Laws 1917, §1202; Va. Code 1924, §610;
W. Va. Code 1923, ch. 145, §14; Wis. Stat. 1925, §4057.

Ordinances setting up examinations: Ala. School Code 1924, art. 3,
§17; Ariz. Rev. Stat. 1913, §2701; Ark. Stat. 1921, §8797; Cal. Pol. Code
1923, §1519a; Col. Comp. Laws 1921, §8263; Del. Laws Spec. Sess. 1920,
ch. 48, §14; Fla. Rev. Stat. 1920, §508; Ga. Annot. Code 1914, §1494;
Idaho Comp. Stat. 1919, §803; Ill. Rev. Stat. 1923, ch. 122, §294; Iowa
Code 1924, §3861; Kan. Rev. Stat. 1923, §7a-1301; Ky. Stat. 1922, §4386;
La. Supple. Stat. 1926, Act 100, §11; Maine Rev. Stat. 1916, p. 385; Md.
Code 1924, art. 77, §16; Mich. Comp. Laws 1915, §5881; Minn. Gen. Stat.
1923, §2907; Miss. Code 1917, §7794; Mo. Rev. Stat. 1919, §11358; Neb.
Comp. Stat. 1922, §6426; Nev. Rev. Laws 1919, §3255; N. H. Public Laws
1926, ch. 116, §24; N. J. Comp. Stat. Supple. 1911-24, §185-29; N. M.
Session Laws 1923, ch. 118, §105; N. Y. Cons. Laws 1918, p. 2211; N. C.
Cons. Stat. 1919, §5643; N. D. Code 1913, §1370; Ohio Code 1926, §§7819,
7726; Okla. Stat. 1921, §10292; Ore. Laws 1920, §4935; Penn. School
Laws 1921, §1310; R. I. Gen. Laws 1923, §1000; S. C. Code 1922, §2549;
S. D. Rev. Stat. 1919, §7386; Tenn. Code Supple. 1920, §1449a-5; Tex. Civil
Stat. 1925, §2878; Utah Code 1917, §4510; Vt. Gen. Laws 1917, §1202;
Va. Code 1924, §610; Wash. Stat. 1922, §4523; W. Va. Code 1923, ch. 45,
§97; Wis. Stat. 1925, §41.57; Wyo. Comp. Stat. 1920, §2356.

*tion and certifying all such applicants for the renewal and
extension of certificates and issuance of life certificates.* The
state board of examiners shall prepare all questions for examinations under this article." [1]

The use made of the authority thus granted varies from
state to state and can be discovered only by a detailed analysis
of the by-laws of each state board or department of education. An extract from a recent school report of Rhode
Island, summarizing the by-laws of the Rhode Island state
board of education in this particular, is perhaps justified as
illustrative of the action which may be taken under the
authority thus bestowed, although it can in no wise be considered typical.

" Since 1898 the law has required that every teacher employed
in a public school shall hold a certificate of qualification issued
by or under the authority of the state board of education.
Under the statutes the board exercises the right to determine
the requirements for certification, and to issue certificates of
various types. . . . In accordance with the general plan, and
under the new rules of the board certificates are now classified
and issued as follows: I. Professional certificates, valid for five
years and renewable, permanent on accredited experience of five
years in teaching and minimum credit for professional improvement. Qualification in Rhode Island education is required for
unconditioned professional certification. . . . These certificates
are classified as follows: (1) Professional certificate valid in
secondary schools; graduation from an approved college or
university, or satisfactory proof of equivalent education, and
two hundred and sixteen hours of professional courses in education. (2) Professional certificates valid in elementary
schools; graduation from an approved normal school requiring
graduation from a four-year high school for entrance. (3)
Professional certificate valid in primary and pre-primary

[1] *Supra.*

schools; graduation from the primary-kindergarten course in an approval normal school requiring graduation from a four year high school for entrance. (4) Limited professional certificates valid only for teaching a special subject or art; accredited academic qualifications and professional study equivalent to requirements for other professional certificates. (5) Conditional professional certificates; an applicant for a certificate who presents evidence of qualifications for a professional certificate except in Rhode Island education may receive a conditional professional certificate valid for one year on condition that he will qualify in Rhode Island education within that time. II. Provisional certificates: (1) Senior provisional certificates renewable and valid for five years in schools and subjects classified as for professional certificates. (a) Academic qualifications as for professional certificates, (b) successful experience of five years in teaching, (c) successful study of one year in normal school or equivalent including Rhode Island education. The holder of a senior provisional certificate may obtain a professional certificate by pursuing courses offered for study and improvement to teachers in service. (2) Junior provisional certificate valid for one year in elementary schools and classified by years from one to five. An initial provisional certificate may be granted to graduates of secondary schools on approved professional study in summer school or extention courses, or on examination. An advanced provisional certificate valid for another year may be granted on successful teaching and continued professional study until the candidate is entitled to a senior provisional certificate. (3) Special provisional certificates. A college graduate or a teacher of accredited experience of five years in public schools may receive a special provisional certificate valid for one year and renewable for one year after the holder has qualified in Rhode Island education.[1]

The peculiar conditions present in each state have prevented uniform development. Lack of space, however, pre-

---

[1] *Rhode Island School Report, 1920*, p. 211 *et seq.*

vents any extended treatment of the subject. Moreover, exceptions have very frequently been made in both the general laws and the ordinances of the state departments of education in this connection also, permitting particular municipalities to set their own standards so that only a detailed study of the special laws in each state could possibly reveal an exact picture of present conditions. Nevertheless, some idea of the general action which may be taken under this grant of authority may, perhaps, be obtained from the Rhode Island report just quoted.

The control of the supervising body over local personnel, however, does not end here. In a number of states the removal or suspension of a teacher by the local authorities is subject to state *review*.[1] In Iowa, for example, not only may a teacher, whose certificate to teach has been revoked by a local superintendent, appeal to the superintendent of public instruction for a hearing, but the revocation of the license does not go into effect until after the decision based upon the hearing has been handed down, and in the case of a life certificate, not until the superintendent's action has been affirmed by the board of examiners after full review. The statute in New York is , likewise, exceedingly explicit. " No teacher shall be removed during a term of employment unless for neglect of duty, incapacity to teach, immoral conduct, or other reason which when appealed to the commissioner of education shall be held by him to be sufficient cause for such dismissal."[2] The removal of teachers, however, is but one of the specific objects singled out for review in the jurisdic-

---

[1] Cal. Pol. Code 1923, §1519a; Col. Comp. Laws 1921, §8339; Idaho Stat. 1919, §973; Ill. Rev. Stat. 1923, §307; Iowa Code 1924, §3895; Minn. Gen. Stat. 1923, §2926; N. H. Public Laws 1926, ch. 117, §28; N. Y. Cons. Laws 1918, p. 218; Ore. Laws 1920, §4956; S. C. Code 1922, §2549; S. D. Rev. Stat. 1919, §7386; W. Va. Code 1923, ch. 45, §57.

[2] *Supra.*

tions making use of the mechanism.   Quite a number of states permit such action in cases of unfair grading.[1]

The use of the mechanism of state *appointment* in this connection seems to be totally unknown except in the case of a few local superintendents of schools; and in certain of these, the state's action is confined to filling vacancies caused by the resignation or death of the locally chosen occupant of the office.[2]

Such is not the case, however, with the process of *removal.*[3]   A surprisingly large number of states make use of the procedure.   For the most part it takes the form of a revocation of the license to teach, which *ipso facto* renders it impossible for the teacher concerned to continue his professional work within the state.   In some jurisdictions full discretion in the use of this power is lodged with the state

[1] Minn. Gen. Stat. 1923, §2926; Ohio Code 1926, §7858; Wis. Stat. 1925, §3927.

[2] Md. Code 1924, art. 77, §5; N. H. Public Laws 1926, ch. 116, §22; N. J. Comp. Stat. Supple. 1911-24, §185-22 (county superintendents only) ; Penn. School Laws 1921, §1011 (to fill vacancies); S. C. Code 1922, §2567 (to fill vacancies); Vt. Laws 1919, no. 55 (The State Board of Education nominates—local directors actually appoint) ; Va. Code 1924, §604.

[3] Ala. School Code 1924, art. 4, §42; Ariz. Rev. Stat. 1913, §2697; Ark. Stat. 1921, §8784; Cal. Pol. Code 1923, §1519a; Col. Comp. Laws 1921, §8264; Conn. Statutes 1921, ch. 238, p. 3230; Fla. Rev. Stat. 1920, §511; Idaho Stat. 1919, §959; Ill. Rev. Stat. 1923, ch. 122, §3; Iowa Code 1924, §3892; Kan. Rev. Stat. 1923, §72-1345; La. Supple. Stat. 1926, Act 100, §42; Mich. Comp. Laws 1915, §5883; Minn. Gen. Stat. 1923, §2926; Mont. Code 1921, §1099; Mo. Rev. Stat. 1919, §11334; Neb. Comp. Stat. 1922, §6434; Nev. Rev. Laws 1919, §3242; N. J. Comp. Stat. Supple. 1911-24, §185-32; N. M. Session Laws 1923, ch. 148, §105; N. Y. Cons. Laws 1918, p. 2212; N. D. Code 1913, §1374; Ohio Code 1926, §§7827, 7808, 7827-1; Okla. Stat. 1921, §10565; Ore. Laws 1920, §4956; Penn. School Laws 1921, §1322; R. I. Gen. Laws 1923, §1002; S. C. Code 1922, §2549; Tenn. Code Supple. 1920, §1449a-13; Tex. Civil Stat. 1925, §2878; Va. Code 1924, §688; Vt. Gen. Laws 1917, §1203; Wash. Stat. 1915, §4654; W. Va. Code 1923, ch. 45, §112; Wyo. Comp. Stat. 1920, §2356.

authorities; in others, certain specific charges must be made. Illustrative of the grant of power bestowed upon the state educational authorities in the states falling into the first category is that made in Iowa where " any certificate or diploma may be revoked by the board for sufficient cause." The superintendent of education in Alabama on the other hand may revoke only the certificates of such teachers as may " be guilty of immoral conduct or unbecoming and indecent behavior." In Montana, such action may be taken " for incompetence or immoral conduct." The line of demarcation between these two categories is obviously rather tenuous. In Michigan " the board of school examiners may suspend or revoke a teacher's license for neglect of duty, incompetence or immorality," but only " after a hearing."

Although the application of this power to those other than the teaching staff is somewhat less frequent, nevertheless the superintendents of public instruction in at least fourteen states are " authorized and empowered to revoke the licenses of any county examiner or superintendent who fails or neglects to perform any of the duties required of him by law." In New York, to multiply examples, " whenever it shall be proved to the satisfaction of the commissioner of education that any trustee, member of a board of education, clerk, collector, treasurer, school commissioner, superintendent of schools, etc., has been guilty of any wilful violation or neglect of duty under this chapter, or any other act pertaining to the common schools or other educational institutions participating in state funds, or wilfully disobeying any decision, order or regulation of the regents or of the commissioner of education, said commissioner may, by an order under his hand and seal, which order shall be recorded in his office, remove such school officer from office." Such in general is the grant of power in the states listed below. In one or two jurisdictions the sweep of authority thus bestowed upon the state administrative officials is very much limited. Attendance officers only are subject to such supervision in Indiana, and in Alabama only district superintendents who neglect the legal requirements in regard to the pay of teachers.[1]

Needless to say action of this character is not taken by the state departments of education save under exceptional circumstances.

CURRICULUM

A second phase of educational activity which has been singled out for special consideration is the content of the school curriculum. Two mechanisms of control have been chiefly used — *ordinance making* and *grants-in-aid*. In those states in which the state departments of education have been empowered to *prescribe* the course of study for the schools, state administrative supervision has, indeed, made headway.[2] Examples might readily be multiplied. The

[1] Ark. Stat. 1915, §360; Del. Laws Spec. Sess. 1920, ch. 48, §89; Fla. School Laws, art. 12, §3; Ga. Annot. Code 1914, §1565; Ind. Stat. 1921, ch. 123; Md. Code 1924, art. 77, §2; Mich. Comp. Laws 1915, §9862; N. H. Public Laws 1926, ch. 116, §22; N. M. Session Laws 1923, ch. 148, §201; N. Y. Cons. Laws 1918, p. 2035; N. C. Cons. Stat. 1919, §5414; Penn. School Laws 1921, §1119; Va. Code 1924, §607; Vt. Laws 1919, no. 55; W. Va. Code 1923, ch. 45, §32.

[2] Ordinances for elementary school course of study: Ala. School Code 1924, art. 3, §15; Ariz. Rev. Stat. 1913, §2697; Ark. Stat. 1921, §8764; Cal. Pol. Code 1923, §1665; Del. Laws Spec. Sess. 1920, ch. 48, §9; Fla. School Laws, §35.78; Ga. Annot. Code 1914, §1565; Idaho Stat. 1919, §803; Ind. School Laws, §§112, 133; Iowa Code 1924, §3831; Kan. Rev. Stat. 1923, §72-102; Ky. Stat. 1922, §4382; La. Acts 1915, §2519; Mich. Comp. Laws 1915, §809; Maine Rev. Stat. 1916, p. 384; Md. Code 1924, art. 77, §14; Miss. Code 1917, §7326; Mont. Code 1921, §941; Nev. Rev. Laws 1919, §3242; N. H. Public Laws 1926, ch. 116, §8; N. J. Comp. Stat. Supple. 1911-1924, §185-21c; N. M. Session Laws 1923, ch. 148, §105; N. D. Code Supple. 1925, §1109; Ohio Code 1926, §7645; Okla. Stat. 1921, §10292; Ore. Laws 1920, §4963; Penn. School Laws 1921, §1607; S. C. Code 1922, §2549; Tex. Civil Stat. 1925, §2811; Utah Code 1917, §4531; Vt. Gen. Laws 1917, §1247; Va. Code 1924, §719; Wash. Stat. 1922, §4529; W. Va.

state department of education in Idaho is directed to " prepare or cause to be prepared a course of study for the public schools of the state, and prescribe the use that shall be made of the same." Similarly the state board of education in Kansas has been empowered " to prescribe courses of study for the public schools of the state including the common or district schools, the graded schools, and the high schools, ... and to revise the several courses of study whenever in their judgment such revision is desirable." In this manner it is possible to attain a unity of curriculum and a standardization of instruction which is probably exceedingly desirable, and at the same time retain a flexibility of program which would be practically impossible were a de-

Code 1923, ch. 45, §9; Wis. Stat. 1919, §40.57; Wyo. Comp. Stat. 1920, §2267.

Ordinances for high school course of study: Ala. School Code 1924, art. 3, §15; Ariz. Rev. Stat. 1913, §2697; Ark. Stat. 1921, §8764; Cal. Pol. Code 1923, §1665; Del. Laws Spec. Sess. 1920, ch. 48, §9; Fla. Rev. Stat. 1920, §537; Ga. Annot. Code 1914, §1565; Idaho Stat. 1919, §803; Iowa Code 1924, §3831; Kan. Rev. Stat. 1923, §72-102; Ky. Stat. 1922, §4526b-2; Maine Rev. Stat. 1916, p. 384; Md. Code 1924, art. 77, §14; Miss. Code 1917, §7326; Mo. Rev. Stat. 1919, §11337; Mont. Code 1921, §836; Nev. Rev. Laws 1919, §3242; N. H. Public Laws 1926, ch. 116, §8; N. J. Comp. Stat. Supple. 1911-24, §185-21c; N. M. Session Laws 1920, ch. 148, §105; N. D. Code Supple. 1925, §1109; Okla. Stat. 1921, §10292; Ohio Code 1926, §7645; Penn. School Laws 1921, §1607; S. C. Code 1922, §2549; Tenn. Code Supple. 1920, §1454a; Tex. Civil Stat. 1925, §2812; Utah Code 1917, §4531; Vt. Gen. Laws 1917, §1237; Va. Code 1924, §719; Wash. Stat. 1922, §4529; W. Va. Code 1923, ch. 45, §9; Wis. Stat. 1925. §40.57; Wyo. Comp. Stat. 1920, §2342.

Ordinances prescribing examinations in elementary schools: Idaho Stat. 1919, §1047; Ind. School Laws, p. 53, §375; Iowa Code 1915, §2634b6; Kan. Rev. Stat. 1923, §72-5104; Ky. Stat. 1922, §4369; Md. Code 1924, art. 77, §14; Mont. School Laws, p. 69, §903; Neb. Comp. Stat. 1922, §6385; N. D. Code Supple. 1925, §1109; Okla. Stat. 1921, §10292; Ore. Laws 1920, §5363; S. C. School Laws, p. 29, §147; Wash. Stat. 1922, §4529.

Ordinances prescribing examinations in high schools: Md. Code 1924, art. 77, §14; Mont. Code 1921, §944; N. Y. Cons. Laws 1918, p. 2016; N. D. Code Supple. 1925, §1109; Wash. Stat. 1922, §5094.

tailed curriculum enacted into law. In some jurisdictions the idea of this flexibility is hinted at in the statutes. The state superintendent of public schools in Maine, for example, is directed to "prescribe the studies to be taught in the common schools, reserving to town committees the right to prescribe additional studies, and the course of studies prescribed by the state superintendent of schools shall be followed in all schools; provided, however, that upon the approval by the state superintendent of any course arranged by the superintending school committee, said course shall be the authorized course for said town." Not only is geographic flexibility thus made possible, but that more important kind of flexibility called for by time and changing circumstances is also present, for it is exceedingly likely that a state board of education fully cognizant of its problems will be more ready to adapt itself to changing needs than a legislative body which (though for the most part depending on the recommendation of the department of education) must in all cases be convinced of the necessity for change.

In addition to this general supervision maintained through the ordinance-making power certain phases of the curriculum have been singled out for special attention—those phases of it particularly which for one reason or another cannot as yet be subjected to the mandatory fiat of the ordinance-making process. The means of supervision chiefly relied upon in this connection is the mechanism of *grant-in-aid* which has been used extensively for the development of courses in agriculture,[1] home economics,[2] industrial training,[3] high

1 Ala. School Code 1924, art. 3, §22; Ariz. Rev. Stat. 1913, §2795; Ark. Stat. 1921, §8769; Cal. Pol. Code 1923, Act 7497; Col. Comp. Laws 1921, §§8134-8136; Conn. Gen. Stat. 1918, §829; Del. Laws Spec. Sess. 1920, ch. 48, §25; Fla. Rev. Stat. 1920, §664; Idaho Comp. Stat. 1919, §1004; Ill. Rev. Stat. 1923, ch. 122, §562; Ind. Stat. 1926, §7051; Iowa Code 1924, §3840; Kan. Rev. Stat. 1923, §72-4301; Ky. Stat. 1922, §4535b-1; La. Supple.

2-3 (*See Notes 2 and 3 on next page.*)

schools,[4] normal training in high schools [5] and special classes for defectives.[6]

It can generally be assumed that auxiliary to or concomitant with a system of grants-in-aid the devices of *reports, inspection, approval* and *ordinance making* will also be called into play. The desirability of a system of reports may, perhaps, be understood from a comment of the state depart-

Stat. 1926, Act 179, §1916; Maine Rev. Stat. 1917, p. 179; Md. Code 1924, art. 77, §258; Mass. Gen. Laws 1921, ch. 74, §9; Mich. Comp. Laws 1915, §5950; Minn. Gen. Stat. 1923, §2986; Mo. Rev. Stat. 1919, §11269; Mont. Code 1921, §1311; Neb. Comp. Stat. 1922, §6417; Nev. Rev. Laws 1919, p. 2960; N. H. Public Laws 1926, ch. 116, §6; N. J. Comp. Stat. Supple. 1911-24, §185-372; N. M. Session Laws 1923, ch. 148, §501; N. Y. Cons. Laws Supple. 1918, p. 543; N. C. Cons. Stat. 1919, §5396; N. D. Code Supple. 1925, §1471b1; Ohio Code 1926, §367-1; Okla. Stat. 1921, §10694; Ore. Laws 1920, §4966; Penn. School Laws 1921, §3414; R. I. Gen. Laws 1923, §957; S. C. Code 1922, §2543; S. D. Rev. Stat. 1919, §7406; Tenn. Code Supple. 1920, §1400a-21; Utah Acts 1919, ch. 86; Vt. Gen. Laws 1917, §1304; Va. Code 1924, §1003e; Wash. Stat. 1922, §4906; W. Va. Code 1923, ch. 45, §14; Wis. Stat. 1925, §41.13; Wyo. Comp. Stat. 1920, §2363.

[2] See footnote immediately preceding.

[3] See footnote immediately preceding.

[4] Ala. School Code 1924, art. 4, §55; Ariz. Rev. Stat. 1913, §2794; Ark. Stat. 1921, §8768; Cal. Pol. Code 1923, Act 1750; Conn. Gen. Stat. 1918, §995; Del. Laws Spec. Sess. 1920, ch. 48, §16; Kan. Rev. Stat. 1923, §72-3201; Maine Rev. Stat. 1916, p. 370; Md. Code 1924, art. 77, §23; Minn. Gen. Stat. 1923, §2990; Mo. Rev. Stat. 1919, §11263; Mont. Code 1921, §1211; Nev. Rev. Laws 1919, §3392; N. Y. Cons. Laws 1918, p. 2070; N. D. Code Supple. 1925, §1433; R. I. Gen. Laws 1923, §1075; S. C. Code 1922, §2721; Tenn. Code Supple. 1920, §1400a-4; Utah Code 1917, §4580; Vt. Gen. Laws 1917, §1288; W. Va. Code 1923, ch. 45, §82; Wis. Stat. 1925, §20.26.

[5] Ark. Stat. 1921, §8768; Fla. Rev. Stat. 1920, §605; Iowa Code 1924, §3902; Kan. Rev. Stat. 1923, §72-4401; Maine Rev. Stat. 1916, p. 365; Md. Code 1924, art. 77, §195; Minn. Gen. Stat. 1923, §3030; Mo. Rev. Stat. 1919, §11310; Mont. Code 1921, §1310b; Neb. Comp. Stat. 1922, §6411; N. Y. Cons. Laws 1918, p. 2262; Ohio Code 1926, §7654-1; S. C. Code 1922, §2723; Vt. Gen. Laws 1917, §1214; W. Va. Code 1923, ch. 45, §80; Wyo. Comp. Stat. 1920, §2427.

[6] Cal. Pol. Code 1923, §1618; Minn. Gen. Stat. 1923, §3031; Mo. Rev. Stat. 1919, §11149; Ohio Code 1926, §7757; Penn. School Laws 1921, §1413.

ment of Kansas for the year 1918.   It seems that the supervising authorities in charge of the high schools had found it impossible with the limited staff they had at their command to visit each of the six hundred schools in the state doing high school work in the course of a year, and had consequently resorted to a system of reports as a substitute means of supervision.   The comment of the state superintendent of education thereon is exceedingly interesting.

As there is . . . frequent change in the teaching staff with a resultant change in the course of study and general policy of the schools, it has been necessary to devise a form of report that will give such information as will make it possible to determine whether or not the school is meeting accredited requirements and what its rating should be.   It is also desirable to have in the superintendent's office such a system of permanent records as will make it possible to determine what progress the high schools of the state are making.   Accordingly at the beginning of the school year blanks for the high school principals are sent to each principal.   The purpose of the questions in this blank is to call attention to the standards for accredited schools and to elicit the information that will show so far as possible whether or not the school can be accredited, and if so, what its rating should be....
On the receipt of these reports early in the school year they are carefully scrutinized and letters are written calling attention to any irregularities that appear and making such suggestions as seem to be called for looking to the improvement of school conditions.[1]

The effectiveness with which this method of control is used varies, of course, from state to state.   In most jurisdictions it is supplemented by the process of *inspection* and *approval*.   In Michigan, for example, " any approved public school, department or part-time class giving instruction in agriculture, industrial or home economic subjects which

[1] *Report of the Superintendent of Education, Kansas 1918*, p. 50.

receives the benefit of federal moneys as herein provided, shall provide suitable buildings and equipment in order to give such instruction, and shall also appropriate for the salaries of the instructors a sum of money equal to one half of the federal allotment to such schools, and the balance necessary for the salaries of such instructors shall be appropriated and distributed to such school districts from the state treasury. . . . *The state board of control shall provide for proper inspection . . . and upon the approval of the work done and the receipt of a satisfactory report . . .* the state superintendent shall certify to the auditor general the amount of such state and federal moneys due each school district."[1] That such supervision is necessary seems to be the general consensus of opinion among state officials. A report of the superintendent of education in Virginia may be quoted merely by way of emphasis.

Before leaving the subject of supervision I call attention to the fact that . . . 24 percent of the amount spent for teachers' salaries in the cities and 65 percent in the counties . . . (is paid by the state). There is no question that some state law in reference to assistant superintendents or supervising teachers is urgently needed to conserve this large investment of state money. *I have repeatedly called attention to the waste of our agricultural funds because it seemed impossible to arouse the legislative mind to the need of providing a state inspector.* To effect the small amount saved by not employing a sufficient number of supervisors, those unnecessary officers, this multiplicity of functionaries—we have lost thousands of dollars by compelling inexperienced teachers to labor without guidance among people sometimes too poorly informed to know, and sometimes too humble or modest to assert rights which seem fundamental in our modern theory of public instruction.[2]

[1] *Michigan Laws 1917*, no. 189, §5.

[2] *Report of Superintendent of Education, Virginia 1916-17*, p. 27.

Given the proper financial arrangements there is little question that the device of grants-in-aid can be used to stimulate the development of neglected aspects of educational activity.   Nor can there be much doubt that in the hands of capable supervising officials a well rounded system of this character can do much toward maintaining these services, once thoroughly rooted, in a state of relative efficiency. Whether it is possible to obtain a set of capable supervising officials, as immune to politics as the necessities of administration demand, is perhaps a moot question.

TEXT BOOKS

Closely allied to the control exercised over the curriculum is that maintained over text books.   For the most part this supervision is exercised through the *ordinance-making* process and consists of the state authorities either drawing up a list of books which must be used by all the schools throughout the state, or drawing up a list from which the local authorities may, in their discretion, make such selections as seem particularly adapted to the peculiar circumstances under which they work.[1]   In California, for example, the state board of education is directed to " compile and enforce the use of state text books throughout the elementary schools of the state."   Similarly the law of

1 Ordinances prescribing a list of possible textbooks: Ala. School Code 1924, art. 3, §16; Ariz. Rev. Stat. 1913, §2697; Ark. Stat. 1921, §9066; Cal. Pol. Code 1923, §1519b; Conn. Gen. Stat. 1918, §826; Del. Laws Spec. Sess. 1920, ch. 48, §9; Fla. Rev. Stat. 1920, §669; Ga. Annot. Code 1914, §1439; Idaho Comp. Stat. 1919, §803; Ind. Stat. 1926, §6480; Kan. Rev. Stat. 1923, §72-4105; Ky. Stat. 1922, §4421a-1; La. Supple. Stat. 1926, Act 100, §§4, 25; Mich. Comp. Laws 1915, §5798; Miss. Code 1917, §7824; Mo. Rev. Stat. 1919, §11371; Mont. Code 1921, §1191; Nev. Rev. Laws 1912, §3253; N. M. Session Laws 1923, ch. 148, §105; N. C. Cons. Stat. 1919, §5691; N. D. Code Supple. 1925, §1109; Ohio Code 1926, §7709; Okla. Stat. 1921, §10247; Ore. Laws 1920, §4963; S. C. Code 1922, §2549; Tenn. Code 1917, §14616-2; Tex. Civil Stat. 1925, §2843; Utah Code 1917, §4557; Va. Code 1924, §610a; W. Va. Code 1923, ch. 45, §11.

Arkansas provides that "it shall be the duty of [the state text book] commission to select and adopt a uniform series of books for use in all the public grade schools of the state . . . . [which shall be] used to the exclusion of all others in the public schools of the state." The grant of power in the Idaho code is somewhat broader.

The state board of education shall determine how and under what regulations text books shall be adopted for the use of such schools, determine whether or not the text books shall be free, and prescribe the regulations under which such books may be provided. The state board of education shall have and is hereby given power to adopt plans, rules and regulations for the adoption of such state text books as to the board seem best and proper.[1]

Thus it is possible for the state authorities to clinch their control over the local curriculum.

SCHOOL LIBRARIES

Somewhat akin to this supervision is that maintained over school libraries. Although the mechanism of *advice* is called into play, the mainstay of this supervision is the device of *grant-in-aid*. The condition most usually imposed is that the locality raise a specified sum of money.[2] In a number of states, however, an additional provision is added to the effect that the municipality must select its books from lists *approved* by the central authorities,[3] and conduct the libraries in a manner *prescribed* by them.[4]

[1] *Supra.*

[2] Cal. Pol. Code 1923, §1712; Conn. Gen. Stat. 1918, §1004; Minn. Gen. Stat. 1923, §3018; Nev. Rev. Laws 1919, §3393; N. Y. Cons. Laws 1918, §2204; S. D. Code 1922, §2686; Wash. Stat. 1922, §756a.

[3] Iowa Code 1924, §4324; Mont. Code 1921, §1186; W. Va. Code 1923, ch. 45, §62.

[4] Ky. Stat. 1922, §4383; La. Stat. 1915, §2666; Nev. Rev. Laws 1919, §3242; Tenn. Code 1917, §1396a113; W. Va. Code 1913, §2067; Wis. Stat. 1919, §40.36.

SCHOOL BUILDINGS

Certain other fields of supervision still remain to be considered; the maintenance of medical service in the schools, school finance, and the condition of school buildings.

Although both the process of *inspection*[1] and the dissemination of *advice*[2] are used in connection with the supervision of school buildings in many jurisdictions, it is in those states which require all plans and specifications for school buildings to be submitted to the state educational authorities for *approval* before construction work may begin that real supervision exists.[3] The argument in favor of such a procedure seems fairly strong. The work of an architect in the average city after all is the building of homes or office buildings. Schools are comparatively rare objects. It is very unlikely consequently that there will be anyone among the local architects who has specialized in school buildings. In all probability, therefore, the local architect who undertakes this work will be somewhat less efficient in handling the peculiar problems of school buildings than a specialist in the

[1] Ark. Stat. 1921, §8764; Cal. Pol. Code 1923, §362g; Del. Laws Spec. Sess. 1920, ch. 48, §9; Maine Rev. Stat. 1916, p. 353; Md. Code 1924, art. 77, §31; Mass. Gen. Laws 1921, ch. 143, §28; N. D. Code 1913, §1490; Ohio Code 1920, §1037; Penn. Code 1920, §4894; Vt. Gen. Laws 1917, §185-21c; Va. Code 1924, §673; Wis. Stat. 1925, §39.02.

[2] Ark. Stat. 1921, §8764; Del. Laws Spec. Sess. 1920, ch. 148, §9; Ill. Rev. Stat. 1923, ch. 122, §3; Ky. Stat. 1922, §4395; Maine Rev. Stat. 1916, p. 353; Md. Code 1924, art. 77, §30; Mass. Gen. Laws 1921, ch. 143, §28; Nev. Rev. Laws 1919, §3242; N. C. Cons. Stat. 1919, §5671; N. D. Code 1913, §1185; Okla. Stat. 1921, §10403; Penn. School Laws 1921, §615; Tex. Civil Stat. 1925, §2659.

[3] Del. Laws Spec. Sess. 1920, ch. 48, §9; Maine Laws 1921, p. 25; Md. Code 1924, art. 77, §30; Mass. Gen. Laws 1921, ch. 143, §15; Mich. Comp. Laws 1919, no. 139; Minn. Gen. Stat. 1913, §2874; Mont. Code 1921, §1174; N. Y. Cons. Laws 1918, p. 2186; N. D. Code 1913, §1492; S. D. Rev. Stat. 1919, §7573; Tex. Civ. Stat. 1914, §4510; Utah Code 1917, §4527; Va. Code 1924, §673.

subject. Nevertheless the average-sized city can certainly not be expected to retain an expert of this variety on its staff, for the amount of work to be done would in no wise justify such a procedure. The state, on the other hand, can very justifiably maintain such an officer, who if the foregoing reasoning is correct can be expected to save considerably more than his salary through suggested changes in the plans submitted to him by local architects. Such, indeed, has been the experience in many of the states, if we are to believe the testimony of the state superintendents of education.

Indeed, so successful has been the work of the supervising architect that a number of states permit their department of education to prescribe such *rules and regulations* relative to the construction of these buildings as seem fitting and proper.[1] The Minnesota statute is, perhaps, the most detailed of its kind, authorizing, as it does, the state superintendent of education to " prescribe rules, and examine all plans and specifications for the erection, enlargement and change of school buildings, which plans and specifications shall first be submitted to him for approval before the contract is let, and no new school building shall be erected or any building enlarged or changed until the plans and specifications have been submitted to and approved by the superintendent of education. He shall include in such rules those made from time to time by the state board of health relative to sanitary standards for toilets, water supply and disposal of sewage in public school buildings."

A comment in a recent Utah report is very interesting in this connection in that it shows both the procedure and the effect of the procedure in at least one state:

[1] Ala. School Code 1924, art. 4, §45; Del. Laws Spec. Sess. 1920, ch. 48, §9; Maine Laws 1921, p. 25; Minn. Gen. Stat. 1913, §2874; N. J. Comp. Stat. 1915, p. 1420, §48; Penn. School Laws 1921, §908; Utah Laws 1921, ch. 94; Va. Code 1924, §786; Wis. Stat. 1925, §39.02.

The new school buildings commission adopted a set of rules for the planning of school buildings and distributed them to boards of education and others interested. The rules describe in detail standards for school sites, requirements of plans and specifications for school buildings, lighting of class roms, heating and ventilating, sanitation, plumbing, fire protection, etc. Since the adoption of these rules the plans and specifications submitted for approval have shown that more thought and attention are being given to health and safety appliances, and to utility in plan arrangement and economic building construction. The commission finds the best results are obtained if the preliminary drawings are submitted for examination and suggestions before the blue prints are made. This saves time both for the commission and for the architect since it permits the making of necessary changes in plans with a minimum of inconvenience. Boards of education have accordingly been urged to have architects submit preliminary drawings before plans are printed.[1]

FINANCE

Comment has already been made in a preceding chapter concerning the supervision maintained by state officials over municipal finance. For the most part this supervision extends to the field of educational activity as well as to all other phases of municipal government. In a number of states in which no general powers of financial supervision have been established, however, school finance has been thought worthy of special attention. The control has, for the most part, taken the form of *inspection* which seemingly has justified itself in this connection, at least in the minds of the supervising officials, as it has in all other aspects of the field of finance.[2]

[1] *Utah State Board of Education, Report 1916*, p. 134.

[2] Ala. Gen. Laws 1923, §736; Ariz. Rev. Stat. 1913, p. 910; Del. Laws 1921, ch. 160, §49; Ga. Annot. Code 1914, §1565; Ky. Stat. 1922, §4398a-3; Mich. Comp. Laws 1922, §5641; S. D. Rev. Stat. 1919, §7505; Tex. Civ. Stat. 1914, §4510; Utah Code 1917, §4519; Vt. Gen. Laws 1917, §185-21c.

In my previous report [says the superintendent of schools in Kentucky] I spoke somewhat at length in regard to the inspection law passed by the legislature in 1912. This law continues to justify its existence in a most gratifying way. Because of it, in one case, the Southern Pacific Railroad has been forced to pay to the Highland Park Graded School District one hundred thousand dollars in back taxes. . . . The work of the inspectors in securing accurate census returns from the counties and cities has gone far toward raising the per capita tax levy to the present amount of $5.25, the highest it has ever been in the history of Kentucky.[1]

Except for the fact that in connection with the mechanism of *grant-in-aid* the state authorities are occasionally permitted to *prescribe* the set-up of books, accounts, etc., this power of audit constitutes the sum-total supervision maintained over school finance.[2]

MEDICAL SERVICE

Mention, at least, should be made of the fact that a limited degree of control is exercised by the state authorities over the maintenance of medical service in the schools. For the most part, however, this supervision is confined to the enactment of such *ordinances* as are necessary to give effect to the mandatory declarations found in many of the statutes concerning the maintenance of such service.[3]

State administrative supervision over education consequently seems to have made considerable headway. Not

---

[1] *Biennial Report of the Superintendent of Public Instruction, Kentucky 1915*, p. vii.

[2] N. J. Comp. Stat. 1915, §1412; Vt. Gen. Laws 1917, §1172; Wis. Stat. 1919, §38.01.

[3] Ala. School Code 1924, art. 4, §50; Ark. Stat. 1921, §8764; Del. Laws Spec. Sess. 1920, ch. 48, §9; Ind. Stat. 1926, §6915; Maine Rev. Stat. 1916, p. 361; N. Y. Cons. Laws 1918, §2224; N. C. Cons. Stat. 1919, §5747; Ohio Code 1926, §7692-2; Va. Code 1924, §724a.

only is a limited degree of supervision maintained over the whole field through the mechanism of reports, inspection, advice and grant-in-aid, but certain phases of the field have been subjected to really intensive control.   Particularly has this been the case in connection with the selection of the teaching personnel, the development of the curriculum and the adoption of text books.   In a somewhat fewer number of jurisdictions the erection of school buildings, the maintenance of school libraries, and the general field of school finance are given similar supervision.

CHAPTER VI

DEPENDENCY AND DELINQUENCY

No exact figures indicating the extent of the problem of poverty in the United States have ever been tabulated. Indeed, the conception of poverty is itself a more or less subjective matter, for what seems dire destitution to one person seems comfort if not affluence to another. Nevertheless, various estimates of the extent of the phenomena have been made. In October, 1921, the United States Commissioner of Industrial Relations declared: " It is evident both from the investigations of this commission and from the reports of all recent governmental bodies that a large portion of our industrial population is, as a result of the combination of low wages and unemployment, living in a condition of actual poverty. How large this proportion is cannot be exactly determined, but it is certain that at least one-third and possibly one-half of the families of wage earners employed in manufacturing and mining communities earn in the course of the year less than enough to support them in anything like comfortable and decent conditions." [1]

J. L. Gillin, one of the leading students of the subject, believes that when we obtain more careful statistics, including not only the recipients of public poor relief, but also those receiving relief from private sources, " we shall probably find that the pauperism rate is from five to eight per cent " of the population. Whether the first or second figure is accurate is immaterial. It is not pleasant to contemplate

[1] *The Cost of Living Among Wage-Earners*, Detroit, Mich. N. J. C. B., New York, Special Report No. 19, Oct., 1921, p. 14.

the spectacle of from five to eight million people underfed, underclothed, and undersheltered in prosperous America.[1]

In so far as the municipalities are concerned, the most fundamental work in connection with the problem has been done by the departments of health and education. The direct attack upon the problem as conducted through the departments of charity has usually been palliative rather than fundamental. In general, their work has been the relief of only the most acute cases of destitution. Two modes of procedure have been followed, institutional care and outdoor relief. The latter, however, is usually in the hands of county officials, although in some states, township, city, county and state officers all participate in its administration.[2] The primary work of the municipalities, nevertheless, has been the maintenance of almshouses of one sort or another.

Their historic failure in this particular is too well known to need repetition. And yet the crusade to rectify this evil, launched by Dorothy Dix almost one hundred years ago, has not been fully effective even yet. Even in the twentieth century reports of extremely revolting conditions continually crop out. At late as 1915 a survey of the poor-houses of Missouri was summarized as follows:

Many of the houses are old, unsanitary and practically unfit for habitation. Some are without foundations, having their rough floors laid directly upon the ground. Roofs are sunken and walls swaying, seemingly about to fall upon the inmates. . . . The superintendent is generally without means of properly segregating the sexes. Almost every one of the larger institutions has in it one or more sexual perverts, irresponsible idiots, insane men or women, some of them dangerously insane. These

[1] Gillin, J. L., *Poverty and Dependency*, New York (1922), p. 37.

[2] In New York, for example, most outdoor relief is administered by town or city poor law officers, wherever the counties maintain the almshouses.

he can keep from acts of brutal immorality only by constant vigilance, beatings and threats of floggings, or by locking them up in separate rooms. One almshouse was observed where an attempt was made to separate the men and women by a high cage fence of barbed wire. Yet like the others, it had its scandalous history of disgraceful happenings and illegitimate births. This failure to control moral conditions and the bringing into existence of unfortunate children in our almshouses is one of the most distressing features of the whole system and one which under the circumstances cannot fairly be charged to the underpaid and overworked superintendents.[1]

Widespread publicity concerning conditions of this character, together with the passing of the belief that indigence is primarily due to an overcharge of original sin, has been chiefly responsible for the establishment of state supervisory bodies dedicated to the purpose of overcoming if possible, the ignorance, indifference, corruption and brutality of the local officials. Such agencies with authority over municipal poor-relief activities have now been created in at least thirty jurisdictions.[2]

Although nearly half of these agencies call for *reports* of one kind or another from the institutions under their

---

[1] Warfield, G. A., *Outdoor Relief in Missouri*, New York (1915), p. 16.

[2] Ala. Code 1923, §4857; Ark. Stat. 1921, §1023; Cal. Gen. Laws 1923, Act 1330, §3; Col. Annot. Stat. 1923, §615; Conn. Gen. Stat. 1918, §1894; Del. Laws, vol. 30, ch. 60, p. 139; Fla. Rev. Stat. 1920, §691, Acts 1921, §8535; Ga. Annot. Code Supple. 1922, §215888; Ill. Rev. Stat. 1923, ch. 24a, §55; Ind. Annot. Stat. 1926, §4297; La. Stat. 1920, p. 209; Maine Rev. Stat. 1916, ch. 147, §3; Mass. Gen. Laws 1921, ch. 121, §39i; Mich. Comp. Stat. Supple. 1922, ch. 64, §1982; Minn. Gen. Stat. 1923, §4448; Mo. Rev. Stat. 1919, §12179; Mont. Rev. Code 1921, §330; Neb. Comp. Stat. 1922, §8272; N. H. Public Laws 1926, ch. 108, §7; N. J. Laws 1918, ch. 147, §125; N. Y. Cons. Laws 1918, p. 7806; N. C. Cons. Stat. 1919, §5006; Ohio Gen. Code 1926, §1352; Okla. Comp. Stat. 1921, §51; Ore. Laws 1920, §8447; Penn. Supple. Stat. 1924, §9056-a-14; S. D. Rev. Code 1919, §10033; Tenn. Acts 1917, ch. 170, §7, 1923, ch. 7, §42; Vt. Gen. Laws 1917, §7317; Wis. Stat. 1925, §46.16.

care,[1] in every jurisdiction without exception central control rests very largely upon central *inspection*.[2]   In many states the grant of authority from the legislature in this connection is broad and unrestricted.   The state inspectors are directed, " to visit, inspect and examine once a year or oftener state, county, municipal and private institutions of an eleemosynary, charitable, correctional or reformatory character." [3]   In others, specific objects or practices are singled

[1] The reports are of two types, those specified in the law and those called for at the discretion of the administrative authorities. In the first class are: Ala. Code 1923, §4871 ; Col. Annot. Stat. 1926, §615; Conn. Gen. Stat. 1918, §1894; Ind. Annot. Stat. 1926, §4355; Maine Rev. Stat. 1916, ch. 147, §3; Mass. Gen. Laws 1921, ch. 121, §39; Minn. Gen. Stat. 1923, §4448; Mo. Rev. Stat. 1919, §12179; N. C. Cons. Stat. 1919, §5008; Penn. Supple. Stat. 1924, §9056a-14; Tenn. Acts 1923, ch. 7, §2; Vt. Gen. Laws 1917, §7314; Wis. Stat. 1925, §46.16. In the second class are: Ala. Code 1923, §4857; Ark. Stat. 1921, §1023; Cal. Gen. Laws 1923, Act 1330, §3; Del. Laws, vol. 30, ch. 64, p. 139, §1004; Fla. Rev. Stat. 1920, §691, Acts 1921, ch. 8535; Ga. Annot. Code Supple. 1922, §2158 gg.; Ind. Annot. Stat. 1926, §4297; Maine Rev. Stat. 1916, ch. 147, §3; Mass. Gen. Laws 1921, ch. 121, §39; Minn. Gen. Stat. 1923, §4448; Neb. Comp. Stat. 1922, §8272; N. H. Public Laws 1926, ch. 108, §7; N. Y. Cons. Laws 1918, p. 7805; N. C. Cons. Stat. 1919, §35008; Ohio Gen. Code 1926, §1352; Penn. Supple. Stat. 1924, §9056a-14; Tenn. Acts 1923, ch. 7, §142-2; Va. Acts 1922, ch. 105; Wis. Stat. 1925, §46.18.

[2] All of the states which maintain systems of supervision make use of the mechanism of inspection.

[3] Ala. Code 1923, §4852; Ark. Stat. 1921, §1023; Cal. Gen. Laws 1923, Act 1330, §3; Conn. Gen. Stat. 1918, §1888; Del. Laws, vol. 30, ch. 64, p. 139, §1004; Ga. Annot. Code Supple. 1922, §2158gg; Ill. Rev. Stat. 1923, ch. 24a, §55; Ind. Annot. Stat. 1926, §4297; La. Stat. 1920, p. 209; Maine Rev. Stat. 1916, ch. 147, §3; Mass. Gen. Laws 1921, ch. 121, §7; Mich. Comp. Laws Supple. 1922, ch. 64, §1982; Minn. Gen. Stat. 1923, §4448; Mo. Rev. Stat. 1919, §12177; Mont. Rev. Code 1921, §330; Neb. Comp. Stat. 1922, §8272; N. H. Public Laws 1926, ch. 108, §8; N. J. Laws 1918, ch. 147, §125; N. Y. Cons. Laws 1918, p. 7806; N. C. Cons. Stat. 1919, §5006; Ohio Code 1926, §1352; Okla. Comp. Stat. 1921, §51; Ore. Laws 1920, §8447; Penn. Supple. Stat. 1924, §9056a-12; S. D. Rev. Code 1919, §10033; Tenn. Acts 1917, ch. 120, §7; Vt. Gen. Laws 1917, §7417; Va. Acts 1922, ch. 105; Wis. Stat. 1925, §46.16.

out for inquiry. In many cases the very selection of these objects and practices indicates all too clearly the evils which state administrative supervision was designed to overcome. In still other states, a combination of the two practices has been used; the administrative authorities are given a broad and unrestricted sweep of authority, and at the same time certain objects are pointed out as worthy of special attention. Chief among these have been sanitary conditions,[1] the treatment of inmates,[2] and the detention of persons who have never been legally committed.

That such a system of inspection may have considerable justification, the Missouri survey referred to above strikingly brings out. And Missouri is by no means unique among the states in this particular. Here and there in the reports of the state boards of charity evidence continuously crops out which reveals that many localities, if left to themselves, would soon permit conditions of a most obnoxious character to develop in connection with these local institutions. Such evidence is to be found even in the most progressive states. The condition of the almshouse hospital in Lawrence, Massachusetts, for example, was recently pro-

[1] Ala. Code 1923, §4852; Conn. Gen. Stat. 1918, §1888; Del. Laws, vol. 30, ch. 64, p. 139, §1004; Ill. Rev. Stat. 1923, ch. 25, §5; Ind. Annot. Stat. 1926, §4297; Maine Rev. Stat. 1916, ch. 147, §3; Mass. Gen. Laws 1921, ch. 121, §7; Mich. Comp. Laws Supple. 1922, ch. 64, §1982; Minn. Gen. Stat. 1923, §4448; Mo. Rev. Stat. 1919, §12177; Mont. Rev. Code 1921, §330; Neb. Comp. Stat. 1922, §8272; N. J. Laws 1918, ch. 147, §125; N. Y. Cons. Laws 1918, p. 7808; N. C. Cons. Stat. 1919, §5006; Penn. Supple. Stat. 1924, §9056a-12; Vt. Gen. Laws 1917, §7317; Wis. Stat. 1925, §46.16.

[2] Ala. Code 1923, §4852; Conn. Gen. Stat. 1918, §1888; Del. Laws, vol. 30, ch. 64, p. 139, §1004; Ill. Rev. Stat. 1923, ch. 25, §5; Ind. Annot. Stat. 1926, §4297; Maine Rev. Stat. 1916, ch. 147, §3; Mass. Gen. Laws 1921, ch. 121, §7; Mich. Comp. Laws Supple. 1922, ch. 64, §1982; Minn. Gen. Stat. 1923, §4448; Mo. Rev. Stat. 1919, §12177; Mont. Rev. Code 1921, §330; Neb. Comp. Stat. 1922, §8272; N. J. Laws 1918, ch. 147, §125; N. Y. Cons. Laws 1918, p. 7808; N. C. Cons. Stat. 1919, §5006; Penn. Supple. Stat. 1924, §9056a-12; Vt. Gen. Laws 1917, §7317; Wis. Stat. 1925, §46.16.

nounced intolerable; and little less scathing was the comment on New Bedford, where it was recommended that either general and extensive improvements be made or a new institution erected.[1] As late as 1922 in Connecticut visits of inspection by the members and secretary of the department of public welfare revealed the existence of loosely managed town farms where matters of sanitary comfort received scant attention, where insufficient separation of the sexes, inadequate facilities for heat and baths, and a total disregard of fire hazards were the rule rather than the exception. Occasionally even the food supply was found to be below standard.[2] Nor was the situation in Indiana, another supposedly progressive state, any better.

Of the ninety-two poor asylum buildings, twenty are built upon modern plans. Those in Benton, Clark, Dekalb and Dubois counties are lighted by oil lamps. The buildings in Brown, Crawford, Harrison, Martin, Ohio, Ripley, Starke and Warwick counties are frame. Those in Martin and Crawford counties are dilapidated and in miserable condition. They are uninhabitable and a disgrace to the counties and the state.[3]

Further illustrations might be multiplied, but sufficient have been adduced to indicate something of the necessity that exists for the maintenance of such supervision.

Closely related to the process of inspection is the practice of disseminating *advice*. In general, five modes of procedure are followed. Suggestions and recommendations are inevitably made by inspectors on their appointed rounds.

[1] *Massachusetts Department of Public Welfare, Report 1923*, p. 113. It should, perhaps, be emphasized that these conditions are exceptional in Massachusetts; nevertheless, their presence in the Commonwealth is indicative of what might take place were the municipalities left unsupervised.

[2] *Connecticut Department of Public Welfare, Report 1921-22*, p. 31.

[3] *Indiana State Board of Charities, Report 1919*, p. 122 *et seq.*

Furthermore, the part played by newspaper publicity concerning notoriously bad conditions is exceedingly important. In addition in at least thirteen states, no city may " erect, add to, or remodel a jail, almshouse, infirmary, house of correction or workhouse " without first submitting the plans and specifications therefor to the board of administration for its criticisms and suggestions.[1] The procedure in this connection in all likelihood closely resembles that followed by the departments of education in the states in which the educational officials have received a similar grant of authority. Strangely enough, in only three states have the supervising boards been specifically granted statutory warrants for calling state-wide conferences of local welfare of officers.[2] Such conferences are actually held, however, on a voluntary basis in the vast majority of jurisdictions. Moreover " numerous inquiries are received," in practically every state in the Union in which supervising agencies exist, " from public officials and executive officers of institutions concerning their duties and responsibilities with reference to particular problems with which they are confronted," all of which must receive careful consideration.

The mechanism of *grant-in-aid* is probably more effective in securing results than the mere dissemination of advice; nevertheless only six states make use of the procedure at all and in five of these it is used primarily in connection with

[1] Cal. Gen. Laws 1923, Act 1330, §3; Ga. Annot. Code Supple, 1922, §2158ii (applicable to new buildings only) ; Ill. Rev. Stat. 1923, ch. 23, §32; Ind. Annot. Stat. 1926, §4297; Maine Rev. Stat. 1916, ch. 147, §4; Mass. Gen. Laws 1921, ch. 121, §38; Minn. Gen. Stat. 1923, §4448; Mo. Rev. Stat. 1919, §12178; N. Y. Cons. Laws 1918, p. 7805; Ohio Gen. Code 1926, §1352; Tenn. Acts 1923, ch. 7, §42-2; Va. Acts 1922, ch. 105; Wis. Stat. 1925, §46.17.

[2] Del. Laws, vol. 30, ch. 64, p. 139, §1004-c; Ill. Rev. Stat. 1923, ch. 23, §31; Ohio Gen. Code 1926, §1357. The practice of holding such conferences, however, is to be found in many more states.

out-door relief.[1] Cities and towns in Massachusetts are reimbursed by the state for the support of non-residents who are so ill that they cannot be moved to the state infirmary. Elsewhere the devise is used exclusively in connection with the support of needy children.   The local boards of mothers' aid in Maine, for example, are reimbursed one-half the amount of their expenditure by the state upon the certification by the state supervisory board that they have performed their function effectively.   The supervisory board may require such reports from the local officers as it deems necessary, determine the character and amount of the aid to be given, and maintain a general oversight of the families receiving aid.   The board or any of its secretariat is given access to all records, and in general determines all questions of policy in connection with the administration of the law. Such, in broad outline, is also the system of supervision as it exists in Massachusetts, Virginia and Wisconsin.   In Connecticut a state agent, appointed for the purpose by the state treasurer, carries on the administration.   For the most part, however, he acts upon the reports and recommendations of the local officials.   At any rate, two-thirds of the expense in connection with the maintenance of the system is borne by the local treasurer.   The California procedure is outlined in the statute itself.

There is hereby appropriated out of any money in the state treasury—to each and every county, city and county, city or town maintaining [any] needy orphans, half-orphans, abandoned children or the child or children of a father who is incapacitated for gainful work by permanent physical disability, or is suffering from tuberculosis in such a stage that he cannot pursue a

[1] Cal. Gen. Laws 1923, Act 1330, §3; Conn. Stat. 1917, ch. 323, 1921, ch. 247; Maine Laws 1917, ch. 222, 1919, ch. 171, §1; Mass. Gen. Laws 1921, ch. 122, §18; Va. Acts 1922, ch. 488; Wis. Stat. 1917, §48.33 (1)-(10), §20.17 (13), 1921, ch. 86.

gainful occupation, or any or all of such classes of persons, aid not in excess of the sum of one hundred twenty dollars per annum for each such orphan, half-orphan, abandoned child, or child of a father who is incapacitated for gainful work . . . provided that in addition to the amount paid by the state for each orphan . . . maintained in a private home or in an institution . . . the city pay for the support of such orphan . . . an amount equal to the sum paid by the state.[1]

Somewhat more drastic than either the dissemination of advice or a system of grants-in-aid is the practice of requiring state *approval* for certain specific actions. The revelation of conditions described earlier in the chapter led to more radical supervision in some states than in others and resulted, in more than half a dozen jurisdictions, in the requirement of administrative approval for particular types of activity. The action most frequently singled out for such scrutiny is building construction and repair. All plans and specifications for new buildings or the reconstruction of old ones must first be submitted to the administrative authorities for approval in these states before any work may begin.[2]

Some notion of the volume of activity which may thus be embraced can be gathered from the development in New York. In 1923 fifty-eight plans for the erection or remodeling of buildings for charitable purposes were sent to Albany; the estimated cost thereof totaled $9,500,000. " This does not include," moreover, " buildings constructed by the state or by the City of New York, the plans for which

---

[1] Cal. Pol. Code 1923, §2283. If in addition a city undertakes a system of widows' pensions, the state administrative authorities are authorized to contribute half the pension up to $120 likewise.

[2] Ala. Code 1923, §4854; Maine Rev. Stat. 1916, ch. 147, §7; Mich. Comp. Laws Supple. 1922, ch. 64, §1982, Acts 1925, no. 146; Minn. Gen. Stat. 1923, §3179; Neb. Laws 1922, §8272; N. C. Cons. Stat. 1919, §5008; Ohio Gen. Code 1926, §1353; Penn. Stat. Supple. 1924, §9056a-16.

are not required under the statutes to be presented to the
board for approval." [1]

A few states round out the authority thus established by
granting their supervising agencies power to issue specific
orders.[2]   In Connecticut and Michigan the powers which
have thus been granted are limited indeed, and in all instances
are subject to the approval of the governor.   Somewhat
more extensive is the authority which has been delegated to
the supervising officials in Alabama.

The prison inspector is authorized to order city councils or other
governing bodies having control of any jail, prison, or almshouse, to put such jail, prison or almshouse and the grounds
around the same in a proper sanitary condition, and to make such
repairs, alterations and additions as he may deem necessary.
Provided, that if additions or new buildings are ordered, the
council may appeal to the governor, who shall have final power
to control the matter.

A somewhat larger number of states make use of the
ordinance-making power,[3] which is directed, for the most

---

[1] *State Board of Charities, New York 1923,* p. 4.

[2] Ala. Code 1923, §4854; Conn. Gen. Stat. 1918, §1889 (Our Connecticut Department of Public Welfare has never attempted any supervision
or even inspection of these places, although it is possible that we might
be authorized to do so under the General Statutes—letter from state
Official); Mich. Comp. Laws 1922, ch. 64, §1982; N. Y. Cons. Laws 1918,
§7805 (Such action relates to the treatment of inmates and is subject
to the authorization of a justice of the supreme court); Okla. Comp.
Stat. 1921, §57; Penn. Stat. Supple. 1924, §9056a-12; Vt. Gen. Laws
1921, p. 226 (Such action relates exclusively to building repairs); Wis.
Stat. 1925, §46.17.

[3] Ala. Code 1923, §§111, 4857; Cal. Gen. Laws 1923, Act 1330, §3; Del.
Laws, vol. 30, ch. 64, p. 139, §1004; Ind. Annot. Stat. 1926, §4297; Maine
Rev. Stat. 1916, ch. 147, §3; Mass. Gen. Laws 1921, ch. 121, §39; Mo. Rev.
Stat. 1919, §12177; Neb. Laws 1922, §8272; N. Y. Cons. Laws 1918, p.
7805; Ore. Laws 1920, §8447; Penn. Stat. Supple. 1924, §9056a-13; Tenn.
Acts 1923, ch. 7, §42-2; Wis. Stat. 1925, §46.18.

part, however, to the prescription of forms of reports, records, etc. In fact, only in Alabama, Oregon and Pennsylvania has any comprehensive use of the mechanism been made. In each of these jurisdictions, the supervisor is empowered " to formulate such rules and regulations as he may deem necessary with reference to hygiene, cleanliness, and healthfulness of all jails and almshouses in the state, including town and city prisons." [1] This, however, constitutes the sum total supervision maintained over this phase of municipal activity.

DELINQUENCY

Accurate data relative to the problem of crime is difficult, if not impossible to obtain. Nevertheless, various estimates of the property loss entailed thereby have been made. These, although they are probably inaccurate to the extent of millions of dollars, may, nevertheless, give some conception of the magnitude of the problem. Lydston and the Institute of Economics place the cost at $5,000,000,000; Bushnell, however, believes that $6,000,000,000 is a more accurate figure.[2] In 1924 the Bankers Protective Association arrived at the conclusion that the loss was nearer $3,500,000,000. These figures, be it noted, do not include the cost of maintaining the law-enforcing agencies (the police, prosecutors, criminal courts, institutions of correction, etc.), nor do they include the loss entailed through the failure of the profes-

[1] In Massachusetts " if the overseers of the poor of any city except Boston or any town, fail to place out any pauper for two months after the date of receiving such child, the state board of charity, to the exclusion of said overseers, shall perform such duty and such child shall, under the direction of said board, be supported by the city or town in the manner as if placed out by the overseers, and shall be subject to visitation by the officer or agents of said board until the board is satisfied that the overseers will properly care for him."

[2] Sutherland, E. H., *Criminology*, Philadelphia (1924), p. 68.

sional criminal to make a normal contribution to society. Consequently, inaccurate though these estimates may be, it is probably true that they err in understating rather than in overstating the cost of crime to society.

That a portion of this crime is peculiarly American, a comparison of criminal statistics at home and abroad strikingly indicates. A report to the American Bar Association by a special committee on law enforcement in 1923 stated that in 1921 there were but 95 robberies in all England and Wales, and only 121 in France (in 1919, the last year for which figures were available), whereas New York reported 1,445 and Chicago 2,417. In the latter year there occurred, furthermore, but 585 murders in France as against 7,850 (so it is estimated) in the United States. To this number should be added, moreover, 6,790 cases of manslaughter and other unlawful killings, thus bringing the grand total of unjustifiable homicides up to 14,640. In 1919 Raymond Fosdick published the results of an intensive study of the police systems of the United States and Europe. By correcting the police records and modifying the reports somewhat to make them more nearly comparable, he reached the conclusion that, in 1917, " Chicago had seventeen times as many murders per hundred thousand population as London, nineteen times as many felonious homicides, seven times as many burglaries, and sixty times as many robberies; New York City had eight times as many homicides as London, five and a half times as many burglaries, and thirty times as many robberies; St. Louis had twenty-eight times as many homicides as London and seventeen times as many burglaries; Detroit had eleven times as many burglaries and Cleveland nineteen times." [1] It may be that because of intricate differences in definition and procedure, these figures are inaccurate; nevertheless, it seems quite certain that the general conclusion

[1] Sutherland, *op. cit.*, p. 56.

which they indicate, to wit, that the crime rate in the United States is relatively much higher than in either England or France, is true.

Some see the explanation of this situation in certain biological forces; others see it in sociological or environmental influences; still others, in the breakdown of our law-enforcing agencies. An element of truth is possibly present in each of these theories. Neither space nor the purpose of our study, however, will permit a digression of sufficient length to determine the relative weight of each.

One thing is certain—our law-enforcing agencies have not been adequate to cope with the situation. Historically, the enforcement of law and the maintenance of justice constitute a function which has resided in the hands of local officials (the sheriff, the county prosecutor, and the courts, supplemented in the more populous counties by the police, municipal prosecutors and municipal courts). Very similar, historically, has been the situation in England. In Great Britain, however, as we have already discovered, the development of modern civilization with the consequent inability on the part of local jurisdictions to handle some of the newer problems, has given rise in certain fields of administration to a system of administrative supervision. One of the fields in which this change has taken place is that of law enforcement. A similar development, consequently, might be expected in the United States. Such, however, has not been the case.

POLICE

Only nine states all told supervise in any way the activities of the local police.[1] This supervision, for the most part,

[1] Ala. Laws 1915, no. 29; N. H. Laws 1913, ch. 148; Mo. Rev. Stat. 1919, §7863; Md. Laws 1920, §559; Mass. Stat. 1906, ch. 291, §7; N. Y. Laws 1920, ch. 8, §270; Maine Laws 1917, ch. 37; R. I. Acts 1913, ch. 99; S. D. Laws 1919, §7011. In Idaho "the Governor has authority to ap-

is of two types: that designed merely to check gross abuse; and that intended to confer upon the supervising agency broad authority and wide discretion.   In the latter class are those states in which the governor has been given power to *appoint* the chief of police; in the former, those in which the governor has been given power merely to make *removals*.   Specifically, Alabama, Maine, Maryland, Massachusetts, New Hampshire and Rhode Island fall into the first category; New York and South Dakota into the second.

In no state of the first class, however, do all the cities of the state fall under this drastic control.   In Massachusetts the police systems of Boston and Fall River alone come under this supervision.   The police commissioner in each of these cities is appointed by the governor for a term of five years. The control is still further developed in Boston by the fact that the selection of all patrolmen is under the jurisdiction of the state civil-service commission.   A similar relationship exists between the Governor of Maryland and the chief of police of Baltimore; the term of the police commissioner in this instance, however, is one year longer than it is in Massachusetts.   Insofar as the first-class cities are concerned, a similar arrangement exists in Missouri; and in those cities having between two and three hundred thousand population, two of the three commissioners who constitute the police board are likewise so appointed, the mayor in these cities being ex-officio the third commissioner.   In New Hampshire, the police forces of Manchester, Nashua, Portsmouth, Somersworth, Dover, Berlin, Laconia and Exeter are under

point law enforcement officers whose police powers are superior to those of municipal or county officers.   At the present time there is but one such state officer operating in the state and he carefully refrains from antagonizing or interfering in the orderly enforcement of the law by local officers.   The mere fact that he has authority to act seems to have a wholesome effect throughout the entire state." (Letter from Secretary to the Governor.)

similar control, as also are the police forces in two other cities in New England, one in Maine,[1] the other in Rhode Island.[2] In the case of both the New Hampshire and Rhode Island cities, a board of three commissioners, one of whom retires each biennium, constitutes the controlling body. The system of supervision in Alabama is somewhat unique. The state senate elects the board of public safety in all cities having a population of between twenty-five and fifty thousand.

In each of these states, of course, the governor may remove any or all of these state-appointed officials.

In New York and South Dakota the power of removal is the only power of supervision granted. Action may be taken in South Dakota only when a police officer wilfully fails or refuses to enforce the prohibition law. In New York, however, the jurisdiction of the governor extends to all situations in which the public welfare is jeopardized.

Although appointment and removal are the only mechanisms of control thus far used in connection with this activity, the nature of the service does not preclude the use of other devices. A central bureau might well disseminate *information and advice* of a very useful character. Indeed a law creating just such an agency was recommended to the New York legislature in 1928. A system of *grants-in-aid,* moreover, is used in England and the *approval* of the central authorities is necessary for the validation of most police ordinances. A descriptive study of this character, however, scarcely gives the author the right to pass judgment on the desirability and applicability of these various devices in any particular service without knowing the local situation in detail.[3]

[1] Lewiston.

[2] Woonsocket.

[3] In addition to the supervision thus indicated, fifteen states have established state constabularies, which, although usually given no juris-

The police, moreover, are by no means our only law-enforcing agency; equally important parts of the machinery which has been established for the maintenance of law and order are the prosecuting officials and the courts. By definition, however, they lie without the scope of our study.

JAILS

More directly related to the problem we are studying is the management of our institutions of correction. Historically, these have occupied pretty much the same position as our almshouses and poor farms; and their administration has, in many instances, been an equal failure. Scathing, indeed, have been the comments concerning these institutions in days past. A legislative investigating commission in Ohio summed up the situation as it existed in the eighties and nineties as follows:

> Children, youth, the middle-aged, the old, all at first simply accused of crime and more or less wrongfully accused are found congregated in our jails. And to perfect the wrong they are crowded often in an ill-ventilated, dirty, dark prison, where the whole being, physical, mental and moral, is soon fitted to receive all uncleanness with greediness. . . . It is a startling and terrible proposition sustained by this report, that Ohio is today supporting at public expense as base seminaries of crime as are to be found in any civilized community.[1]

Such were the conditions which called forth a drive on the part of humanitarian forces in America to rectify the administration of these institutions. And well might such a

diction within metropolitan areas, since they are chiefly designed to give the rural districts more adequate protection, do nevertheless supplement with their activities the efforts of the local police. This, however, can hardly be characterized as supervision in the sense in which the word has thus far been used throughout this book.

[1] Orth, K. P., *Centralization of Administration in Ohio*, New York (1903), p. 115.

drive be launched, for even today the conditions reputed to exist in the jails throughout the country are by no means flattering to an enlightened republic. J. F. Fishman, former federal inspector of prisons, defines a jail as:

An unbelievably filthy institution in which are confined men and women serving sentence for misdemeanors and crimes, and men and women not under sentence who are simply awaiting trial. With few exceptions, having no segregation of the unconvicted from the convicted, the well from the diseased, the youngest and most impressionable from the most degraded and hardened. Usually swarming with bedbugs, roaches, lice and other vermin, it has an odor of disinfectant and filth which is appalling; supports in complete idleness countless thousands of able bodied men and women, and generally affords ample time and opportunity to assure inmates a complete course in every kind of viciousness and crime. A melting pot in which the worst elements of the raw material in the criminal world are brought forth, blended and turned out in absolute perfection.[1]

And that the definition is not a gross exaggeration many recent state reports bear witness. A 1923 bulletin of the North Carolina State Board of Charities and Public Welfare contains the following comment:

The modern reader of history is often horrified at the accounts of living conditions in the English jails of the middle ages, where disease was rife, and where the dungeon, the thumbscrew and the rack were favorite methods of torture. But the reader would be more horrified still if he knew that many of these conditions exist in the county jails of our state today, and these conditions are allowed to exist because the people do not know what is going on behind prison bars.

In a recent study of some thirty county jails in our state four dungeons were found, three of which had been used within the past few weeks. One of these dungeons had concrete walls,

[1] Fishman, Joseph F., *Crucibles of Crime, New York 1923*, p. 13.

concrete ceiling and floor, and a heavy iron door with no window and no light or ventilation whatsoever, except such as might find its way through the narrow crack under the door. In this concrete vault 6 x 8 x 10 feet, only a few months ago seventeen negroes were confined at one time by the jailor, according to his own statement. The prisoners were too crowded to sit down and were compelled to stand. That classic illustration of prison cruelty, the Black Hole of Calcutta, where one hundred and twenty-three English prisoners lost their lives through suffocation, had two small windows in it. This dungeon has none. It is still being used as a place of punishment. No bedding is furnished. A prisoner confined in it is usually kept in total darkness for two days at a time with nothing to sleep on but the concrete floor. Please bear in mind that this punishment is not inflicted by a court, but by the jailor, who assumes such authority to himself without any basis in law. . . . In another jail dungeon, not quite totally dark, a prisoner was confined for four months for fighting another prisoner. . . . Two jails recently visited had only one apartment, so that there were no provisions whatever for separation of races or sexes. And so the revolting details unfold.[1]

The psychological reaction which these conditions produce, or at least may produce, upon the inmates is strikingly set forth in a conversation between Thomas Mott Osborne and a convict whose term was about to expire.

Do you know how a man feels when he leaves an institution of this kind? I'll tell you how I felt at the end of my first term. . . . I hated everybody and everything; and I made up my mind that I'd get even.[2]

The fact that the illustrations which have been used have been drawn primarily from county rather than municipal

---

[1] *Bulletin, North Carolina Board of Charities and Public Welfare,* January-March, 1923, pp. 6, 7.

[2] Osborne, T. M., *Prisons and Common Sense,* Philadelphia (1924), p. 28.

institutions does not make them any less relevant. The county jail is frequently used for municipal purposes. Furthermore, situations equally vile have without question existed in city jails and lockups. It may be, however, that the picture thus presented is an exaggeration of the situation which exists in the average municipal institution of a cor-rectional character. Nevertheless, J. F. Fishman, who was quoted above, maintains that " the exceptions are so few and far between that they stand out like patches of snow in a street of swirling mud." [1]

The fact that conditions of this character have existed in times past goes a long way toward explaining the develop-ment of state administrative supervision in the field of criminology, and the possibility of their return justifies its retention in the minds of those who believe in the efficacy of such control.

The further fact that from two-thirds to three-fourths of all convicted criminals serve out their sentences in the three thousand-odd jails scattered throughout the country, and that generally speaking the jail is the detention house of all those whom the authorities wish to detain, including those wrongfully accused of crime and important witnesses (not a small number by any means) as well as those held for trans-portation to a penitentiary, merely intensifies the belief of the exponents of administrative supervision in the necessity for such control.

About twenty-nine states, all told, have established super-visory agencies.[2] The extent to which they have been

---

[1] Fishman, J. F., *op. cit.*, p. 15.

[2] Ala. Code 1923, §4857; Ark. Stat. 1921, §1023; Cal. Gen. Laws 1923, Act 1330, §3; Col. Annot. Stat. 1926, §615; Conn. Gen. Stat. 1918, §1888; Del. Laws, vol. 30, ch. 64, p. 139; Ga. Annot. Code Supple. 1922, §2158g; Idaho Comp. Stat. 1918, ch. 24a, §55; Ind. Annot. Stat. 1926, §4297; La. Stat. 1920, p. 209; Maine Rev. Stat. 1916, ch. 147, §3; Mass. Gen. Laws 1921, ch. 124, §9; Mich. Comp. Laws Supple. 1922, ch. 64, §1982; Minn.

granted power for the accomplishment of their purposes varies from jurisdiction to jurisdiction. Although thirteen states make use of the mechanism of *reports,* the chief reliance of this supervision in the overwhelming majority of jurisdictions is a system of *inspection.* Indeed, all of the states maintaining such systems of supervision at all make use of the process. In the vast majority of these the grant of power is couched in very general terms and permits the state authorities wide discretion.[1] The board of charities and corrections in Virginia, for example, is "empowered, authorized and enjoined to visit, inspect and examine, once a year or oftener, state, county, municipal and private institutions which are of an eleemosynary, charitable, correctional or reformatory character, or which are for the care, custody or training of the defective, delinquent or criminal classes." In addition, in this connection as well as in connection with the inspection of institutions of a charitable character, reference is made in the laws of many states to certain specific objects

Gen. Stat. 1923, §4448; Mo. Rev. Stat. 1919, §12178; Mont. Rev. Code 1921, §331; Neb. Laws 1922, §8272; N. H. Public Laws 1926, ch. 108, §8; N. J. Laws 1918, ch. 147, §125; N. Y. Cons. Laws 1918, p. 7805; N. C. Cons. Stat. 1919, §5006; Ohio Gen. Code 1926, §1352; Okla. Comp. Stat. 1921, §51; Penn. Stat. Supple. 1924, §9056a-14; S. D. Rev. Code 1919, §10033; Tenn. Acts 1917, ch. 170, §7; Va. Acts 1922, ch. 105; Vt. Acts 1919, p. 328; Wis. Stat. 1925, §46.16.

1 Ala. Code 1923, §4852; Ark. Stat. 1921, §1023; Cal. Gen. Laws 1923, Act 1330, §3; Conn. Gen. Stat. 1918, §1888; Del. Laws, vol. 30, ch. 64, p. 139, §1004; Ga. Annot. Code Supple. 1922, §2158gg; Idaho Comp. Stat. 1918, ch. 24a, §55; Ind. Annot. Stat. 1926, §4297; La. Stat. 1920, p. 209; Maine Rev. Stat. 1916, ch. 147, §3; Mass. Gen. Laws 1921, ch. 124, §2; Mich. Comp. Laws 1921, ch. 64, §1982; Minn. Gen. Stat. 1923, §4448; Mo. Rev. Stat. 1919, §12177; Mont. Rev. Code 1921, §331; Neb. Laws 1922, §8272; N. H. Public Laws 1926, ch. 108, §8; N. J. Laws 1918, ch. 147, §125; N. Y. Cons. Laws 1918, §78.5; N. C. Cons. Stat. 1919, §5006; Ohio Gen. Code 1926, §1352; Okla. Comp. Stat. 1921, §51; Penn. Stat. Supple. 1924, §9056a-12; S. D. Rev. Code 1919, §10033; Tenn. Acts 1917, ch. 170, §7; Va. Acts 1922, ch. 105; Vt. Acts 1919, p. 328; Wis. Stat. 1925, §46.16.

of inquiry, such as sanitary conditions, the treatment of inmates, the detention of persons who have never been committed, and the management and discipline of the institutions.

How effective has the use of the mechanism been? To it, possibly more than to any other single cause, must be accredited such improvements as have taken place. And considerable strides have assuredly been made in certain specific communities. In New York, for example, according to a report of the state supervisory body, the jails have been brought to the point where, for the most part, they may be pronounced habitable. Plain, wholesome food is served three times a day in all but six counties; the fee system has been abolished and at least a minimum of cleanliness introduced; separation of the convicted from the unconvicted has been pretty generally effected, and the segregation of the sexes is the rule. In some jurisdictions more frequent sessions of the grand jury have been obtained, with a consequent speedier release of the innocent; padded cells have been pretty generally provided for violent prisoners; and the retention of insane persons is no longer permitted. Even outdoor exercise has been introduced in a few jurisdictions where the jail yards make such an innovation possible. Changes have come gradually and often reluctantly; nevertheless they have come, and considerable credit for bringing them about must be given to the mechanism of inspection.

Equally widespread among the states is the practice of disseminating *advice*. Much more limited, however, is the statutory authorization therefor. In fact, specific reference to the procedure is to be found in the laws of only eighteen states.[1] These usually provide that " no city shall erect, add

[1] Ala. Code 1923, §4852; Cal. Gen. Laws 1923, Act 1330; Del. Laws, vol. 30, ch. 64, p. 139, §41004-c; Ga. Annot. Code Supple. 1922, §2158jj; Idaho Comp. Stat. 1919, ch. 24a, §55; Ind. Annot. Stat. 1926, §4297; Maine Rev.

to or remodel a jail, almshouse, infirmary, house of correction or workhouse without first submitting the plans and specifications therefor to the board of administration for its criticisms and suggestions." The absence of specific directions in the law has not, however, restricted the mechanism either in method or in scope. The media of inspectors, newspaper publicity, conferences, correspondence and the submission of plans and specifications are all used extensively, irrespective of the wording of the statute, and the scope of the mechanism is bounded only by the four points of the compass and the energy and capacity of the supervising officials.

Somewhat more stringent is the control exercised through the requirement of *approval,* although its action is considerably more limited. Nevertheless, at least eleven states require all plans and specifications relative to new buildings or extensive alterations in existing structures to be submitted to the administrative authority for its approval before construction work may actually begin.[1]

In an approximately equal number of jurisdictions the power of enacting *rules and regulations* governing certain aspects of the maintenance of these local penal institutions has been granted the supervising agency.[2] In a

Stat. 1916, ch. 147, §7; Minn. Gen. Stat. 1923, §4414; Mo. Rev. Stat. 1919, §12178; N. J. Laws 1918, ch. 147, §125; N. Y. Cons. Laws 1918, p. 7805; N. C. Cons. Stat. 1919, §5006; Ohio Gen. Code 1926, §1352; Okla. Comp. Stat. 1921, §51; Penn. Stat. Supple. 1924, §9056a-11; Tenn. Acts 1923, ch. 7, §42-2; Va. Acts 1922, ch. 105; Wis. Stat. 1925, §46.17.

[1] Ala. Code 1923, §4854; Maine Rev. Stat. 1916, ch. 147, §7; Mass. Gen. Laws 1921, ch. 134, §14; Mich. Comp. Laws Supple. 1922, ch. 64, §1982; Minn. Gen. Stat. 1923, §10875; Neb. Laws 1922, §8292; N. C. Cons. Stat. 1919, §5008; Ohio Gen. Code 1926, §1353; Penn. Stat. Supple. 1924, §9056a-16; Va. Acts 1922, ch. 105; Wis. Stat. 1925, §46.17.

[2] Ala. Code 1923, §4854; Conn. Gen. Stat. 1918, §1889. ("Our Connecticut Department of Public Welfare has never attempted any supervision or even inspection of these places, although it is possible that we

majority of these the operation of the mechanism has been confined to the prescription of forms of reports, etc. Such is not the case, however, in five states: Alabama, Massachusetts, New York, Pennsylvania and Wisconsin. In the state first named the state prison inspector has been given authority to " formulate such rules and regulations as he may deem necessary with reference to hygiene, sanitation, cleanliness and healthfulness of all jails and almshouses in the state including town and city prisons," and very similar powers have been granted the supervising authorities in each of the other jurisdictions.

In seven states, furthermore, the administrative agency may issue such specific *orders* relative to the enforcement of these general ordinances as may seem necessary. In a number of these states, should any such order entail building alterations or repairs, an appeal may be taken by the municipality to the governor, whose decision is usually final.

It appears, therefore, that state administrative supervision over municipal activity in the field of dependency and delinquency is primarily confined to an effort to maintain the institutions for the care of the destitute and confinement of the delinquent on a reasonable level of efficiency. In a few states the municipal police force is subject to similar supervision.

might be authorized to do so under the General Statutes section 1883—" letter) ; Mich. Comp. Laws 1922, ch. 64, §1982; Minn. Gen. Stat. 1923, §9361; N. Y. Cons. Laws 1918, p. 7805; Okla. Comp. Stat. 1921, §57; Penn. Stat. Supple. 1924, §9056a-12.

CHAPTER VII

MUNICIPALLY OWNED UTILITIES

THE movement for the regulation of public utilities and the reasons therefor have long since become matters of public record. Applied at first merely to railroads, the principle has been extended to cover utilities of every form and variety. The first of the railroad commissions appeared in New England, when in 1844 New Hampshire and Rhode Island each set up supervising bodies. In the following decade Maine, Vermont, Connecticut and New York all followed their example. The duties of these commissions were exceedingly limited, being confined for the most part to the collection of information and the enforcement of the safety provisions of the law. Not until 1885 was a state commission given jurisdiction over local utility activities. At first limited in jurisdiction to gas companies, then given authority over electric light companies, the Massachusetts commission stands as a pioneer in commission regulation of public utilities. Aside from the ground-breaking work of this commission, however, modern regulatory methods may be said to have begun in 1907, when the states of Wisconsin and New York established such commissions and granted them broad jurisdiction over all forms of public utilities operating within the state.[1] The path thus blazed has been followed to a greater or less extent by every state in the Union save only Delaware.

[1] Nash, L. R., *Economics of Public Utilities*, New York (1925), p. 94; King, C. L., *The Regulation of Municipal Utilities*, New York (1912), p. 253.

In the course of this development two questions of interest to our discussion arose: first, should the principle of home rule prevail or did the operation of utilities make a system of regulation by municipal commissions inherently impracticable, if not impossible; and second, should municipally owned utilities be included within the jurisdiction of the state commissions even where these commissions were given state-wide authority?

The principal arguments in favor of home rule were and are that local officials are more completely familiar with the conditions affecting their local utilities and with the local sentiment relative thereto than it is possible for state utility commissions to be, no matter how efficient; and, consequently, that they are in a position to deal with the problem of regulating the local utilities more effectively than can state officials who lack this intimate contact with the local situation. Moreover, since these utilities make use of local streets, enjoy the benefits of local franchises, receive the support of the local populace, and all in all depend for their development upon the future growth of the locality, it seems logical that the unit of government which should regulate their conduct is the municipality.

On the other hand, the assertion is made that only a state commission can secure the data essential to intelligent regulation for no single city, with a few exceptions, can afford to hire a suitable staff for the purpose of collecting and collating the necessary information. Nor are the advantages of uniform comparative statistics inconsequential. Furthermore, an exceedingly large number of utilities no longer limit the geographic scope of their activities to the confines of a single city. And last but not least, the obnoxious influence of local politics on a local regulatory body is thereby removed.

In some states the advocates of home rule still hold the

day; in others, the exponents of state supervision. In still others a compromise has been effected between these two positions and a system of supervision based upon this compromise is in vogue.

The question of including municipally owned utilities within a scheme of state supervision has arisen, naturally enough, only in those states in which a system of state utility regulation of local utility enterprises has been established. Within these states there is a distinct division of opinion as to the proper policy. In Wisconsin the movement for the inclusion of *municipally owned utilities* within the jurisdiction of the state commission has gone so far that a municipality may not erect or acquire a plant of a character similar to any already in operation within its jurisdiction without the commission's approval. And should the commission give its consent to the construction or acquisition of any such utility, the right to review all schedules of rates and services connected with the operation thereof, and to make such changes in said schedules as seem fitting and proper, remains with the commission. Moreover, the form of all books and accounts, and the content of all reports, are likewise subject to the commission's determination. The objects sought by this supervision are obvious. The primary argument on its behalf is that only thus is it possible to develop a well-rounded system of utilities and to prevent the economic waste which unwise municipal activity would entail. Opposed to this is the feeling, shared by many, that the utilities of a city should lie within its own control; that a system of state supervision of this character is not really essential since the profits motive (the source of a large proportion of the ills of municipal utilities under private ownership) is absent. Nor is this belief rendered less dynamic by the fact that its conclusions are identical with the natural desire of local politicians for the fullest sweep of power.

The importance of this question has been considerably enhanced in recent years by the tremendous development of *municipally owned utilities* throughout the country. Over seven thousand cities, towns and villages now own and operate their own waterworks, all but nine of the cities over 100,000 being included among them. Approximately two thousand five hundred municipal electric light and power plants have likewise developed. In at least one hundred and nine jurisdictions, furthermore, the manufacture and distribution of gas has fallen under similar control. Mention, at least, should be made of the other fields of governmental invasion: street railways, municipal fuel yards, ice plants, street paving and repair plants, municipal ports, piers and terminals, ferries, baths, markets and abattoirs.

A survey, therefore, of the extent to which *municipally owned and operated utilities* have come under state control is not, perhaps, uncalled for nor unimportant. Some supervision of these municipally owned enterprises is exercised in almost half of the states. In some the supervision extends to *all* municipally owned utilities; in others, only to those utilities specifically indicated in the statutes, chief among which are wharves and other waterfront developments, dams, levies, waterworks, bridges etc. Both the construction and maintenance of these utilities are objects of the state's solicitude. The extent of this supervision, however, varies from utility to utility and from state to state. In some jurisdictions the control is nominal, in others, drastic.

MUNICIPALLY OWNED UTILITIES GENERALLY

In nineteen of the states which maintain a system of state supervision over municipally owned and operated utilities generally, *reports* may be called for by the supervising authorities at such times as may be specified in the statutes, and in at least eighteen of these at such other times as the supervising agencies deem necessary.[1] The requirement of reports has for its end in this connection pretty much the same objectives as are to be found in the fields hitherto discussed. Most outstanding among these, perhaps, is the amassing of information as a basis for the determination of both future policy and future administrative action.

In seventeen jurisdictions these reports must include such information relative to the operation and management of these various utilities as the commission may desire. To use the language of the Arizona statute, " every public service corporation shall furnish to the commission in such form and detail as the commission shall prescribe all tabulations, computations and other information required by it to carry into effect any of the provisions of the chapter, and shall make specific answer to all questions." In an approximately equal number of jurisdictions the law provides that copies of all schedules of rates and charges shall be filed with the supervising agency.[2] In addition, certain

---

[1] Ariz. Rev. Stat. 1913, §2304 (applicable only to municipally owned utilities when they extend their activities beyond the city limits) ; Ind. Public Service Com. Act (as amended 1926), §55; Maine Rev. Stat. 1916, ch. 55, §6; Md. Annot. Code 1924, art. 23, §371; Mich. Act no. 38, Public Acts 1925 (applicable to gas, electric and water utilities) ; Mo. Rev. Stat. 1919, §10453 (water works excepted) ; Mont. Rev. Code 1921, §3886; Nev. Rev. Laws 1912, §4520; N. J. Laws 1911, ch. 195 (as amended 1925), §17e; N. Y. Pub. Serv. Com. Act. §66; Penn. Stat. 1920, §18066; R. I. Gen. Laws 1923, §3721 (water works and water service specifically exempted) ; S. D. Rev. Code 1919, §9526 (telephone services only) ; Utah Comp. Laws 1917, §4795; Vt. Gen. Laws 1917 (amended 1919, 1921, 1923, 1925), §5058; W. Va. Annot. Code 1923, ch. 150, §5; Wis. Stat. 1925, §196.07; Wyo. Comp. Stat. 1920, §549.6.

[2] Ariz. Rev. Stat. 1914, §2290a (see footnote, *supra*) ; Ind. Pub. Serv. Com. Act (as amended 1926) §41; Maine Rev. Stat. 1916, ch. 55, §25; Md. Annot. Code 1924, art. 23, §364; Mo. Rev. Stat. 1919, §10453 (water-works excepted) ; Mont. Rev. Code 1921, §3891; Nev. Rev. Laws 1912, §4520; N. J. Laws 1911, ch. 195, §16d; N. Y. Pub. Serv. Com. Act, §66;

other specific information is called for in the laws of at least fifteen states.[1] A like number of jurisdictions require the prompt reporting of any accidents that may occur in connection with the operation of these utilities.[2]

On the basis of the information thus amassed, it is hoped that a comparison between private and municipal enterprise may be made possible, that such defects in operation and management as have developed may be discovered and corrected, and — in those states in which rates and charges are subject to state control — that satisfactory conclusions as to the reasonableness of the rates charged and the schedules of service maintained may thus be arrived at.

Supplementary to the requirement of reports from all municipally owned and operated utilities is the process of *inspection.* In general, this mechanism is devoted to the investigation of accidents, the audit of books, a survey of

R. I. Gen. Laws 1923, §3711 (waterworks specifically exempted); S. D. Rev. Code 1919, §9512; Utah Comp. Laws 1917, §4784; Vt. Gen. Laws 1917 (amended 1919, 1921, 1923, 1925), §5067; W. Va. Annot. Code 1923, ch. 150, §5; Wis. Stat. 1925, §196.19; Wyo. Comp. Stat. 1920, §5488.

[1] Ariz. Rev. Stat. 1913, §2290b; (see footnote, p. 216); Ind. Pub. Serv. Com. Act (as amended 1926), §13; Maine Rev. Stat. 1916, ch. 55, §6; Md. Annot. Code 1924, art. 23, §364; Mo. Rev. Stat. 1919, §10453 (waterworks specifically exempted); Mont. Rev. Code 1921, §3886; Nev. Rev. Laws 1912, §4520; N. J. Laws 1911, ch. 195 (as amended 1925), §25; N. Y. Pub. Serv. Com. Act, §66; S. D. Rev. Code 1919, §9512 (telephones only); Utah Comp. Laws 1917, §4786; Vt. Gen. Laws 1917 (amended 1919, 1921, 1923, 1925), §5057; W. Va. Annot. Code 1923, ch. 150, §5; Wis. Stat. 1925, §196.07; Wyo. Comp. Stat. 1920, §5496.

[2] Ariz. Rev. Stat. 1913, §2320 (see footnote, p. 216); Maine Rev. Stat. 1916, ch. 55, §35; Md. Code 1924, art. 23, §372; Mo. Rev. Stat. 1919, §10454 (waterworks specifically exempted); Mont. Rev. Code 1921, §3907; Nev. Rev. Laws 1912, §4520; N. J. Laws 1911, ch. 195 (as amended 1925), §17g; N. Y. Pub. Serv. Com. Act, §47; R. I. Gen. Laws 1923, §3712 (waterworks specifically exempted); Utah Comp. Laws 1917, §4812; Vt. Gen. Laws 1917 (amended 1919, 1923, 1925), §5059; Va. Code 1924, §3737; Wash. Code 1922, §10399; Wis. Stat. 1925, §196.72; Wyo. Comp. Stat. 1920, §5496.

plants and facilities, and an inquiry into the process and methods of management. In those states in which the device has been directed toward the investigation of accidents, it has for its purpose in part at least the allocation of blame, and in part the discovery of those defects of plants or management which were responsible for the catastrophe. All told, fifteen states make use of the mechanism in this connection.[1]

In at least seventeen jurisdictions, moreover, all books and papers relative to the operation of these utilities are subject to the demand of state inspectors and must be placed at their disposal.[2] Thus the information acquired through the medium of reports may be checked and the accuracy of local accounts made doubly sure. Needless to say, also, an analysis of these accounts is necessary both in connection with the determination of tariff schedules, and in connection with any attempt to arrive at a fair valuation.

The scope of the mechanism in at least fourteen states, however, is not confined to the mere audit of books, but in-

[1] Ariz. Rev. Stat. 1913, §2320 (see footnote, p. 216); Maine Rev. Stat. 1916, ch. 55, §35; Md. Annot. Code 1924, art. 23, §372; Mo. Rev. Stat. 1919, §10454 (waterworks excepted); Mont. Rev. Code 1921, §3907; Nev. Rev. Laws 1912, §4541; N. J. Laws 1911, ch. 195 (amended 1925), §17g; N. Y. Pub. Ser. Com. Act, §47; R. I. Gen. Laws 1923, §3723; Utah Comp. Laws 1917, §4812; Vt. Gen. Laws 1917 (amended 1919, 1921, 1923, 1925), §5059; Wash. Code 1922, §10399; W. Va. Code 1923, ch. 150, §5; Wis. Stat. 1925, §196.72; Wyo. Comp. Stat. 1920, §5496.

[2] Ariz. Rev. Stat. 1913, §2334 (see footnote, p. 216); Ind. Pub. Ser. Com. Act (amended 1926), §20; Maine Rev. Stat. 1916, ch. 55, §§5, 23; Md. Annot. Code 1924, art. 23, §362; Mo. Rev. Stat. 1919, §10452 (waterworks excepted); Mont. Rev. Code 1921, §3887; N. J. Laws, 1911, ch. 195, (as amended 1925), §166; N. Y. Pub. Ser. Com. Act, §§45, 66; Ohio Gen. Code 1925, §499-14; R. I. Gen. Laws 1923, §4825 (waterworks excepted); S. D. Rev. Code 1919, §9505 (telephone utilities only); Utah Comp. Laws 1917, §4799; Vt. Gen. Laws 1917 (as amended 1919, 1921, 1923, 1925), §5058; Wash. Code 1922, §10415; W. Va. Annot. Code 1923, ch. 150, §5; Wis. Stat. 1925, §196.08; Wyo. Comp. Stat. 1920, §5466.

cludes also the right to survey all the physical facilities used in connection with these utilities.[1] The members of the commission and the staff connected therewith are, in the language of the statutes, authorized " to enter the offices, depots, cars and right of way of any person or corporation or railroad within the state, and to enter the offices, plants, exchanges, stations, land or lines of any other utility company within the state for purposes of inspection." The necessity for such authority, if the utility commission is to determine the fair valuation of any utility or regulate the services of the same, is apparent on slightest reflection. Even greater is the range of effectiveness of the mechanism in those jurisdictions which include the methods of operation and management within its scope.[2] In the language of the Indiana code, " the commission shall have authority to inquire into the management of the business of all public utilities and shall keep itself informed as to the manner and method in which the same is conducted, and shall have the right to obtain from any public utility all necessary information to enable the commission to perform its duties."

[1] Ariz. Rev. Stat. 1913, §2322b (see footnote, p. 216); Ind. Pub. Ser. Com. Act (as amended 1926), §40; Maine Rev. Stat. 1916, ch. 55, §4; Md. Annot. Code 1924, art. 23, §362; Mo. Rev. Stat. 1919, §10452 (waterworks excepted); Mont. Rev. Code 1921, §3890; N. J. Laws 1911, ch. 195 (amended 1925), §16a; N. Y. Pub. Ser. Com. Act, §§45, 66; R. I. Gen. Laws 1923, §677 (waterworks excepted); Utah Comp. Laws 1917, §4799; Vt. Gen. Laws 1917 (amended 1919, 1921, 1923, 1925), §5056; W. Va. Annot. Code 1923, ch. 150, §5; Wis. Stat. 1925, §196.18; Wyo. Comp. Stat. 1920, §5470.

[2] Ariz. Rev. Stat. 1913, §2311 (see footnote, p. 216); Ind. Pub. Ser. Com. Act (as amended 1926), §§36, 51; Maine Rev. Stat. 1916, ch. 55, §4; Md. Annot. Code 1924, art. 23, §362; Mo. Rev. Stat. 1919, §10452 (waterworks excepted); Mont. Rev. Code 1921, §3890; N. J. Laws 1911, ch. 195 (as amended 1925), §16i; N. Y. Pub. Ser. Com. Act 1924, §§45, 66; S. D. Rev. Code 1919, §9517 (telephone utilities only); Utah Comp. Laws 1917, §4799; Vt. Gen. Laws 1917 (amended 1919, 1921, 1923, 1925), §5061; W. Va. Annot. Code 1923, ch. 150, §5; Wis. Stat. 1925, §196.02; Wyo. Comp. Stat. 1920, §5470.

A glimpse of the actual procedure followed in the conduct of these investigations may be caught here and there in the reports of the state utility commissions.

In Illinois, for example when complaints relative to the operation of gas plants (to chose a specific utility) are received by the commerce commission, it is usual to send the chief of the gas division or his assistants to make the investigation, helped, if need be, by assistants from the service division who are temporarily assigned to the particular task. In conducting an investigation of gas conditions in a given municipality, it is usual first to ascertain whether the managers of the utility as a result of a complaint by the consumers, have made any serious and immediate attempt to rectify the trouble. If nothing has been done in this direction, then the engineer of the commission tries by suggestion or by advice, but never by an order or direct instruction, to impress upon the managers of the utility the advisability of at once taking steps to improve the service conditions. The investigation is then directed to the complete operations of the utility concerned in an effort to ascertain where the fault or faults arose and to eliminate the possibility of a similar set of circumstances resulting in equally poor results in the future. According to the rules of the commission, each utility must keep on file in its office a written record of all complaints received, the date on which they were handled, and the means taken to dispose of them. The engineers make a list of these complaints, thoroughly analyze them, and then tabulate them according to their nature, so that the more important faults in the system can be recognized and taken care of, if necessary, by an order of the commission. Where the heating quality of the gas is the primary point at issue, it becomes necessary to begin the investigation in the production plant itself. For this purpose, the daily records are very thoroughly examined. Tables are made of the operating conditions which show (in the case of a water-gas plant, for instance) the method of operating and the amount of production material used. If the records that are usually found on the daily file of an efficiently managed gas utility are consistently kept by the plant superintendent, very little difficulty is encountered in tracing the fault in the gas quality to its source; and, when that is done, little trouble remains in arranging the plant operations for the future, so that the trouble need not occur again.

It cannot be pretended, of course, that the procedure followed here is typical of that followed elsewhere. Methods of inspection vary both from state to state and from utility to utility, and no illustration, however carefully chosen, can claim to be typical.

Much less widespread than usual, if one were to judge from the statutes alone, is the practice of disseminating *advice* in the field of utility regulation. Indeed, in Kansas only do the statutes make mandatory the establishment of a formal procedure.

Upon application to the proper authorities first, second and third class cities of this prairie state may receive such assistance as the utility commission is equipped to give. Among the more important cases in which such advice and assistance actually were given in 1921, was the Great Bend, Ottawa, Garnett and Independence telephone cases, the establishment of electric rates for Atchison, and of a municipal water rate for Concordia. Technical service was also rendered in the town last mentioned in connection with the construction and operation of its water-works plant. The valuation of a private electric plant for the City of Cedar Vale, and the valuation of the municipal electric plant and transmission line of the City of Burlingame for the purpose of establishing a rate basis for current sold to Scranton, were likewise included among the commission's activities. In connection with the services thus rendered, the technical skill of both accountants and engineers was called upon; but, although the law provides for extensive assistance of this character, its provisions have never been fully carried out because of the limited staff made necessary by the meagerness of the appropriations to the commission.

In a number of other jurisdictions, needless to say, although no specific warrant to do so is found in the law, advice relative to both the construction and maintenance of these utilities is nevertheless given. A recent letter from the Railroad Commission of Wisconsin, for example, contains the following paragraph. " The municipally owned utilities of Wisconsin, with few exceptions, operate in close cooperation with the commission and the technical staff of the commission is called upon frequently for informal advice in the disposition of problems which arise." Such a development, in fact, is almost inevitable in those states in which the processes of approval and review are called into play.

In at least eight jurisdictions certificates of *necessity and convenience* must be secured by all public utilities, whether municipally owned and operated or not, before construction work may be begun.[1] The statutory grant of authority found in Arizona is fairly typical. " A municipal corporation may embark in any industry for which it may issue a franchise . . . (but) . . . no municipal corporation being served by any public utility under the control of the corporation commission may construct, operate and maintain any such public utility without having first obtained from said

[1] Ariz. Rev. Stat. 1913, §2326 (see footnote, p. 216); Ind. Pub. Ser. Com. Act (as amended 1926), §98; Md. Annot. Code 1924, art. 23, §379; Mo. Rev. Stat. 1919, §10462 (waterworks excepted); N. Y. Pub. Ser. Com. Act, §§53, 68; Penn. Stat. 1920, §18150 (The approval of the commission is not required in Pennsylvania where the municipality will not compete with a private corporation); Wis. Stat. 1925, §196.52; Wyo. Comp. Stat. 1920, §5497.

corporation commission a certificate of necessity and convenience as provided by the Public Service Commission Act." It is thought the economic waste of a duplication of public utilities may thus be avoided. The municipalities in a number of states are, in fact, required to buy out the existing utilities rather than establish competing plants. In each case of this character, the purchase price of the utility concerned is subject to the state utility commission's *approval*. Indeed, the use of the mechanism of approval in this connection, extends to more than half of all the states maintaining any supervision whatever.[1] Closely allied to this is the control which is exercised in some seven jurisdictions over all bonds issued in connection with the erection or acquisition of these utilities.[2]

In at least nine states, moreover, the *approval* of the commission is necessary before any changes may be made by any municipality in tariff rates or schedules.[3] Action of this character in the field of utility regulation, however, so closely blends into the process of *review*, that it is exceed-

[1] Ariz. Rev. Stat. 1913, §2327 (see footnote, p. 216); Ind. Pub. Ser. Com. Act (as amended 1926), §95; Maine Rev. Stat. 1918, ch. 55, §40; Md. Annot. Code 1924, art. 23, §379; Mo. Rev. Stat. 1919, §10464 (waterworks specifically excepted); N. J. Laws 1911, ch. 195 (amended 1925), §18h; N. Y. Pub. Ser. Com. Act §§54, 68; Penn. Stat. 1920, §18150; Wis. Stat. 1925, §196.52; Wyo. Comp. Stat. 1920, §5497.

[2] Ariz. Rev. Stat. 1913, §2328 (see footnote, p. 216); Ind. Pub. Ser. Com. Act 1926, §89; Maine Rev. Stat. 1916, ch. 55, §37; Md. Annot. Code 1924, art. 23, §381; Mo. Rev. Stat. 1919, §10466 (waterworks specifically excepted); N. J. Laws 1911, ch. 195 (as amended 1925), §18e; N. Y. Pub. Ser. Com. Act, §§55, 69.

[3] Ariz. Rev. Stat. 1913, §2291 (see footnote, p. 216); Ind. Pub. Ser. Com. Act (as amended 1926), §45; Mo. Rev. Stat. 1919, §10440 (waterworks specifically excepted); Mont. Rev. Code 1921, §3891; N. J. Laws 1911, ch. 195 (amended 1925), §17b; N. Y. Pub. Ser. Com. Act §29; S. D. Rev. Code 1919 (telephone utilities only), §9512; Vt. Gen. Laws 1917 (amended 1919, 1921, 1923, 1925), §5066; W. Va. Annot. Code 1923, ch. 150, §9.

ingly difficult if not impossible for the analyst to differ-
entiate between them with any degree of certainty. The
line of demarcation is merely that in the case of approval
the positive sanction of the commission must be obtained
before the rates have effectiveness; whereas, in those jurisdictions in which only the power of review has been granted
the supervising agency, the new rates stand (although usually
they cannot go into effect until after thirty days have
elapsed) unless challenged by a consumer or by the utility
commission itself, in which case a hearing, frequently subject to specified rules of procedure, must be held before any
decision can be handed down. Seventeen states in all make
use of this latter process both in connection with the rates
to be charged and also in connection with the services to be
rendered.[1] The scope of authority thus bestowed upon the
utility commissions may best be seen in the statutes, themselves. That of Arizona may again be taken as typical:
" Whenever the commission, after a hearing had upon its
own motion or upon complaint, shall find that the rates,
fares, tolls, rentals, charges or classification, or any of them,
demanded, observed, charged or collected by any public
service corporation . . . are unjust or unreasonable, dis-
criminatory or preferential, or in any wise in violation of
any provision of law " it shall correct the same.[2]

[1] Ariz. Rev. Stat. 1913, §2309 a & b (see footnote, p. 216); Ind. Pub.
Ser. Com. Act (as amended 1926), §57; Maine Rev. Stat. 1916, ch. 55, §43;
Md. Annot. Code 1924, art. 23, §373: Mo. Rev. Stat. 1919, §10456 (waterworks specifically excepted); Mont. Rev. Code 1921, §3897; Nev. Rev. Laws
1912, §4533; N. J. Laws 1911, ch. 195, §17h; N. M. Acts 1921, ch. 93, §7;
N. Y. Pub. Ser. Com. Act, §§49, 72; R. I. Gen. Laws 1923, §3681 (waterworks specifically exempted); S. D. Rev. Code 1919, §9520 (telephone
utilities only); Utah Comp. Laws 1917, §4803; Vt. Gen. Laws 1917
(amended 1919, 1921, 1923, 1925), §5062; W. Va. Code 1923, ch. 150,
§11; Wis. Stat. 1925, §196.26; Wyo. Comp. Stat. 1920, §5469.

[2] Ariz. Rev. Stat. 1913, §2308a (see footnote, p. 216).

It might be interesting to examine in detail the procedure followed by these state agencies in arriving at their decisions.

Regular sessions of these commissions, for hearing and deciding contested cases, are usually held on a stated day of each month and continued as long as necessary. During the sessions any person who feels aggrieved by any act or omission to act on the part of any utility contrary to the utility laws of the state may lodge a complaint or petition for relief. In most jurisdictions all such complaints or applications must be made in writing by the complainant or his attorney, and must contain not only the name of the party complained of but also a brief statement of the facts on which the application for relief is based. In the preparation of these papers the secretary of the commission is usually instructed to give such advice as to the form thereof as seems necessary, and to furnish any information from the records of the commission as will be conducive to a full presentation and a speedy disposal of the matters in controversy. All such complaints are filed in their proper place on the docket and taken up in due order. Before a notice relative to a hearing is issued in some jurisdictions, however, the secretary of the commission is instructed to notify the utility complained of concerning the nature of the complaint and the party making the same, so that, if possible, an adjustment may be made without the expense of a formal trial or hearing. In the event that no such action is possible, a formal notice of the petition fixing both the time and place of the hearing must be issued. The utility so notified must file an answer to the complaint at least five days before the date of the hearing and a copy of this answer must be immediately forwarded to the complainant. The actual procedure at the hearing is very frequently modeled after that of one of the courts of the state.

So great is the variation among the states, however, that

it is impossible to generalize with any degree of accuracy concerning the operation of this mechanism. In Virginia, for example, the regular sessions of the commission are held each year in Richmond on the second Monday in January, April, June, September and November. Each complaint must be in writing, must distinctly and plainly set forth the grounds of the complaint, and must be supported in each case by an affidavit. Two copies of each of these petitions, furthermore, must be filed with the commission unless there is more than one defendant, in which case two additional copies must be filed for each additional defendant. Upon the filing of each such complaint or petition with the commission, a notice in the form of a writ is issued by the clerk according to the law which directs the bailiff of the commission or other proper officer to summon the defendant or defendants to appear before the commission on the day named therein, at which time the defendant must file an answer in writing (with two additional copies thereof), specifically admitting or denying item by item the material allegations of the complaint, and setting forth the facts which will be relied upon to support any such denial. The answer likewise must be verified by affidavit and signed by the attorney or counsel if such there be. (It should be mentioned parenthetically that amendments to either the complaint or the answer thereto may be allowed at any time by the commission upon application of either party). Furthermore, if the parties to the dispute are able to agree upon the facts or any portion thereof, these facts shall be accepted as evidence in the proceedings. Should both parties be ready upon the filing of the answer, the commission may proceed at once to hear the matter. If either party, however, is not prepared for the hearing, an adjournment may be had and a day for the hearing fixed. Instead of answering the complaint, however, the defendant may, if he chooses, demur.

At the hearing witnesses are examined orally unless testimony as otherwise provided in the rules of procedure is agreed upon. In each case the petitioner or complainant must prove the existence of the facts complained of unless they be admitted, or unless the defendant be in default by failing to answer. Facts alleged in the answer must likewise be proved by the defendant unless admitted by the plaintiff. In cases of failure to answer, the commission may take such proof of the charge as is deemed reasonable and proper and may make such order thereon as the circumstances of the case seem to require.

Both complainant and defendant are entitled to process to compel the attendance of witnesses or the production of books and papers before the commission. All such processes may be issued by the clerk of the commission upon the application of any party to the proceedings. When depositions are taken, they must be returned to the clerk of the commission.[1]

Needless to say, in each of the states in which the process of review is used to supervise either the rates charged or the services rendered, the state commission is empowered to issue specific *orders* correcting such malpractices as may have been brought to light as a result of an investigation and hearing.[2] Indeed, in many states they may substitute their

---

[1] *Virginia State Corporation Commission, Report 1924*, pp. 1-4.

[2] Ariz. Rev. Stat. 1913, §§2308a, 2311 (see footnote, p. 216); Ind. Pub. Ser. Com. Act (as amended 1926), §§28, 72; Maine Rev. Stat. 1916, ch. 55, §43; Md. Annot. Code 1924, art. 23, §373; Mo. Rev. Stat. 1919, §10456 (waterworks specifically excepted); Mont. Rev. Code 1921, §3899; N. J. Laws 1911, ch. 195 (as amended 1925), §16c; N. M. Acts 1921, ch. 93, §7; N. Y. Pub. Ser. Com. Act, §§49, 66; R. I. Gen. Laws 1923, §3686 (waterworks specifically excepted); S. D. Rev. Code (telephone utilities only), §9522; Utah Comp. Laws 1917, §4800; Vt. Gen. Laws 1917 (amended 1919, 1921, 1923, 1925), §5061; W. Va. Annot. Code 1923, ch. 150, §§5, 23; Wis. Stat. 1925, §196.37; Wyo. Comp. Stat. 1920, §5473. In some seven states in which municipal councils retain the right in

own *rules and regulations* regarding the schedule of rates and charges, or regarding the operation of the utility for those of the municipality.[1]

For the most part, however, the ordinance-making power has been confined in its operation to the determination of the form and content of the reports to be made by the utilities to the various commissions,[2] to the enactment of such rules and regulations as are deemed necessary to insure the safety of both employees and the public,[3] and the prescription of

their dealings with privately owned and operated utilities to fix through their franchise grants or local ordinances the rates of charge or schedules of service, the state commissions have been granted the specific right to overrule such action. In New Jersey no such ordinance takes effect until after it has the full approval of the state utilities commission. Ind. Pub. Ser. Com. Act 1925, §110; Ohio Gen. Code 1926, §614-44; Ore. Laws 1920, §6090; R. I. Gen. Laws 1923, §3716 (waterworks specifically excepted); Vt. Gen. Laws 1917 (amended 1925), §§5064, 5267; Wis. Stat. 1925, §196.58; Wyo. Comp Stat. 1920, §5497.

[1] Ariz. Rev. Stat. 1913, §2308b (see footnote, p. 216); Ind. Pub. Serv. Com. Act 1926, §§28, 35; Maine Rev. Stat. 1916, ch. 55, §46; Md. Annot. Code 1924, art. 23, §373; Mo. Rev. Stat. 1919, §10478 (waterworks specifically excepted); Mont. Rev. Code 1921, §3890 (units of service, etc.); N. J. Laws 1911, ch. 95 (as amended 1925), §16f; N. Y. Pub. Ser. Com. Act, §66; R. I. Gen. Laws 1923, §3685 (waterworks specifically excepted); S. D. Rev. Code 1919, §9520 (telephones utilities only); Utah Comp. Laws 1917, §4803; Vt. Gen. Laws 1917 (amended 1925), §5061; W. Va. Annot. Code 1923, ch. 150, §§5, 22; Wis. Stat. 1925, §196.15; Wyo. Comp. Stat. 1920, §5473.

[2] Ariz. Rev. Stat. 1913, §2304 (see footnote, p. 216); Ind. Pub. Ser. Com. Act (as amended 1926), §13; Maine Rev. Stat. 1916, ch. 55, §22; Md. Annot. Code 1914, art. 23, §371; Mich. Public Acts 1925, no. 38; Mo. Rev. Stat. 1919, §10453 (waterworks specifically excepted); Mont. Rev. Code 1921, §3886; Nev. Rev. Laws 1912, §4521; N. J. Laws 1911, ch. 195 (as amended 1925), §25; N. Y. Pub. Ser. Com. Act, §46; Penn. Stat. 1920, §18066; R. I. Gen. Laws 1923, §3721 (waterworks specifically excepted); S. D. Rev. Code 1919, §9526 (telephone utilities only); Utah Comp. Laws 1917, §4795; Vt. Gen. Laws 1915 (as amended 1925), §5058; W. Va. Annot. Code 1923, ch. 150, §5; Wis. Stat. 1925, §196.07; Wyo. Comp. Stat. 1920, §5496.

[3] Ariz. Rev. Stat. 1913, §2311 (see footnote, p. 216); Md. Annot. Code

the form in which the books and accounts of these various and sundry corporations must be kept.

All told, sixteen jurisdictions prescribe the set-up of accounts.[1] The New Jersey statute is, perhaps, typical. " Every municipality operating any form of public utility service shall keep the accounts thereof in the manner prescribed by the board for the accounting of similar public utilities and shall file with said board such statement thereof as it may be directed to do by the public utilities board." The procedure which is followed in the various states in arriving at a proper system of accounts varies, of course, from jurisdiction to jurisdiction. Very frequently the statutes suggest that, in those utilities in which it is practicable, systems of accounts similar to those prescribed by the interstate commerce commission be used. In those industries in which national associations have worked out uniform systems of accounts, the systems thus recommended are often used.

The activity of the utility commission in Connecticut in determining a uniform classification of accounts for the electric and gas industry may throw some light on the procedure.

That the views of the utilities affected might be fully pre-

1924, art. 23, §373; N. Y. Pub. Ser. Com. Act §50; R. I. Gen. Laws 1923, §3685; Utah Comp. Laws 1917, §4803; Vt. Gen. Laws 1917 (amended 1925), §5061; W. Va. Annot. Code 1923, ch. 150, §§5, 23; Wis. Stat. 1925, §196.37; Wyo. Comp. Stat. 1920, §5473.

[1] Ariz. Rev. Stat. 1913, §2324 (see footnote, p. 216); Ind. Pub. Serv. Com. Act (as amended 1926), §13; Maine Rev. Stat. 1916, ch. 55, §17; Md. Annot. Code 1924, art. 23, §378; Mich. Act no. 38, Public Acts 1925; Mo. Rev. Stat. 1919, §10461 (waterworks specifically excepted); Mont. Rev. Code 1921, §3885; N. J. Laws 1911, ch. 195 (amended 1925), §17d; N. Y. Pub. Ser. Com. Act, §§52, 66; Ohio Gen. Code 1926, §499-14; Penn. Stat. 1920, §18066; R. I. Gen. Laws 1923, §3721 (waterworks specifically excepted); Utah Comp. Laws 1917, §4816; W. Va. Annot. Code 1923, ch. 150, §26; Wis. Stat. 1925, §196.06; Wyo. Comp. Stat. 1920, §5496.

sented and the advantages that might be derived therefrom made use of before any accounting system was prescribed, the two state organizations representing these industries were asked to appoint committees to work in conjunction with the commission in formulating such a system. These committees gave much time and thought to the subject and used as a basis for their consideration the uniform systems of accounts prescribed by the committee on statistics and accounts of public utilities of the National Association of Railway and Utilities Commissioners, and recommended for adoption by state commissions at the annual meeting held in Detroit, Michigan, in November, 1922.

Both committees favored the adoption of this classification of accounts with certain changes designed to meet local conditions more directly or to conform more closely with accounting features which were thought better adapted for the industries in this state. At a conference of the committees with the commission, when the subject was fully discussed, it was agreed that, while some changes or amendments to the systems recommended by the National Association might be desirable, nevertheless since a large number of state commissions had adopted the classification as recommended by the National Association without change, and since the main object of a system of accounts was to bring about a uniformity of accounting, the " Uniform Classification of Accounts " for electric and gas companies, recommended by the National Association of Railway and Utilities Commissioners should be adopted.

The maintenance of such a system of accounts makes possible a comparative study of the relative efficiency of private and municipal management which would otherwise be impossible.

SUPERVISION OVER SPECIFIC UTILITIES

In addition to this supervision over municipally owned utilities generally, a limited oversight is maintained in a few jurisdictions over certain utilities specifically mentioned in the statutes. Chief among these are wharves and water-front developments, dams and water works, and in one or two jurisdictions gas and electric plants. All of these utilities, be it said, frequently come under the general supervision maintained in the states previously discussed.

Although the processes of *inspection, advice* and *approval* are all brought into action in connection with the supervision of municipally owned wharves and waterfront developments, the chief burden of control falls upon the last named mechanism. Indeed, the process of inspection is specifically mentioned in the law only in Iowa,[1] and the dissemination of advice is made mandatory only in New Jersey.[2] Considerable variation is to be found in the laws of the states in which state approval is required before work may begin on a wharve or harbor development project, caused chiefly by the varying geographic situation of the different states.[3] In Iowa, the river front improvement commission of each city is empowered to adopt such plans and specifications for the improvement of the river channel and banks, and the reclaiming of land between the meandered stream lines, as it deems best; but before actual work may begin, all such plans and specifications must be approved by the executive council of the state. In Pennsylvania the law authorizes cities which happen to be located on navigable waters to " purchase, alter and modify all properties extending into navigable

[1] Iowa Code 1924, §5821.

[2] N. J. Public Laws 1915, p. 432.

[3] Ala. Gen. Acts 1915, p. 689; Iowa Code 1924, §5821; Maine Rev. Stat. 1903, p. 86; Mass. Acts 1911, ch. 748, §15, Rev. Laws 1902, p. 823; R. I. Gen. Laws 1909, pp. 515-16.

streams, but only with the approval of, in pursuance to, and in conformity with the recommendations of the board of harbor commissioners, approved by the board of port wardens." In New Jersey, likewise, all plans for the development of any waterfront upon any navigable water must first be submitted to the state supervising authorities, and no such development or improvement may be commenced without their approval. Needless to say, in all of these states *advice and direction* are given the local authorities in connection with the discussion of the plans thus submitted.

State supervision over the construction and maintenance of dams and waterworks is maintained in a somewhat larger number of jurisdictions. All plans for the erection of any such project are objects of administrative solicitude in at least nine states, and in four jurisdictions a system of state inspection is maintained.[1] Exemplary of the statutory authorization found in these latter commonwealths is that portion of the New Hampshire statutes which provides that " it shall be the duty of the commission from time to time to cause all dams in the state of a height in excess of twenty-five feet, and all other dams which by reason of their height and location would be a menace to the public safety if improperly constructed or maintained, to be inspected by competent engineers. If such inspection shall indicate that the public safety demands the repairing or reconstruction

[1] Cal. Pol. Code 1923, Act 9109; Col. Annot. Stat. 1921, §1685; Kan. Rev. Stat. 1923, §68-1502, 3, 4; Iowa Code 1924, §§5821, 7767; Maine Rev. Stat. 1916, p. 1333; N. H. Public Laws 1926, p. 849; N. J. Public Laws 1915, p. 432; N. M. Laws 1915, §§5690, 5692; R. I. Laws 1923, §2536. In addition, it should be remembered that the control exercised over electric power plants frequently carries with it control over such dams as are constructed in connection therewith. It should further be remembered that the control exercised by the state boards of health over municipal waterworks and sewage systems likewise brings many of these projects under state control.

of any such dam, the commission shall order the owner of such dam to make the requisite repairs."

Somewhat more varied is the phraseology of law which bestows the right of approval upon the state administrative agencies. In New Jersey, " no municipal corporation may without the consent of the state water supply commission build any reservoir or construct any dam on any river or stream in this state . . . . which will raise the waters of such river or stream more than five feet above their usual mean low-water height, nor repair, alter or improve dams now existing which so raise the water, without such consent, but this shall not affect streams where the area shall be less than one square mile in extent." In Kansas, " if the mayor and council, or board of commissioners of a second or third class city . . . . shall deem it necessary to improve the system of water works, by enlarging, extending, repairing and improving the same, the city engineer shall prepare the plans and specifications. These shall be presented to the public utilities commission . . . . for approval; and if approved by such commission, the same shall be returned to the city clerk showing approval; no bonds to pay the cost for any improvement provided in this act shall be issued by the mayor and council until the plans and specifications, and an estimate of the cost thereof, provided therein, shall have been approved by the utilities commission, the cost of such improvement shall in no case exceed the cost of such approved estimate."

Another variation in procedure to which attention should possibly be called exists in Indiana. Should the state public service commission refuse to approve the issuance of bonds for the purchase or other acquisition of any water-works system in any municipality throughout the state a referendum may be taken upon the matter. The decision of the local electorate is final.

A unique situation exists in New Jersey in that any municipality which so desires may turn the task of furnishing the city with an adequate water supply over to the state water commission. All expenses incurred by the state commission in connection with any such enterprise are, of course, chargeable to the municipality.[1]

Finally, mention at least should be made of the fact that in three states in which no general supervision is maintained over electric utilities, " all municipal corporations which now own or operate, or which may hereafter own or operate electric light, power or water plants are authorized, upon procuring the consent of the public service commission therefor to furnish service to the people outside." [2]

Thus it appears that state administrative control over municipally owned or operated utilities extends in at least eighteen states to all such utilities generally, whereas in a more limited number of jurisdictions it is confined to certain municipally owned utilities specified in the statutes. The supervision which is maintained over the utilities in the first group of states varies, of course, from jurisdiction to jurisdiction. In fifteen or sixteen states, however, the control is quite extensive.

[1] N. J. Public Laws 1915, p. 1610, §2.

[2] N. J. Public Laws 1915, p. 87, §98; Mass. Gen. Laws 1921, ch. 164, §47; Ind. Stat. 1918, §8924b.

CHAPTER VIII

OTHER FUNCTIONS

THERE still remain to be considered a number of services over which a more limited control is exercised—more limited in the sense that the supervision of these activities is less stringent than that maintained in the services thus far discussed, and in the sense that the control exists in fewer states. Most prominent among the functions thus supervised are those which deal with the control of fires and fire hazards, the local civil service, municipal libraries, local ports and harbors.

FIRES AND FIRE HAZARDS

Approximately half a billion dollars is lost each year in the United States through fire, a considerable proportion of which in all probability is totally unnecessary. The contrast between our loss from this source and that of England is striking. In 1920 the loss due to fire in Great Britain was but $42,000,000, whereas that in the United States was $477,886,677. The British loss in 1921 was $48,000,000; the American $495,406,012. In 1922 the contrast was even greater, for in that year the loss in Great Britain amounted to only $30,000,000, while that in the United States totalled $521,860,000. When the figures for this latter year are translated into per capita terms, it appears that the per capita loss in England was 72c., whereas that in the United States was $4.75. Although it is probable that a certain portion of the difference between the two countries can be explained on the ground that the per capita valuation of perishable property is not as high in England as it is in the

235

United States, and also by the fact that many more buildings here are constructed of wood than is the case abroad, nevertheless such an explanation is in no way a justification. The loss of half a billion dollars yearly in this manner, if any of it is preventable, simply cannot be justified. The added fact that fifteen thousand lives are lost each year in these conflagrations makes a bad situation even worse.

In approximately three-fourths of the states, consequently, the legislatures have thought the matter serious enough to take action, with the result that state agencies for the purpose of supervising and supplementing local activity have been established in each of these jurisdictions.[1]

In general, two lines of attack upon the problem have been followed, fire prevention and fire fighting. In the overwhelming majority of states, however, greater emphasis has been laid upon the former rather than the latter, every effort being made to eliminate incendiarism and to reduce fire hazards.

INCENDIARISM

The number of conflagrations due to the cause first named is surprisingly large. An official of one of the leading fire insurance companies estimates that forty-five per cent of all

[1] Ala. Code 1923, §960; Ark. Digest 1921, §5952; Conn. Gen. Rev. Stat. 1918, §2283; Ga. Annot. Code 1914, §2412(k); Ill. Rev. Stat. 1923, ch. 13, §111; Ind. Annot. Stat. 1926, §11765; Iowa Code 1924, §1625; Kans. Rev. Stat. 1923, §§31-201; Ky. Acts 1920, ch. 16, §10; La. Stat. 1920, p. 998; Maine Rev. Stat. 1916, p. 570; Md. Code 1924, art. 48A; Mass. Gen. Laws 1921, ch. 148, §3; Mich. Act no. 178 of 1915 (as amended by Acts 168-283 of 1919), §2; Minn. Gen. Stat. 1923, §5955; Miss. Code 1917, §5126; Mont. Laws 1911, ch. 148, §7; Neb. Session Laws 43rd Sess. S. F. no. 145; N. H. (letter); N. C. Cons. Stat. 1919, §6074; N. D. Comp. Laws 1913, §204; Ohio Code 1924, §825; Okla. Annot. Stat. 1921, ch. 1, art. 9, §95; Ore. Gen. Laws 1921, ch. 169, §5; Penn. Stat. 1920, §10926; R. I. Gen. Laws 1923, §2787; S. C. Code 1922, §4112; S. D. Code 1919, §9122; Tenn. Code 1917, §3079a-270; Tex. Rev. Civ. Stat. 1925, §4896; Vt. Session Laws of 1919, no. 147, §5; Va. Code 1924, §4185; Washington (letter); W. Va. Code 1923, p. 1002; Wis. Code 1923, §2394-52.

fires in the year 1922 were incendiary in character. Other authorities place their estimates at from twenty-five to thirty per cent.

The necessity for prompt *reporting*, if an effective investigation of these fires is to be made, is quite apparent. A provision to that effect, consequently, has found its way into the laws of thirty of the states maintaining this supervision.[1] More or less typical of the grant of power thus bestowed upon the supervising authorities is the paragraph which follows:

The department of trade and commerce, the chief of the fire department of every city or village in which a fire department is established, and the mayor of every city and the chairman of the board of trustees of every village in which no fire department exists, shall investigate the cause, origin and circumstances of every fire occurring in such city or village. Such investigation shall be begun within two days, not including Sundays, after the occurrence of the fire. The officer making the investigation shall forthwith notify the department of trade and commerce and shall within one week of the occurrence of the fire furnish to the department a written statement of all facts relating to the cause and origin of the fire, and such other information as may be called for by the blanks provided by the department.

The details of these statutes vary greatly, of course, from state to state. In some, as in Tennessee, the local officials are allowed ten days in which to file returns; in others, five; in still others, three. In a number of states, moreover, the investigations on which these reports are based are at all times under the supervision of and subject to the direction of the state authorities.[2]

[1] Only Arkansas, Georgia, Maryland and South Carolina fail to have such a requirement in their laws.

[2] Maine Rev. Stat. 1916, p. 570; Minn. Gen. Stat. 1923, §5955; Miss.

The *investigation* of suspicious fires is, perhaps, the most important phase of the state fire marshal's activities, as a long record of successful prosecutions based on evidence amassed by the state authorities readily indicates.[1]   In 1922 in Iowa, for example, two hundred and twenty-four cases of suspicious fires were investigated by the state marshal with the result that eighteen indictments were secured.   In two cases the prisoners were given thirty years imprisonment each, two were given ten years, one was sent to a reform school, and ten, on account of their age, were paroled.   The other cases were still pending at the time of this investigation.

FIRE HAZARDS

More fundamental than the punishment of incendiarism is the elimination of fire hazards.   To this end, at least seven states make use of the mechanism of *reports,* requiring the local authorities thereby to indicate any conditions which might be conducive to conflagration whenever and wherever

Code 1917, §5126; Mont. Laws of 1911, ch. 148, §6; Neb. Session Laws 43rd Session S. F. no. 145, §6; N. C. Cons. Stat. 1919, §6074; Ohio Code 1924, §825; Okla. Annot. Stat. 1921, ch. 1, art. 9, §95; Ore. Gen. Session Laws 1921, ch. 169, §5; S. D. Code 1919, §9122; Wis. Code 1923, §2394-71.

[1] Ala. Code 1923, §959; Ark. Digest 1921, §5952; Conn. Gen. Rev. Stat. 1916, §2282; Ga. Annot. Code 1914, §2412(k); Ill. Rev. Stat. 1923, ch. 73, §111; Ind. Annot. Stat. 1926, §11768; Iowa Code 1924, §1628; Kan. Rev. Stat. 1923, §31-201; Ky. Acts 1920, ch. 16, §7; La. Stat. 1920, §998; Maine Rev. Stat. 1916, p. 571; Md. Code 1924, art. 48a, §55; Mass. Gen. Laws 1921, ch. 148, §3; Mich. Act 178 of 1915 (as amended by Acts 168 and 283 of 1919), §3; Minn. Gen. Stat. 1923, §5956; Miss. Code 1917, §5126; Mont. Laws of 1911, ch. 148, §9; Neb. Session Laws 43rd Session, S. F. no. 145, §6; N. C. Cons. Stat. 1919, §6075; N. D. Comp. Laws 1913, §205; Ohio Code 1924, §827; Okla. Annot. Stat. 1921, ch. 1, art. 9, §96; Ore. Gen. Laws 1921, ch. 169, §10; Penn. Stat. 1920, §10929; S. C. Code 1922, §4112; S. D. Code 1919, §9123; Tenn. Code 1917, §3079a-285; Tex. Rev. Civ. Stat. 1925, §4896; Vt. Session Laws 1919, no. 147, §5; Va. Code 1924, §4186; W. Va. Code 1923, p. 1003; Wis. Code 1923, §2394-50.

discovered.[1] In general, the statutes provide that wherever any of the local fire chiefs "find any building or other structure either private or public, which for want of repairs, lack of or insufficient fire-escapes, automatic or other fire alarm apparatus or fire extinguishing equipment, or by reason of age or dilapidated condition, or from other cause, is especially liable to fire and which is so situated as to endanger other property or which is so occupied that fire would endanger the persons or property therein, he shall forthwith report the facts and conditions so found to the state fire marshal, giving the ownership and location of the building or buildings so examined, the particular conditions noted, a general description of such building or buildings, the purpose or purposes for which used, the character of other buildings so near as to be endangered from fire and a recommendation as to whether such buildings so examined should be repaired or completely torn down and removed."

In a number of cases further action concerning conditions of this character seems to lie within the province of both the state and the local authorities; in others, it seems to be left entirely to the state fire marshal. In seventeen of the jurisdictions which bestow the right of further action upon the municipal authorities, moreover, their action is at all times subject to state *review*.[2] A typical grant of statutory authority in this connection follows:

[1] Conn. Gen. Rev. Stat. 1918, §2283; Ind. Annot. Stat. 1926, §11765; Kan. Rev. Stat. 1923, §31-108; Ky. Acts 1920, ch. 16, §14; Mich. Act 178 of 1915 (as amended by Acts 168 and 283 of 1919), §6; N. C. Cons. Stat. 1919, §6077; S. C. Code 1922, §4595.

[2] Ill. Rev. Stat. 1923, ch. 73, §114; Iowa Code 1924, §1634; Kan. Rev. Stat. 1923, §31-205; Ky. Acts 1920, ch. 16, §14; La. Stat. 1920, p. 999; Maine Rev. Stat. 1916, p. 570; Mass. Gen. Laws 1921, ch. 145, §6; Mont. Laws of 1911, ch. 148, §16; N. C. Cons. Stat. 1919, §6077; N. J. Comp. Laws 1913, §206; Ohio Code 1924, §835; Okla. Annot. Stat. 1921, ch. 1, art. 9, §98; Ore. Laws 1921, ch. 169, §7; Penn. Stat. 1920, §10927; S. C. Code 1922, §4114; Tenn. Code 1917, §3079-276; W. Va. Code 1923, p. 1004.

Whenever (the local) officers shall find any building or other structure which, for want of repair, or by reason of age and dilapidated condition, or for any other cause, is especially liable to fire, and which is so situated as to endanger other property, or so occupied that fire would endanger persons or property therein, and whenever any such officers shall find in any building, or upon any premises combustible or explosive material or inflammable conditions dangerous to the safety of said buildings or premises they shall order the same to be removed or remedied and such order shall forthwith be complied with by the owner or occupants of said building or premises. Provided, however, that if the said occupant or owner shall deem himself aggrieved by such order, he may, within ten days, appeal to the State Fire Marshal and the cause of complaint shall at once be investigated by the direction of the latter, and unless by his authority the order is revoked such order shall remain in force and be forthwith complied with by said owner or occupant.

Supplementing this local activity are the *investigations* conducted by the state administrative authorities themselves.[1] In Illinois, for example, five thousand inspections are being made by state officers each month. The effectiveness of this activity varies of course from jurisdiction to jurisdiction. Nevertheless, the fact that state inspections are being carried

[1] Ala. Code 1923, §967; Conn. Gen. Rev. Stat. 1918, §2282; Ill. Rev. Stat. 1923, ch. 13, §114; Ind. Annot. Stat. 1926, §11767; Iowa Code 1924, §1632; Kan. Rev. Stat. 1923, §31-110; Ky. Acts 1920, ch. 16, §7; La. Stat. 1920, p. 999; Maine Rev. Stat. 1916, p. 570; Md. Code 1924, art. 48A, §57 (public buildings only); Mass. Gen. Laws 1921, ch. 145, §6; Mich. Act 178 of 1915 (amended 1919), §6; Minn. Gen. Stat. 1923, §5960; Miss. Code 1917, §5129; Mont. Laws of 1911, ch. 148, §16; Neb. Session Laws 43rd Session, S. F. no. 145, §12; N. C. Cons. Stat. 1919, §6077; N. D. Comp. Laws 1913, §206; Ohio Code 1924, §834; Okla. Annot. Stat. 1921, ch. 1, art. 9, §98; Ore. Gen. Laws 1921, ch. 169, §6; Penn. Stat. 1920, §10927; S. C. Code 1922, §4114; S. D. Code 1919, §9125; Tenn. Code 1917, §3079a.274; Tex. Rev. Civ. Stat. 1925, §4897; Vt. Session Laws 1919, no. 147; Va. Code 1924, §4190; W. Va. Code 1923, p. 1004; Wis. Code 1923, §2394-52.

on in at least thirty-one different jurisdictions means, in all probability, a considerable reduction of the fire hazard.

The practice of inspection is perhaps most effective in securing results when combined with the power to issue specific *orders*.[1] In twenty-eight states, consequently, such a combination has been made. Wherever possible, it is the practice to permit owners to put their buildings into a safe state of repairs, but when this can not be done the buildings are simply condemned.

Less specifically connected with the process of inspection than has usually been the case in the functions hitherto discussed is the practice of disseminating *advice* which in this connection is, for the most part, designed to awaken a realization on the part of the body politic to the danger of fire hazards. The channels used to accomplish this purpose are numerous and sundry. Most common, perhaps, is the distribution of printed material. During 1916-17, for example,

---

[1] Not, however, until the interested parties have had due notice, and ample opportunity given them to be heard, has this been done. After the finding has been made by personally inspecting the building, the owner is sent a notice of the finding which notifies him just what must be done with his property and the amount of time allowed for compliance. After the time for compliance has expired and the owner refuses or ignores the order, the papers are placed in the hands of the county attorney with instructions to commence prosecution. Nebraska State Fire Marshal, Report 1921, p. 4 *et seq.*

Ala. Code 1923, §967; Ark. Digest 1921, §5950; Conn. Gen. Rev. Stat. 1918, §2282; Ill. Rev. Stat. 1923, ch. 73, §114; Ind. Annot. Stat. 1926, §11767; Iowa Code 1924, §1633; Ky. Acts 1920, ch. 16, §14; La. Stat. 1920, p. 999; Maine Rev. Stat. 1916, p. 570; Mass. Gen. Laws 1921, ch. 145, §6; Mich. Act 178 of 1915 (amended 1919), §6; Minn. Gen. Stat. 1923, §5962; Miss. Code 1917, §5129; Mont. Laws 1911, ch. 148, §16; Neb. Sessions Laws 43rd Session S. F. no. 145, §12; N. D. Comp. Laws 1913, §206; Ohio Code 1924, §835; Okla. Annot. Stat. 1921, ch. 1, art. 9, §98; Ore. Gen. Laws 1921, ch. 169, §6; Penn. Stat. 1920, §10927; S. C. Code 1922, §4114; S. D. Code 1919, §9125; Tenn. Code 1917, §3079a.274; Tex. Rev. Civ. Stat. 1925, §4897; Vt. Session Laws 1919, no. 147, §13; Va. Code 1924, §4190; W. Va. Code 1923, p. 1004; Wis. Code 1923, §2394-52.

more than seven hundred thousand pieces of literature dealing with fire prevention were distributed throughout Pennsylvania, not to mention the many pieces of "boiler-plate" likewise made use of.   Here, too, however, there is an immense variation in procedure among the different jurisdictions.   In many states, bureaus are maintained for the purpose of placing speakers on fire-prevention subjects before farm organizations, commercial clubs, insurance gatherings, city councils, schools, etc., whenever and wherever possible.   In Iowa two sets of motion-picture film, "The Danger Which Never Sleeps," have been procured and are in constant use.   An endeavor has been made to organize local fire-prevention committees in every municipality in Minnesota, thus forming a nucleus which will take an active interest in matters pertaining to fire prevention.   A further effort to stimulate this interest has been made by holding fire-prevention meetings in each municipality every year during which a general inspection of the city or town is carried on.

The control which the state authorities exercise by virtue of their *ordinance-making* power is confined for the most part to the designation of forms of reports, records, etc.[1] There are, nevertheless, a few exceptions.[2]   A provision in

[1] Ala. Code 1923, §960; Conn. Gen. Stat. 1918, §2283; Ill. Rev. Stat. 1923, ch. 13, §111; Ind. Annot. Stat. 1926, §11764; Iowa Code 1922, §1652; Kan. Rev. Stat. 1923, §31-201; Ky. Acts 1920, ch. 16, §9; La. Stat. 1920, p. 998; Maine Stat. 1926, p. 570; Mass. Gen. Laws 1921, ch. 148, §3; Mich. Act 178 of 1915 (amended 1919), §2; Minn. Gen. Stat. 1923, §5955; Miss. Code 1917, §5127; Mont. Laws 1911, ch. 148, §7; Neb. Session Laws 43rd Session S. F. no. 145, §16; N. C. Cons. Stat. 1919, §6074; N. D. Comp. Laws 1913, §204; Ohio Code 1924, §825; Okla. Annot. Stat. 1921, ch. 1, art. 9, §95; Ore. Gen. Laws 1921, ch. 169, §5; Penn. Stat. 1920, §10926; S. D. Code 1919, §9122; Tenn. Code 1917, §3079a269; Va. Code 1924, §4185; W. Va. Code 1923, p. 502.

[2] Ala. Code 1923, §958; Cal. Rev. Stat. 1919, §2741; Ill. Rev. Stat. 1923, ch. 73, §114; Ind. Annot. Stat. 1926, §11764; Ky. Acts 1920, ch. 16, §19; La. Stat. 1920, p. 998; N. D. Code 1913, §215; Tex. Rev. Civ. Stat. 1925, §4915.

the North Dakota code empowers the commissioners of insurance, together with the fire marshal, to make such rules for the prevention of fires as are necessary, and directs that all such rules be fully explained to the state, county, and city officials concerned.[1] In California all local fire chiefs are required to perform such duties " as may be required by state law, city or town ordinances, or by the commissioner of insurance." [2] In at least ten states, moreover, the state fire marshal may draw up such rules and regulations concerning the transport and storage of combustible materials, or the maintenance of inflammable conditions, as seem to him fitting and proper.[3] These, however, are the exceptions rather than the rule. Nevertheless, it is difficult to see what is to prevent the state authorities, in jurisdictions where they have both the power to review the actions of all subordinate fire chiefs and the right to enter all buildings and premises for the purpose of eliminating fire hazards, from drawing up a set of rules and regulations for the guidance of their own inspectors which will also apply to all municipal authorities.

FIRE FIGHTING

The supervision thus maintained over fire prevention is not, however, the only control which is exercised. Mention should also be made of the practice, to be found in a limited number of jurisdictions at least, of disseminating *advice* relative to fire fighting and fire-fighting equipment. In some states annual conferences of local fire chiefs are held; in

---

[1] N. D. Comp. Laws 1913, §215.

[2] Cal. Rev. Stat. 1919, §2741.

[3] Ala. Code 1923, §966; Conn. Acts 1921, §3334; Ill. Rev. Stat. 1923, ch. 13, §114; Ind. Annot. Stat. 1926, §11764; Kan. Rev. Stat. 1923, §31-207; Ky. Acts 1920, ch. 16, §19; Mass. Gen. Laws 1921, ch. 148, §10; Mich. Act 178 of 1915, §5; Penn. Stat. 1920, §10925; Tenn. Code 1917, §3079a-273.

others, state inspectors go over local apparatus and advise as to its care and operation; in still others, suggestions for additional equipment are made. Perhaps the most highly developed procedure for the dissemination of this technical information is that which exists in Minnesota, where a state fire college is held for the purpose of instructing firemen in modern methods of fire fighting and fire prevention. The course includes physical drill, first aid and rescue work, fire study, the study of the proper names of all tools used in fire fighting, hose and ladder exercises, the tying of various knots used in fire department work, the use of the life net, of gas masks and oxygen helmets, of oxyacetylene cutting devices, etc.

Only one state has pushed its supervision further, North Dakota. The North Dakota law provides that:

The state auditor shall issue and deliver to the treasurer of any city having an organized fire department, his warrant upon the state treasurer for an amount equal to two per cent of the premium received upon policies issued on property in said city, town or village, and such warrant shall be paid by the state treasurer to the treasurer of such city upon presentation thereof. No city, town or village having one or more organized fire companies therein shall be entitled to any of the benefits arising from this article, unless the fire department or companies shall have been in actual existence eight months prior to the filing of the certificate, and unless such fire department or company shall have had for such period, as part of its equipment, at least one steam, hand or other fire engine, truck or hose cart, with a membership of at least fifteen persons for said period of eight months.

Slight as these minimum requirements are, they indicate a method by which the state, if it so desires, may raise the standard of efficiency in the local fire departments.

CIVIL SERVICE

Much more limited in geographic extent is the control exercised over the local personnel problem. In fact, only four states maintain any supervision whatever.[1] In New York and Ohio the control is exceedingly light; in New Jersey and Massachusetts, however, it is rather stringent. So great is the divergence between the laws that each deserves individual consideration.

Should the mayor of a municipality in New York fail to appoint a local civil service commission, the state commission is empowered to make the appointment in his stead. Furthermore, at any time should it become apparent that a municipal civil service commissioner is incompetent or neglectful of his duty, the state commission may, by unanimous vote and with the written approval of the governor, remove the commissioner. In such an exigency, moreover, the state commission rather than the mayor of the city concerned is empowered to fill the vacancy created. In addition, all ordinances enacted by the local civil service commissions are subject to the approval of the supervising agency, and may at any time by unanimous vote be amended or rescinded by it. Moreover, should a municipal commission by any chance fail to draw up a set of rules and regulations governing its activities, the state commission may present it with a set of the commission's own making which must be followed by all local authorities concerned. Needless to say the supervising agency may from time to time require such reports as it deems fit from the municipal commissions relative to their activity and make such inquiries as appear to it to be necessary.

The situation in Ohio in many particulars resembles that found in New York; in others, it is very different. The

Ohio commission, for example, is empowered, as is the supervising agency in New York, to require such reports and make such investigations as it may deem necessary; it may also make appointments to fill all vacancies which have existed for more than sixty days on the local commissions. No authority to make removals, however, has been lodged with it; indeed, its only weapon is publicity.

Quite different is the situation in Massachusetts. The power granted the state civil service commission of appointing the local examining boards, of preparing rules and regulations relative to the selection of local personnel (subject to the approval of the governor), and of holding up the compensation of persons illegally appointed, gives the state commission practically complete control over the municipal personnel problem throughout the commonwealth.

Even greater is the concentration of power in the hands of the New Jersey civil service commission, in so far as those cities which vote to come under its jurisdiction are concerned. It enacts all rules and regulations governing entrance into the service, holds all examinations, and may review all dismissals; in fact, although it has no statutory authority to do so, it has even attempted to standardize salaries by drawing up and recommending uniform schedules for certain specified services.

LIBRARIES

The supervision maintained over public libraries for the most part takes the form of encouragement and advice. To the end that this service may the more effectively be directed, at least fifteen states attempt to keep themselves informed as to library conditions in the various municipalities throughout the state by means of the process of *reports*.[1] In all

[1] California, Illinois, Iowa, Kentucky, Louisiana, Maryland, Michigan, Minnesota, New Hampshire, North Carolina, North Dakota, Pennsylvania, South Dakota, Texas and Utah. (This information was obtained through correspondence with state officials.)

twenty-six states in which any supervision is maintained, the mechanism of advice is called into play,[1] operating chiefly through a system of correspondence. In at least nine states, however, field workers are maintained to *assist* in the establishment of new libraries and to stimulate the improvement of old ones.[2] Some idea of their duties and functions can be obtained from a recent report from the state of Washington which declares that one of the most important means employed by the commission in giving assistance to libraries is to send a field worker over the state.

This representative from the state office may spend an hour or a fortnight in a local library, giving instruction to an inexperienced librarian, aiding in the preliminary work for opening a new library, in reorganizing an old one, in starting the library's work with schools, or she may be called to a local library to adjust some difficulty with the library board. . . . Whether her stay be long or short . . . such a representative can do wonders in setting right a library institution, in urging the appointment of a capable librarian, in influencing the local library board to pay proper salaries, provide proper hours of work, vacations, sick leave, etc.[3]

In a number of states [4] the central authorities render still

[1] California, Connecticut, Georgia, Illinois, Iowa, Kentucky, Louisiana, Maryland, Massachusetts, Minnesota, Missouri, Nebraska, New Hampshire, North Carolina, North Dakota, Ohio, Oklahoma, Oregon, Pennsylvania, South Dakota, Tennessee, Texas, Utah, Vermont, Washington and Wisconsin. (This information was obtained through correspondence with state officials.)

[2] Neb. Comp. Stat. 1913, §3810; N. H. Public Laws 1901, p. 193; Ohio Code 1924, §793; Ore. Laws 1920, §5489; Penn. Code 1920, §13824; Tenn. Code 1917, §1387a3; Vt. Gen. Laws 1917, §1453; Wis. Stat. 1919, §43.09; Wash. Stat. 1915, §6960.72.

[3] *Washington Report on Library Extension.*

[4] California, Georgia, Illinois, Kentucky, Minnesota, Nebraska, Oregon and Wisconsin. (This information was obtained through correspondence with state officials.)

further assistance by lending books to the local centers. These books remain the property of the state library but are obtainable by the municipal institutions upon request.   Only in Connecticut and Washington, however, has any monetary assistance on the part of the state been offered.   In the latter, a system of *grants-in-aid* has been established through which the localities receive a sum " not to exceed ten cents per volume in circulation " on condition that they maintain standards set by the state library commission.

This supervision is rendered even more effective in at least three states by the further requirement that all librarians employed in public libraries throughout the state must possess certificates of approval from the state authorities.[1]

PORTS AND HARBORS

In twelve jurisdictions state administrative supervision has developed in connection with the administration of local ports.   Nine very important ports of the country are under state control: Boston, Hampton Roads, Portland (Me.), Portland (Ore.), Providence, New London, Mobile, New Orleans and San Francisco.[2]   Boards appointed exclusively by the governors of the respective states are in control of five of them.   In Portland (Me.) and New London, however, the mayor is permitted to serve as an ex-officio member. In Portland (Ore.) the port authorities are elected by the State Assembly and are responsible to it.

In addition, a somewhat less comprehensive type of control has been established in a number of other commonwealths.[3]   Illustrative, if not typical, is the provision of law

[1] Oklahoma, Texas, Utah. (This information was obtained through correspondence with state officials.)

[2] Brown, Edmund, *Shore Control and Port Administration*, Washington (1923), ch. 8; Acts of Virginia, 1926, ch. 230.

[3] Cal. Stat. 1915, §2575 (applicable to San Diego and Eureka); Fla. Laws 1914, §1322; Illinois (letter from the secretary to the governor);

in Florida which empowers the governor to appoint, by and with the consent of the senate, all the harbor masters required for the several ports of the state to hold office for a term of two years unless sooner removed by the governor. Another variation in governmental relationships exists in Pennsylvania.

Such portions of the port of Philadelphia as are outside of the City and County of Philadelphia are under the jurisdiction of the board of commissioners of navigation for the River Delaware and its Navigable Tributaries—a state body. This board has full harbor master authority within the limits of the three counties, and exercises supervision over the construction of wharves and other maritime structures. The commissioners have full charge of the state pilots licensed under the laws of the state.[1]

In Illinois the jurisdiction of the state includes: (a) the control and management of the Illinois and Michigan Canal and the proposed Illinois waterway, (b) the supervision over the plans and construction of the proposed Lake Calumet Deep Water Harbor, (c) prevention of obstructions, encroachments and pollution, (d) supervision of the plans and construction of water structures, (e) protection of the rights of the public with reference to docks, wharves and landings and with reference to access to and egress from navigable waters, and, finally, the preservation and beautifying of public waters. Somewhat similar is the control maintained in the other states aforementioned.[1]

La. Stat. 1915, §5447; Mass. Gen. Laws 1902, p. 604, §19; N. H. Public Laws 1901, p. 375; N. Y. Cons. Laws 1918, p. 5533; Oregon (letter from the secretary to the governor) ; R. I. Laws 1909, p. 511 ; S. C. Laws 1912, §§695, 2470; Va. Session Laws 1926, ch. 230.

[1] (Letter from a state official.)

[2] It sometimes happens that the building of roads by state highway departments brings state officials into contact with municipalities. At

THE INCORPORATION OF MUNICIPALITIES

In a few states the action of state officials is necessary for the incorporation of municipalities.[1] For the most part such action is nominal. It is usually the secretary of state, although occasionally it may be the governor, who is called upon to act. Generally the procedure consists merely in the presentation of a petition signed by the required number of voters, fifty to seventy-five per cent of the inhabitants of the town, as the law may require. Upon the presentation of such a petition the secretary of state or the governor, as the case may be, investigates the facts therein set forth to see that all the legal requirements have been complied with, and, if they have, he issues a proclamation declaring said city to be incorporated.[2]

least six states make provision for such contact. (Cal. Stat. 1915, ch. 78; Ind. Stat. 1919, ch. 53, §22; Iowa Code 1919, §2945; La. Stat. 1915, §6581, p. 2336; Minn. Stat. 1913, §2505; Maine Rev. Stat. 1916, ch. 25, §17.) In Iowa the State Highway Commission acts as a court of review for disputes between city and county officials as to the apportionment of the cost of road building. Colorado, Louisiana, Maine and Minnesota provide for a system of state aid for streets which form connecting links in state roads. Indiana assumes the full cost of improving such streets to the same grade as the state highway.

[1] Mich. Acts 1919, §84; N. C. Cons. Stat. 1919, §2779; N. J. Comp. Laws 1910, p. 398, §5; Tenn. Stat. 1917, §1895; Wisconsin (letter).

[2] Even more automatic is the action of state officials in regard to the classification of cities. The provision contained in the Mississippi Code will serve to illustrate. "Whenever by a census taken under an act of Congress or of the legislature it shall be shown that the population of a city, town or village has increased or diminished so as to take or place such city, town or village out of the class to which heretofore it has belonged or whenever the same is shown by a census of such city, town or village taken under the direction of the municipal authorities and approved by them as correct, the municipal authorities thereof shall certify the facts to the Governor, who shall investigate the matter, and if he find the municipality to be wrongly classified he shall issue his proclamation in accordance with the facts, and shall correctly classify it, transmitting a copy of the procla-

Although not directly supervisory in its nature, the requirement in several states that all state, county, district and city officers must furnish the commissioner of labor, upon his request, all statistical information relating to labor which may be in their possession as such officers, should not be omitted from mention; nor, indeed, should the further requirement, found in both Massachusetts and Montana that " whenever it is made to appear to the mayor of any city that a strike or lockout is seriously threatened or actually occurs, the mayor of said city shall at once notify the state board (of arbitration) of the fact," be overlooked.

Equally interesting is the provision of law in Pennsylvania which establishes a bureau of municipalities providing that:

The said bureau shall gather, classify, index and make available, and disseminate data, statistical information, and advice that may be helpful in improving the methods of administration and municipal development in the several municipalities of the Commonwealth; and shall maintain for the benefit of the municipalities a publicity service, to install or assist in the installing and establishment of modern systems of accounting in the various municipalities of the state, and in order to promote a comprehensive plan or series of plans for the probable future requirements of cities in respect to a system of traffic, thoroughfares, and other highways or main highways, transportation of every sort, suitable coordinated sites for public buildings, parks, parkways, playgrounds and other public uses, the preservation of natural historic features, and any and all public improvements tending to the advantage of municipalities or townships affected, tending to their advantage as a place of business and residence, and to either make or secure in making or securing the necessary surveys, plans and information.

mation to the mayor of such city, town or village." In cases where the population drops below a prescribed minimum the corporation in most states is automatically abrogated.

GENERAL ADMINISTRATIVE SUPERVISION

In addition to the supervision exercised over these specific fields there exist on a limited scale in a limited number of jurisdictions occasional manifestations of what may be called general executive control. More specifically, in six states the governor may, subject to such limitations as are imposed in the statutes, remove certain specified municipal officials from office whenever and wherever he deems it desirable. When the chief executive of either Michigan, Minnesota or New York for example is convinced from evidence submitted to him that an executive officer of any city or village in the state " is incompetent to properly execute the duties of his office, or has been guilty of official misconduct, or of wilful neglect of duty, or of extortion, or of habitual drunkenness," he may at any time remove said official for the good of the service. In Ohio " the governor has authority to remove mayors of municipalities for any form of official dereliction. All other local administrative officials may be removed by the governor for failure to enforce the prohibition law and for no other reason." The grant in South Dakota is much more limited, being confined to the enforcement of prohibition, and in Wisconsin confined only to the municipal judiciary.

Equally limited and equally circumscribed is the practice of state appointment. " The constitution of California provides that the governor may make an appointment to any office when a vacancy occurs in those cases where there is no specific provision of law for filling the vacancy." In New Mexico, whenever any municipal officer has been removed by a court, the governor must immediately appoint his successor. A similar provision in the Arkansas law confines the operation of the mechanism to the chief executives of the municipalities. The statute in Alabama is essentially the same in principle. It is confined in its operation, however, to vacancies on commissions in cities between twenty five and fifty thousand in population. In the case of certain municipalities in Idaho, Pennsylvania and Tennessee, the responsibility of filling certain elective offices made vacant by death is likewise thrown upon the governor of the state. In Oregon the law of municipal organization provides that the first commissioners of all municipal organizations shall be appointed by the governor. Mention should perhaps be made of the fact that the governor of Illinois appoints park commissioners for two parks in the city of Chicago.

The practice of state appointment to fill vacancies caused by resignation, removal, or death on the municipal bench, however, is more common. At least six states make use of the procedure. In each case the appointment is temporary, terminating with the next election. Vermont constitutes an outstanding exception, for the statutes of the State provide that "the governor shall bienially appoint and commission for the term of two years the judges of municipal and city courts, and shall fill all vacancies occasioned by the death, resignation, removal or permanent inability to serve on the part of any such judge."

NOTE: Louisiana has an interesting provision which permits the mayor and aldermen or council of specified cities to amend the city charter in certain particulars with the approval of the governor; but if more than one-tenth of the qualified electors of the city protest, such approval shall not be given until after the amendment has been decided by referendum. There is a further quaint provision in this state that in municipalities of less than twenty five hundred inhabitants the governor must approve any change of corporate name. (La. Stat. 1919, p. 1754.)

CHAPTER IX

SUMMARY AND CONCLUSION

THUS it appears that a system of state administrative supervision over cities has evolved in the United States which resembles in many particulars that which has developed in Europe. In very few states, however, has any " general supervision " been granted the state administrative authorities. For the most part their attention has been confined to special fields of activity: finance, health, education, dependency and delinquency, and municipally owned or operated utilities; in a more limited number of jurisdictions it has been extended to fire, personnel, public libraries, ports, roads, and so forth.

FINANCE

The control over finance is most sweeping. Nevertheless, extensive though it may seem in comparison with the supervision exercised over the other functions, this oversight does not even approximate that maintained in Europe. One or two states only may be said to constitute even the slightest exception to this general rule. For the most part, at the present time, state administrative supervision of municipal finance is directed into four channels: taxation, accounts, budgets and indebtedness.

Most widespread geographically and most thorough in its application is the supervision exercised over the field of taxation. In at least three-fourths of the states systems of reports and inspection are maintained, and needless to say, in each of these provision is made for the dissemination of

254

such advice as seems essential to the administrative authorities. Much more important in this connection, of course, is the process of review which is to be found in an equal number of commonwealths. In thirty-five jurisdictions its action is directed toward the equalization of property valuations between the different taxing units. In a slightly smaller number, thirty-one to be exact, this adjudication is extended to include classes of property, and in a still smaller number, twenty in all, its scope includes individual pieces of property. Supplementary to this, and likewise exceedingly effective as an instrument of control is the power given state officials in twenty eight states to order the reassessment of property whenever and wherever irregularities in the original assessment may appear. It is in those states in which the process of review is given full sweep, and those in which the supervising authorities have been empowered to issue orders, needless to say, that state administrative control of local taxation is really maintained. The supervising officials in at least thirty-six commonwealths, moreover, are empowered to prescribe the set-up of all books, forms of reports, etc. used in this connection, and in a somewhat smaller number of jurisdictions they may even promulgate such general rules and regulations relative to procedure in the assessment of property as they deem necessary. This, for any considerable number of states, constitutes practically all the control maintained. In some seven jurisdictions state appointment of local assessors has replaced the historic system of local election, and in an equally small number of states the administrative authorities have been given the right to make such removals as may be necessary for the good of the service.

Second in the extent of its geographic application is the supervision maintained over local accounts. To this end the power of inspection or audit has been granted the central authorities in at least thirty-five jurisdictions. In this manner a check may be made upon the legality and honesty of all local expenditures.   In addition to the control thus established, the state departments in at least twenty states exercise a measure of additional supervision through their power to prescribe the system of accounts which must be installed.   In Minnesota only has the control been pushed further.   The governor in Minnesota is empowered to suspend or remove any financial official from office when it has been made to appear to him that such officer has been delinquent in the performance of his duties.

Less widespread geographicaly, but equally important is the control which is exercised over municipal indebtedness. A total of twenty-two states maintain at least a limited supervision in this connection.   In each of these a system for the collection of such information relative to indebtedness as is deemed necessary has been established.   These reports, in addition to being a source of information are a necessary part of the process of approval in at least fifteen states.   The procedure in the majority of these commonwealths is about as follows: Before any bond issued for a municipal purpose may be negotiated it must first be presented to the attorney general or state auditor who must certify on the bond a statement to the effect that all the requirements of law have been complied with—if such has been the case.   Somewhat fuller sweep has been given the mechanism in Arizona, Kansas and Nevada.   Should a municipality in any one of these states find it necessary to issue bonds or warrants for an emergency not contemplated in the annual budget, it must first obtain permission to do so from the state tax commission.   Even more stringent is the control in Indiana and Iowa, where no municipal corporation may issue any bonds whatever without the consent and approval of the state board of tax commissioners, if the issuance thereof is protested by ten or more taxpayers.

Much more limited indeed is the control which is exercised over municipal budgets. On the basis of the information amassed in regard to municipal indebtedness, the state auditor or some other supervising official in at least four jurisdictions makes the necessary calculations as to the rate of tax levy which will adequately meet the carrying charges on the obligations thus incurred in the various municipalities throughout the state and transmits the same to the proper local officials. Moreover, should any city in Idaho or Oklahoma fail to levy adequate taxes to meet its obligations the state financial authorities of each of these commonwealths have been empowered to remedy the oversight. In some six jurisdictions only, however, has the control thus lodged with the state officials been really thorough-going. The mainstay of the supervision in these states is the requirement of state approval before any budgetary action on the part of the local authorities becomes final. In two jurisdictions its action is confined to situations in which the municipal council deems it necessary to exceed the statutory limitation on the rate of levy. In Iowa it is limited to those items involving contracts. In the other three, however, it includes all items in the municipal budgets, although in Oregon its action is confined to a particular group of cities.

Of only half a dozen states in the United States, therefore, can it be said that there exists a system of financial control similar to that which exists in Europe, for in each of the European countries examined extensive supervision was maintained both over the issuance of municipal bonds and over the maintenance of local accounts, and, on the Continent at least, over the form and content of municipal budgets. Nevertheless, the fact remains that state administrative supervision over municipal finance has made considerable headway in the United States and that the tendency at the present time is to follow in the footsteps of Europe.

HEALTH

No less extensive than the control over municipal finance is that exercised over public health. A certain limited supervision over general sanitary conditions exists almost everywhere. And as this phase and that of the local health situation has become acute, the supervisory power of the state administrative agencies has been increased so that today these agencies have very extensive powers indeed, over particular phases of municipal health activity—principally over personnel, vital statistics, municipal water works and sewage disposal systems.

The degree of supervision over general sanitary conditions varies from state to state. In practically every jurisdiction the state health authorities are empowered to collect certain items of information prescribed by law and in most states they may collect such additional information as they may deem desirable. Equally widespread is the general grant of the power of inspection under which agents of the state may investigate local sanitary conditions in any city in the commonwealth. Closely allied to this is the practice of disseminating advice relative to public health activities generally which is to be found in the vast majority of jurisdictions. Through the ordinance-making power, however, the main lines of local health activity are laid down and local practice directed. Only one state fails to grant its supervising officers the full sweep of authority in this connection; the remaining forty-seven grant their state boards of health power to enact such health ordinances as may seem necessary. The control thus established is still further buttressed in some twenty-six commonwealths by the fact that the power to issue specific orders relative to particular conditions or to particular cities has also been lodged with the supervising authorities. Through the use of these mechanisms it is thought that the state boards of health can maintain a certain limited supervision over sanitary conditions generally.

In addition to the limited oversight thus maintained over the general field of public health, certain phases of that field have been singled out for more intensive control. One of these is the selection and direction of the local personnel. Naturally enough, the information collected through the medium of reports and inspection is used in connection with the supervision of the local health officials, and much of the advice disseminated through the channels hitherto discussed is intended for their guidance. Needless to say, furthermore, almost all ordinances enacted by the state boards of health directly or indirectly affect their activities. The enforcement of these state policies is made certain, however, and the control over the local health personnel made effective through the mechanisms of removal and substitute administration. In some twenty-three jurisdictions the state authorities have been empowered to remove any and every local health official who fails to perform satisfactorily the duties of his office. Of a somewhat different character but very similar in its sum-total effect is the provision to be found in forty-two states which permits the supervising authorities to take over the complete administration of the local health service any time they so desire.

In a number of jurisdictions the state health authorities round out their control by participating in the selection of the local personnel. This participation is confined in one or two states to the requirement that all local authorities must be approved by the state administrative authorities. A more widely used mechanism of supervision in this connection, however, is state appointment. State boards of health in exactly twenty-four of the states have been granted the right to appoint all local registrars of vital statistics, and in eight the use of the mechanism has been extended to include regular health officers.   The extent of the power thus granted within each state, however, varies from jurisdiction to jurisdiction.

Particular attention has likewise been given in a goodly number of states to the enactment of local health ordinances. In at least eighteen jurisdictions all municipal ordinances of this character must first be submitted to the state authorities for approval before they may become effective, and in at least nineteen states similar action must be taken in connection with quarantine regulations.   Supplementary to the control thus established is the supervision maintained through the mechanism of review which may be found in operation in at least twenty-six states.   In nine of these its action is confined to quarantine regulations; in the remaining jurisdictions, however, it includes within its scope all health ordinances of whatever character.   That ordinances of the state board of health in those fields over which the state board has been given jurisdiction supersede locally enacted ones goes without saying.   Nor need much stress be laid upon the equally obvious fact that during those periods when the state health authorities have taken over the administration of a local health department because of local inefficiency or the existence of emergency conditions, state ordinances are paramount.

Equally intensive is the supervision maintained by the state authorities over the collection of vital statistics.   Municipal corporations are used as units of registration in at least forty-five states.   In these the local registrars are required to send in their reports either through the medium of some regional supervisor or directly to state headquarters. In all but one of these jurisdictions, furthermore, the contents of these returns may, within limits, be prescribed by the supervising authorities, and in at least forty-two the procedure to be used in their collection and tabulation is subject to similar supervision.

A fourth phase of municipal activity which has been thought worthy of special attention in some forty commonwealths is the maintenance of efficient systems of water supply. Although reports are required in twelve jurisdictions, the mainstay of this supervision is the process of inspection. Supplementary to this is the practice of disseminating advice which is to be found in some thirty-five or thirty-six jurisdictions, although statutory warrant for the procedure may be found in only twenty-three. In at least thirty-one states, moreover, state approval of all plans and specifications relative to the construction of any water supply system is necessary before any construction work may begin, and in at least twenty-two states the continued operation of these systems is at all times subject to such approval. The power to issue specific orders relative to the operation of these systems has been lodged with the state authorities in at least thirty-three jurisdictions, thus strengthening their control very considerably. This control has been still further fortified in as many as twenty-six states by the grant of an extensive ordinance-making power in this connection.

Closely allied to the problem of maintaining a pure water supply is that of maintaining an efficient sewage system. Consequently this phase of municipal activity likewise has been placed under the supervision of the state authorities. As in the case of the control maintained over water supplies, a large portion of the oversight exercised over municipal sewage systems lies in the right of the state authorities in three-fourths of the states to maintain a system of inspection over these utilities and to disseminate such advice as seems to be called for. The fact that in at least thirty-one jurisdictions, moreover, state approval of all sewer construction work is likewise required is also pertinent. Topping off the supervision thus set up is the power enjoyed by the supervising officials in twenty-six states of issuing orders relative to the construction and operation of these systems, and their further right in at least twenty-four jurisdictions of enacting such a code of ordinances as seems necessary.

In addition to the supervision thus maintained over these, the major aspects of public health work, a number of miscellaneous activities have been subjected to similar control. Chief among these is the maintenance of swimming pools, hospitals, and places of public assembly.

Extensive as the control over this phase of municipal activity may seem, it is by no means as thorough-going as that maintained either on the Continent or in England. The device of provisional orders, for example, by means of which the Ministry of Public Health in England may alter the territorial boundaries of a district, endow it with particular powers, require it to undertake certain services, or even modify the details of the health codes is nowhere found in America. Much more limited, indeed, is the use which is made here of the mechanism of grant-in-aid. .And equally foreign to the practice in the vast majority of American states is the requirement that the nomination of all local health officers shall be confirmed by the central agency. Nevertheless, a reading of the record indicates very clearly that in the field of public health as in the field of finance state administrative supervision has made very substantial progress, and the probabilities are that the passing years will see little or no change in the present centralizing tendency in this field.

EDUCATION

More intensive, if anything, than the supervision over public health, is the oversight which is exercised by the state authorities in the realm of education. Slowly but surely the forces which have been making for centralization have been carrying the day. Indeed there are now few aspects of elementary or secondary education which are not somewhere, somehow subject to state administrative supervision. In many states practically all local educational activities have to a limited degree at least been placed under the guidance of state officials. In certain fields this supervision is much more stringent than in others. Chief among these is the selection of the teaching personnel, the determination of the school curriculum, and the selection of text books on the basis of which the instruction is to be developed. In addition, in practically every state in the Union special attention has been paid to the development of courses in agriculture, home economics, and industrial training, as well as special classes for defectives. School libraries, normal training, high schools, school attendance, the length of school terms and the condition of school buildings have also been singled out for consideration.

In the maintenance of the general supervision over the local educational activities referred to above, the mechanisms of reports, inspection, advice and grant-in-aid are those most widely used. Extended comment on the oversight which may be attained through this medium seems hardly necessary. The prevailing conception of education as a state function has called for more drastic means of control. For the most part this more stringent supervision has been confined to particular phases of educational activity, nevertheless in a number of jurisdictions the mechanisms of review and ordinance making have been called into full play. More than half the states, for example, permit their state educational authorities full discretion in prescribing the blanks for reports, records, etc. And a surprisingly large number—at least eighteen—seem to have granted these authorities the full sweep of the ordinance-making power within the limits set up by the state constitution and the statutes. In a slightly smaller number of jurisdictions all controversies arising under the school laws of the state are subject to adjudication by the same authorities.

In addition to the control thus exercised over educational activities generally certain phases of this activity, as has already been indicated, have been singled out for special supervision. Of these the matter of teaching personnel is, perhaps, the most outstanding. Not only has admission to the teaching profession been subjected to extensive regulation, but the conduct of the teaching force in office has likewise been made a matter of state concern. The part played by the mechanisms of reports, inspection and advice in this connection needs no elaboration. The use made of the process of grants-in-aid should, perhaps, be commented upon, although it is not extensively used. By arranging the state grant in such a way that it is less profitable for a community to pay a salary below a certain minimum and thereby lose the grant than it is to pay the salary and obtain the subsidy, the device—in at least five jurisdictions—has been used to raise teaching salaries, and incidentally to attract into the profession a higher type of individual than would otherwise be willing to make teaching a life work. The mechanism has been used in a similar manner in at least seven states to raise the general level of educational attainment on the part of the teaching profession, and in eleven to secure an adequate staff to carry the teaching load.

Much more drastic and direct, however, is the control which is maintained over the teaching personnel in at least forty-four jurisdictions through the process of examination and certification. The obvious purpose of the examination is to furnish the educational authorities with adequate information relative to the various candidates upon which they may base their judgment as to the candidate's capacity as a teacher, and, in the event they are satisfied with the intellectual attainments thus revealed, issue a certificate.

The content of these examinations is for the most part left to the state educational authorities. In twenty-four states, moreover, not only have the supervising officials been granted the power to make up these examinations but they have been specifically authorized to set up such standards for admission to the teaching profession as seem to them reasonable and wise. The control of the supervising agency over local personnel, however, does not end here. In some eleven states the suspension or removal of a teacher by the local authorities is subject to state review. In a surprisingly large number of jurisdictions, moreover, thirty-five to be exact, the mechanism of removal has been placed at the disposal of the supervising authorities. For the most part the process of removal takes the form of a revocation of the license to teach, which *ipso facto* renders it impossible for the teacher concerned to continue his professional work within the state. In some jurisdictions full discretion in the use of this power is lodged with the state authorities; in others, certain specific charges must first be made. Needless to say, action of this character is not taken by the state departments of education save under exceptional circumstances.

A second phase of educational activity which has been singled out for special consideration is the content of the school curriculum. Two mechanisms of control have been chiefly used—ordinance-making and grant-in-aid. In the thirty or more states in which the state departments of education have been empowered to prescribe the course of study for the schools state administrative supervision has indeed made headway, and resembles in many particulars that maintained abroad. Whether the local authorities live up to the curriculum thus outlined is, of course, another question. And without doubt practical considerations such as lack of facilities and the financial resources with which to obtain facilities on the part of many a school district limit the supervising officials in their use of this power.   Nevertheless the mere grant of this authority is sweeping indeed.   In addition to the general supervision maintained through the ordinance-making power, certain phases of the curriculum have been singled out for special attention—those phases of it particularly which for one reason or another cannot as yet be subjected to the mandatory fiat of ordinances.   The means of supervision chiefly used in this connection is the mechanism of grant-in-aid.   It has been used for the most part in the development of courses in agriculture, home economics, industrial training, high schools, normal training in high schools and special classes for defectives.

Closely allied to this control is that maintained in some twenty-nine jurisdictions over the choice of text books.   For the most part this supervision is exercised through the ordinance-making process and consists of the state authorities either drawing up a list of books which must be used by all the schools throughout the state, or drawing up a list from which the local authorities may, in their discretion, make such selections as seem particularly adapted to the peculiar circumstances under which they work.

Very much akin to this is the supervision exercised over school libraries.   The mechanisms of control most frequently used in this connection are the dissemination of advice and grant-in-aid.   The condition most usually imposed in this last connection is the raising of a specified sum on the part of the municipality.   In a number of states, however, an additional provision is added to the effect that the municipality must select its books from a list approved by the central authorities, and conduct the libraries in a manner prescribed by them.

Sweeping as the grant of supervisory authority thus bestowed upon the state educational agencies throughout the

United States may seem, the system of administrative supervision which has been built up in the average American state has by no means attained the scope of power or the degree of centralization that exists in Europe. Nevertheless the comment which was evoked in both the field of finance and that of public health is apropos here—state administrative control in the realm of education has indeed made considerable headway, and many signs point to an increase rather than a decrease in the degree of the supervision which will be maintained.

DEPENDENCY AND DELINQUENCY

In connection with the care of the dependent emphasis has been primarily placed upon the supervision of municipal poor houses and homes for the aged. Although two-thirds of the states maintaining any supervision whatever require reports, chief reliance is placed upon the mechanism of inspection which is to be found in each of the thirty states involved. Equally widespread is the process of disseminating advice, which without question has played a very considerable part in eliminating or at least minimizing the deplorable conditions which at one time were so rife in practically every state in the Union. Strangely enough, save in a relatively few jurisdictions, the supervision exercised through these mechanisms is the only control maintained over these institutions. In some half dozen states a system of grants-in-aid is brought into play, and in a slightly larger number all plans and specifications relative to new buildings or extensive alterations in old ones must be submitted to the state authorities for approval. Somewhat more extensive geographically is the use made of the power to enact ordinances; nevertheless, in only three of the thirteen states which have been granted this power does it go beyond the prescription of the content of reports or the set-up of accounts.

Needless to say the supervision thus maintained resembles in only slight degree the control which is exercised in Europe.

Equally limited is the oversight granted the state authorities in the United States over municipal officials in connection with crime. Nine states only supervise the activities of the local police. For the most part this supervision can be divided into two classes: that designed to permit the state authorities to interfere in the event of gross abuse, and that intended to confer upon the supervising agencies broad powers of scrutiny and guidance. Two states fall into the first category; in each the governor has been granted authority to remove any and every chief of police guilty of misconduct in office. The control in the remaining states, although much more drastic, in no case extends to all the cities in the state but is confined to specified municipalities, frequently only the metropoli.

The police, however, are by no means the only administrative agency which deals with the problem of delinquency. Of equal importance in the problem of crime and its prevention is the management of our institutions of correction. In each of the twenty-nine states maintaining a system of supervision over these institutions, the process of inspection plays a major part. Needless to say, along with the process of inspection has gone the practice of disseminating advice. Some eleven states, furthermore, require that all plans and specifications relative to new buildings or to extensive alterations in old structures be submitted to the administrative authorities for their approval before construction work may actually begin. And in a considerably smaller number of jurisdictions the power of enacting rules and regulations governing certain aspects of the maintenance of these institutions has likewise been granted the supervising agency. In at least half of these, moreover, the operation of the mechanism has been confined to the prescription of the form of reports. In seven states the administrative agency may issue such specific orders relative to the management of these penal institutions as seems necessary.

Much more stringent, needless to say, is the control exercised by the central authorities over the problem of delinquency both on the Continent and in England. To such an extent is this the case in fact that by comparison the supervision exercised in the United States seems slight indeed.

MUNICIPALLY-OWNED UTILITIES

In approximately half the states in the Union municipally owned and operated utilities fall under state supervision. In some this supervision extends to all municipally owned utilities, in others to utilties specifically named in the statutes. At least nineteen states permit the supervising authorities to demand reports from all utilties in the state; in eighteen they may include such information relative to the operation and management of these enterprises as the commission deems desirable. Supplementary to this is the process of inspection which, in general, is concerned with the investigation of accidents, the audit of books, the survey of plants and facilities and the analysis of the methods and processes of management. Fifteen states in all make use of the mechanism in connection with accidents; seventeen in connection with the audit of books; fourteen in connection with the survey of physical facilities; and an equal number in connection with investigations into the processes and methods of management.

In at least eight states, moreover, certificates of necessity and convenience must be obtained from the state authorities by all utilities, whether or not municipally owned and operated, before any construction work may begin. The approval of the commission, furthermore, is necessary in at least nine jurisdictions before any changes may be made in tariff charges or schedules of service. In a somewhat larger number of jurisdictions—seventeen to be exact—the process of review is called into play. Needless to say, in each of these states the supervising agencies are empowered to issue such specific orders as may seem necessary to correct such malpractices as may be brought to light in the course of any investigation or hearing. Indeed in many cases they may substitute service and tariff schedules of their own devising in lieu of those of the public service corporation. For the most part, however, the ordinance-making power has been confined in its operation to the determination of the form and content of the reports to be made by the utilities, to the enactment of such rules and regulations as are deemed necessary to insure the safety of both employees and the public, and to the prescription of the form in which the books and accounts of these various and sundry corporations must be kept. A total of sixteen jurisdictions prescribe the set-up of accounts, and eighteen prescribe the form and content of reports. Little need be said about the power to enact such ordinances as may be necessary to insure the safety of both employees and the public which, although specifically granted in but nine states, is usually included in a general grant of power to the utility commission.

In addition to this general control, extending as it does to all municipally owned or operated utilities in the jurisdictions indicated, certain utilities have been singled out for similar attention in a number of states maintaining no such general supervision. Chief among these projects are wharves and waterfront developments, dams and water works, and in an even more limited number of jurisdictions, gas and electric plants.

Extensive though this control may seem, it is certainly no more extensive than that maintained in England where the sanction of the Board of Trade or the Ministry of Transport is usually necessary before a local authority may undertake the construction or operation of a public utility; nor is it nearly as stringent as that exercised in France where all power relative to national highways, whether it be construction, repairing, policing, or what-not, resides in the national or departmental authorities.

OTHER FUNCTIONS

There still remain to be considered a number of services over which a more limited control is exercised—more limited in the sense that the supervision of these activities is less stringent than that maintained in the services thus far discussed, and in the sense that the control has a much narrower geographic application. Most prominent among the functions thus supervised are those dealing with the control of fires and fire hazards. In general, two lines of attack have been followed, fire prevention and fire fighting. In the overwhelming majority of instances, however, greater emphasis has been laid upon the former, every effort being made to eliminate incendiarism and to reduce fire hazards. To this end a system of reports has been established in at least thirty-four jurisdictions, and a system of inspection in at least thirty. Equally widespread is the practice of disseminating advice which is intended for the most part to awaken a realization of the danger of allowing fire hazards to develop among the body politic.

Second in the geographic extent of the supervision thus exercised is that maintained over public libraries. The supervision takes the form, for the most part, of encouragement and advice. The channel chiefly used for the dissemination of this advice in each of the twenty-six states exercising such supervision is a system of correspondence. In nine jurisdictions, however, field workers are also maintained, and in three, all librarians working in these institutions must obtain certificates of approval from the state authorities.

Much more limited in geographic extent is the control exercised over the local civil service. In fact, only four states maintain any supervision whatever. In Massachusetts and New Jersey, this control is fairly extensive; in New York and Ohio, however, it is quite limited, being confined in the last named state to such supervision as " pitiless publicity " makes possible.

The principle of state administrative supervision has been adopted in connection with port administration in some twelve jurisdictions with the result that at the present time at least nine very important ports of the country are under state control, not to mention others of lesser importance.

Finally, in a limited number of jurisdictions there appear occasional manifestations on a limited scale of what may be called general executive power. More specifically, in six states the governor may, subject to such limitations as are imposed in the statutes, remove certain specified municipal officials from office whenever and wherever he deems it desirable. Moreover, in approximately the same number of states he may, where vacancies occur in municipal positions, make the necessary appointments to office.

Reviewing the matter as a whole, therefore, it appears that the forecasts contained in the introductory chapter, based though they were on an exceedingly cursory examination of the system of administrative supervision as it has developed in Europe have, on the whole, been borne out by the facts of further investigation. Although it is true that at the present time in the United States legislative control over municipalities is still the order of the day, nevertheless state administrative supervision has been making rapid headway indeed.   Administrative officers are everywhere being called upon as a supplementary means of control.   Such also, it will be recalled, was the course of events in England, the outcome of which was portrayed in the first chapter.   Administrative supervision in England, it is safe to say, no longer supplements legislative supervision over cities; it has in large measure supplanted it.

Similarly, as one might have expected, the functions which have been singled out for consideration here are those which have received special attention abroad: finance, education, public health, public utilities, delinquency, dependency and so forth.   There was, of course, some variation in the emphasis placed upon the supervision maintained over these different fields in each of the European countries examined, and there is, of course, considerable variation in that emphasis among the sundry states here.   Nevertheless the fact remains that those aspects of municipal activity which were subject to special treatment abroad have been the phases of that activity given special consideration here.

In like manner further investigation seems to have substantiated the belief that a closer similarity would be found between the system of control which has developed here and that which exists in England than that which exists on the Continent.   As has already been pointed out, the emphasis in the English system of supervision is emphatically on what might be called the persuasive mechanisms of control.   The devices most commonly used are reports, inspection, advice and grants-in-aid.   Very much less frequently, although much more so of recent years, do the words approval, review, orders, ordinances, appointment or removal appear in the statutes.   Such is also the case in the United States, although of course these latter mechanisms of supervision have been used whenever necessity has seemed to arise.

Thus, despite the tendency toward home rule in the

United States, state administrative supervision over cities has been making considerable headway. The same forces which have been responsible for its development abroad seem to be at work here. It is not consequently hazarding an altogether unwarranted prophecy to say that the process of centralization may, in the nature of things, be expected to continue and that within the next fifty years we may expect to see greater and greater state administrative supervision over municipalities.

INDEX

Accidents, see public utilities

Accounts, see finance

Administrative supervision, 14, 35

Advice, 19, 43, 44, 45, 46, 58, 59; relative to taxation, 71-74; accounts, 94; general sanitary conditions, 111-114; local health personnel, 115; waterworks, 126, 127; sewage systems, 133; general supervision over education, 151-159; the teaching personnel, 164; school libraries, 183; school buildings, 184; destitution, 194, 195; jails, 209; specifically mentioned utilities, 231; fire hazards, 241; fire fighting, 243, 244; libraries, 247

Agricultural courses, 178

Alabama, Finance: taxation, 61n, 64n, 65n, 66n, 67n, 70n, 71n, 72n, 74n, 75n, 84n, 86n, 90n, 91n; municipal accounts, 91n, 92n. Health: general sanitary conditions, 110n, 113n, 114n; personnel, 116n, 117n, 119n, 121n; municipal health ordinances, 122n; waterworks, 124n, 125n, 126n, 128n, 129n, 131n; sewage systems, 132n, 133n, 134n, 136n; vital statistics, 137n; miscellany, 140n. Education: general supervision, 148n, 149n, 150n, 153n, 155n, 157n, 162n, 163n; personnel, 165n, 166n, 169n, 170n, 174n; curriculum, 176n, 177n, 178n, 179n; textbooks, 182n; school buildings, 185n; finance, 186n; medical service, 187n. Dependency and Delinquency: dependency, 191n, 192n, 193n, 197n, 198n; police, 201n; jails, 207n, 208n, 209n, 210n. Utilities: specific utilities, 231n. Incendiarism, 236n, 238n. Fire hazards, 240n, 241n, 242n, 243n. Odds and ends, 252n

Almshouses, see dependency

Appointment, 16, 17, 23, 56-59; of local tax officials, 87-89; registrars of vital statistics, 137; local educational officials, 174; local police officials, 202, 203; to vacancies on municipal civil service commissions in New York, 245

Appropriations, see finance

Approval, 7, 16, 19-22, 28-30, 32, 50, 51, 58, 59; of matters in incidental connection with taxation, 74; bond issues, 98-100; budgets, 101-104; local health personnel 119; municipal health ordinances, 122; waterworks, 127-129; sewage systems, 133-135; the teaching personnel, examination and certification, 165-169; the operation of school libraries, 183; the construction of school buildings, 184; almshouse construction, 197, 198; jail construction and jail conditions, 210; the construction of utilities, 222, 223; rates and schedules, 223; specifically named municipal utilities, 231-234

Arizona, Finance: taxation, 64n, 65n, 66n, 67n, 71n, 72n, 74n, 75n, 84n, 86n, 90n, 91n; municipal accounts, 91n, 92n; municipal indebtedness, 99n; municipal budgets, 104n. Health: general sanitary conditions, 114n; municipal health ordinances, 122n. Education: general supervision, 148n, 149n, 153n, 155n, 157n, 162n; personnel, 165n, 166n, 170n, 174n; curriculum, 176n, 177n, 178n, 179n; textbooks, 182n; finance, 186n. Municipally owned utilities, 216n, 217n, 218n, 219n, 222n, 223n, 224n, 227n, 228n, 229n

Arkansas, Finance: taxation, 64n, 65n, 66n, 67n, 71n, 72n, 75n, 76n,

84n, 86n, 90n, 91n. Health: general sanitary conditions, 110n, 113n, 114n; personnel, 116n, 117n, 119n, 121n; municipal health ordinances, 122n, 123n; waterworks, 124n, 130n, 131n; sewage systems, 132n, 133n, 136n; vital statistics, 137n, 138n. Education: general supervision, 148n, 149n, 152n, 155n, 162n; personnel, 165n, 166n, 170n, 174n, 176n; curriculum, 176n, 177n, 178n, 179n; textbooks, 182n; school buildings, 184n; medical service, 187n. Dependency and Delinquency: dependency, 191n, 192n; jails, 207n, 208n. Incendiarism, 236n, 238n. Fire hazards, 241n. Odds and ends, 252n

Assessment, see finance
Audit, see finance

Books, see finance
Borrowing, see finance

California, Finance: taxation, 64n, 65n, 66n, 67n, 68n, 71n, 75n, 86n, 90n; municipal accounts, 91n, 95n; municipal indebtedness, 96n; municipal budgets, 101n, 104n. Health: general sanitary conditions, 110n, 113n, 114n; personnel, 117n; waterworks, 125n, 126n; sewage systems, 132n, 133n, 136n; vital statistics, 137n; miscellany, 139n. Education: general supervision, 148n, 149n, 150n, 152n, 153n, 157n, 162n; personnel, 165n, 166n, 170n, 173n, 174n; curriculum, 176n, 177n, 178n, 179n; textbooks, 182n; school libraries, 183n; school buildings, 184n. Dependency and Delinquency: dependency, 191n, 192n, 195n, 196n, 197n, 198n; jails, 207n, 208n, 209n. Specific utilities, 232n. Libraries, 246n, 247n; Ports and harbors, 248n; Odds and ends, 250n, 252n

Centralization _vs._ decentralization, 11-14, 17, 23, 24, 34, 36, 37, 60-64, 107-109, 142-146, 190-191, 205-207, 212-215, 272-274

Centralization _vs._ decentralization in delinquency, 199-201, 204-207
Centralization _vs._ decentralization in dependency, 189-191
Centralization _vs._ decentralization in health, 106-110
Centralization _vs._ decentralization in finance, 60-64
Centralization _vs._ decentralization in education, 143-147
Certificates of necessity and convenience, 222
Charities, see dependency
Child welfare, 301
Childrens' aid, 195
Civil service, 245, 246, 272
Colorado, Finance: taxation, 64n, 65n, 66n, 67n, 68n, 71n, 72n, 73n, 74n, 75n, 76n, 83n, 86n, 89n, 90n, 91n; municipal accounts, 95n; municipal indebtedness, 96n; municipal budgets, 101n, 102n. Health: general sanitary conditions, 110n, 114n; personnel, 116n, 117n, 119n, 121n; waterworks, 125n, 126n, 128n, 129n, 131n; vital statistics, 137n; miscellany, 140n. Education: general supervision, 148n, 149n, 155n, 157n, 162n; personnel, 165n, 170n, 173n, 174n; curriculum, 178n. Dependency and Delinquency: dependency, 191n, 192n; jails, 207n. Specific utilities, 232n
Common carriers, see finance
Commissioner of education, see education
Conferences, 45; in connection with taxation, 71, 72, 74; in connection with health activity, 111, 114; in connection with education, 153-155; teachers' institutes, 156; in connection with destitution, 195
Connecticut, Finance: taxation, 64n, 66n, 67n, 68n, 71n, 72n, 75n, 86n, 90n; municipal accounts, 91n; municipal indebtedness, 96n. Health: general sanitary conditions, 110n, 113n, 114n; personnel, 116n, 117n; municipal health ordinances, 122n; waterworks, 125n, 126n, 128n, 129n, 130n; sewage systems, 132n, 133n, 135n; vital statistics, 137n; miscellany,

140n. Education: general supervision, 148n, 149n, 155n, 157n, 162n; personnel, 165n, 166n, 174n; curriculum, 178n, 179n; textbooks, 182n; school libraries, 183n. Dependency and Delinquency: dependency, 191n, 192n, 193n, 194n, 196n; jails, 207n, 208n, 210n. Incendiarism, 236n, 238n. Fire hazards, 239n, 240n, 241n, 242n, 243n, Libraries, 247n

Contagious disease, see health

Correspondence, 6, 44; in connection with taxation, 71, 72; in connection with health activity, 111; in connection with education, 156, 157; in connection with destitution, 195

Crime, see delinquency

Curriculum, see education

Deaths, 106n

Debts, see finance

Delaware, Finance: taxation, 87n, 90n; municipal accounts, 91n, 92n. Health: general sanitary conditions, 110n, 114n; personnel, 116n, 117n, 119n; waterworks, 125n, 126n; sewage systems, 132n, 133n; vital statistics, 137n; miscellany, 140n. Education: general supervision, 148n, 149n, 151n, 152n, 153n, 155n, 157n, 163n; personnel, 165n, 166n, 170n, 176n; curriculum, 176n, 177n, 178n, 179n; textbooks, 182n; school buildings, 184n, 185n; finance, 186n; medical service, 187n. Dependency and Delinquency: dependency, 191n, 192n, 193n, 195n, 198n; jails, 207n, 208n, 209n

Delinquency, 12, 16-18, 20-22, 32, 33, 36, 199-211, 268; the problem of crime, 199-201; police, 16-18, 20-22, 32, 33, 36, 201-204; appointments in connection with police, 202, 203; removal, 202, 203; jails, 204-211; the problem, 204-207; reports relative to, 208; inspection, 208; advice, 209; approval, 210; rules and regulations, 210; orders, 211

Dependency, 17, 19, 25-27, 36, 189-199, 267; the problem, 189, 190; reports relative to, 191; inspection, 192-194; advice, 194, 195;

grant-in-aid, 195, 196; approval of almshouse construction, 197, 198; orders relative to condition of almshouses, 198; ordinance-making, 198

Destitution, see dependency

Devices of control, see each specific mechanism

Education, 7, 12, 17, 18, 20, 22, 23, 33, 36, 142-188, 262-267; the size and nature of the problem, 142-146; centralization *vs.* decentralization, 142-147; general supervision, 147-164; reports, 147, 149; inspection, 149-151; advice, 151-159; grants-in-aid, 159-162; ordinance making, 162, 163; review, 163, 164; the teaching personnel, 147, 164-176; reports, 164; inspection, 164; advice, 164; grants-in-aid, 164, 165; examination and certification, 165-169; ordinances, 169-173; review, 173, 174; apointment, 174; removal, 174-176; the school curriculum, 147, 176-182; ordinances prescribing, 176, 177, 178; grants-in-aid for the development of courses in agriculture, home economics, industrial training, etc., 178-182; text books, 147, 182-185; school libraries, 185; school buildings, 184-188; advice, 184; inspection, 184; approval of construction work, 184; rules and regulations, 185, 186; finance, 186, 187; medical service, 187

England, 24-38, 257, 262, 267, 269, 271; Ministry of Public Health, 26-31; Home Office, 26, 32, 33; Board of Education, 26, 32, 33; Board of Trade, 26, 32, 33; Ministry of Transport, 26, 32, 33

Epidemics, 118

Equalization, see finance

Examination and certification of teachers, see education

Expenditures, see finance

Filtration plants, 126, 127

Finance, 17, 19, 20, 26, 30, 31, 35, 60-104, 254-258; taxation, 5, 20, 60, 64-91; state tax commissions, 61, 62; tax equalization, 61, 64-91; tax reports, 64, 65; inspection, 66-

71; advice, 71-74; conferences, 72-74; approval, 74; review, 74-82; orders, 83-86; ordinances, 86, 87; removal of local tax officials, 89; appointment of local tax officials, 87-89; evaluation of the property of common carriers, etc., 90; accounts, 30, 91-96, 255, 256; audit, 31, 63, 64, 91-93; assistance in installation, 94; prescription of, 95, 96; removal of accounting officials, 96; debts, 19, 21, 30, 31, 35, 64, 96-100, 256; certification of tax levies to meet interest, 97; approval of bond issues, 98-100; budgets, 5, 6, 17, 19, 20, 62-64, 100-105, 257

Fire fighting, see fires and fire hazards

Fires and fire hazards, 235-244, 271; the problem, 235, 236; incendiarism, 236, 237; reporting, 237; investigation, 238; fire hazards, 238; reports, 238; review, 239; investigations, 240; orders, 241; advice, 241; ordinances, 242, 243; fire fighting, 243; advice, 243, 244; grant-in-aid, 244

Florida, Finance: taxation, 60n, 90n; municipal accounts, 91n; municipal indebtedness, 98n. Health: general sanitary conditions, 110n, 112n, 113n, 114n; personnel, 116n, 117n, 119n; municipal health ordinances, 122n, 123n; waterworks, 125n, 128n, 130n; sewage systems, 132n, 133n, 135n, 136n; vital statistics, 137n; miscellany, 140n. Education: general supervision, 148n, 149n, 152n, 153n, 155n, 157n, 162n, 163n; personnel, 165n, 166n, 170n, 174n, 176n; curriculum, 176n, 177n, 178n, 179n; textbooks, 182n. Dependency, 191n, 192n. Ports and harbors, 284n

France, 18-24, 35-38, 257, 262, 267-269, 271; communes, 19; prefects, 18, 23, 24; Minister of Interior, 18, 23, 24

General administrative supervision, 36, 252, 253, 272

Georgia, Finance: taxation, 73n, 75n, 90n; municipal accounts, 91n,

92n; municipal indebtedness, 98n. Health: general sanitary conditions, 110n; personnel, 116n, 117n, 119n; waterworks, 125n, 126n; sewage systems, 132n; vital statistics, 137n. Education: general supervision, 148n, 149n, 150n, 155n, 157n, 162n; personnel, 165n, 166n, 170n, 176n; curriculum, 176n, 177n; textbooks, 182n; finance, 186n. Dependency and Delinquency: dependency, 191n, 192n, 195n; jails, 207n, 208n, 209n. Incendiarism, 236n, 238n. Libraries, 247

Grants-in-aid, 28, 32, 33, 47, 48, 49, 58, 59; hospitals, 139, 140; education, general supervision over, 159-162; education, the teaching personnel, 164, 165; education, for the development of courses in agriculture, home economics, industrial training, etc., 178-182; education, school libraries, 183; for poor relief, 195, 196; fire fighting apparatus, 244; libraries, 248

Health, 5, 12, 17, 18, 27-29, 36, 106-141, 258-262; size of the problem, 106; state boards, 107-109; local boards, 106-109; general sanitary conditions, 109-115, 258, 259; reports, 110; inspection, 110, 111; advice, 111-114; ordinances, 114, 115; local personnel, 109, 115-121, 259-260; reports, 115; inspection, 115; advice, 115; ordinances, 115; orders, 116; removal, 116; substitute administration, 117, 118; approval, 119; appointments, 119; municipal health ordinances, 109, 122-124, 260; approval, 122; review, 122, 123; ordinances, 124; vital statistics, 136-138, 260; necessity for, 136; reports, 137; ordinances regulating form, etc., 137; removal of local registrars, 138; appointment of local registrars, 137; waterworks, 109, 124-131, 261; danger in inefficient operation, 124; reports, 124; inspection, 125; advice, 126, 127; approval of both construction and operation, 127-129; orders, 129, 130; ordinances,

131; removal, 131; sewage systems, 109, 131-136, 261; reports, 131, 132; inspection, 132; advice, 133; approval, 133-135; orders, 136; swimming pools, 138, 139; hospitals, 139, 140

Health personnel, see health

Highways, 18-21

High schools, 179; see also education

Home economics courses, 178

Home rule, see centralization *vs.* decentralization

Hospitals, see health

Housing, 26, 30

Idaho, Finance: taxation, 61n, 64n, 75n, 82n, 86n, 90n; municipal accounts, 91n, 95n. Health: general sanitary conditions, 110n; personnel, 116n, 117n, 119n; municipal health ordinances, 122n, 123n; waterworks, 130n; vital statistics, 137n. Education: general supervision, 148n, 149n, 150n, 153n, 155n, 157n, 162n; personnel, 165n, 166n, 170n, 173n, 174n; curriculum, 176n, 177n, 178n; textbooks, 182n. Dependency and Delinquency: police, 201n; jails, 207n, 208n, 209n. Odds and ends, 253n

Illinois, Finance: taxation, 64n, 65n, 66n, 67n, 68n, 71n, 72n, 74n, 75n, 84n, 86n, 87n, 90n, 91n. Health: general sanitary conditions, 110n; personnel, 116n, 117n, 119n; municipal health ordinances, 122n; sewage systems, 132n, 133n, 135n; vital statistics, 137n, 138n; miscellany, 140n. Education: general supervision, 148n, 149n, 153n, 155n, 157n, 163n; personnel, 165n, 166n, 170n, 173n, 174n; curriculum, 178n; school buildings, 184n. Dependency, 191n, 192n, 193n, 195n. Incendiarism, 236n, 238n. Fire hazards, 239n, 240n, 241n, 242n, 243n. Libraries, 246n, 247n. Ports and harbors, 248n. Odds and ends, 253n

Illiterates, 142

Incendiarism, see fires and fire hazards

Incorporation of municipalities, 250

Indebtedness, see finance

Indiana, Finance: taxation, 64n, 65n, 66n, 67n, 68n, 71n, 74n, 75n, 76n, 79n, 86n, 89n, 90n, 91n; municipal accounts, 91n, 94n, 95n; municipal indebtedness, 96n, 98n, 99n, 100n; municipal budgets, 102n, 104n. Health: general sanitary conditions, 110n, 114n; personnel, 116n, 117n; municipal health ordinances, 122n; waterworks, 125n, 126n, 128n, 129n, 131n; sewage systems, 132n, 133n, 136n; vital statistics, 137n, 138n; miscellany, 140. Education: general supervision, 148n, 149n, 150n, 152n, 157n, 162n, 163n; personnel, 165n, 166n, 170n, 176n; curriculum, 176n, 177n, 178n; textbooks, 182n; medical service, 187n. Dependency and Deliquency: dependency, 191n, 192n, 193n, 194n, 195n, 198n; jails, 207n, 208n, 209n. Utilities: municipally owned utilities, 216n, 217n, 218n, 219n, 222n, 223n, 224n, 227n, 228n, 229n; specific utilities, 234. Incendiarism, 236n, 238n. Fire hazards, 239n, 240n, 241n, 242n, 243n. Odds and ends, 250n

Industrial training, 178

Inspection, 26, 27, 41-43, 58, 59; relative to taxation, 66-71; accounts, 31, 63, 64, 91-93; general sanitary conditions, 110, 111; local health personnel, 115; waterworks, 125; sewage systems, 132; swimming pools, 138, 139; general supervision over education, 149-151; teaching personnel, 164; school buildings, 184; school finance, 186; almshouses, 192-194; jails, 208; municipally owned utilities, 217-222; specifically mentioned utilities, 231; incendiarism, 238; fire hazards, 240

Iowa, Finance: taxation, 61n, 64n, 75n, 86n, 88n, 90n; municipal accounts, 91n, 92n, 93n, 94n, 95n; municipal indebtedness, 96n, 98n, 99n, 100n; municipal budgets, 100n, 102n, 104n. Health: general sanitary conditions, 110n, 112n; personnel, 116n, 117n; municipal health ordinances, 123n; waterworks, 125n, 126n, 128n, 129n, 131n; sewage systems, 132n, 133n,

134n, 135n, 136n; vital statistics, 137n, 138n. Education: general supervision, 148n, 149n, 150n, 153n, 155n, 157n, 162n, 163n; personnel, 165n, 166n, 170n, 173n, 174n; curriculum, 176n, 177n, 178n, 179n; school libraries, 183n. Utilities: specific utilities, 231n, 232n. Incendiarism, 236n, 238n. Fire hazards, 239n, 240n, 241n, 242n. Libraries, 246n, 247n. Odds and ends, 250n

Jails, see delinquency
Judicial supervision, 13

Kansas, Finance: taxation, 64n, 66n, 67n, 68n, 71n, 72n, 74n, 75n, 76n, 77n, 80n, 81n, 84n, 86n, 90n, 91n; municipal accounts, 95n; municipal indebtedness, 96n, 99n; municipal budgets, 101n, 102n. Health: general sanitary conditions, 110n, 114n; personnel, 116n, 117n, 119n, 121n; municipal health ordinances, 122n, 123n; waterworks, 124n, 125n, 126n, 128n, 129n; sewage systems, 131n, 132n, 133n, 135n; vital statistics, 137n, 138n. Education: general supervision, 148n, 149n, 150n, 155n; personnel, 165n, 166n, 170n, 174n; curriculum, 176n, 177n, 178n, 179n, 180n; textbooks, 182n. Utilities: specific utilities, 232. Incendiarism, 236n, 238n. Fire hazards, 239n, 240n, 242n, 243n
Kentucky, Finance: taxation, 64n, 65n, 66n, 67n, 68n, 71n, 72n, 75n, 76n, 84n, 86n, 90n, 91n; municipal accounts, 91n, 92n. Health: general sanitary conditions, 110n, 112n, 114n; personnel, 116n, 119n, 121n; municipal health ordinances, 122n, 123n; waterworks, 125n, 126n, 128n, 130n, 131n; sewage systems, 132n, 133n, 134n, 136n; vital statistics, 137n, 138n. Education: general supervision, 148n, 149n, 150n, 153n, 155n, 157n, 162n, 163n; personnel, 165n, 166n, 170n; curriculum, 176n, 177n, 178n; textbooks, 182n; school libraries, 183n; school buildings, 184n; finance, 186n, 187n. Incendiarism

236n, 238n. Fire hazards, 239n, 240n, 241n, 242n, 243n. Libraries, 246n, 247n

Legislative supervision, 13, 14, 35
Libraries, 246, 247, 271
Lock-ups, see delinquency
Louisiana, Finance: taxation, 60n, 61n, 64n, 65n, 66n, 67n, 68n, 70n, 71n, 72n, 75n, 76n, 84n, 86n, 87n, 90n, 91n; municipal accounts, 91n, 92n, 94n. Health: general sanitary conditions, 110n, 112n, 113n, 114n; personnel, 116n, 117n, 119n, 121n; municipal health ordinances, 122n; waterworks, 125n, 126n, 128n, 131n; sewage systems, 132n, 133n, 134n, 135n, 136n; vital statistics, 136n, 137n, 138n. Education: general supervision, 148n, 149n, 153n, 155n, 157n, 163n; personnel, 165n, 166n, 170n, 174n; curriculum, 176n, 178n; textbooks, 182n; school libraries, 183n. Dependency and Delinquency: dependency, 191n, 192n; jails, 207n, 208n. Incendiarism, 236n, 238n. Fire hazards, 239n, 240n, 241n, 242n. Libraries, 246n, 247n. Ports and harbors, 249n. Odds and ends, 250n, 253n

Maine, Finance: taxation, 64n, 65n, 66n, 67n, 68n, 71n, 72n, 75n, 84n, 90n, 91n; municipal accounts, 91n, 92n, 94n, 95n. Health: general sanitary conditions, 110n, 112n, 113n, 114n; personnel, 116n, 117n, 119n, 121n; municipal health ordinances, 122n, 123n; waterworks, 125n, 126n, 128n, 130n; sewage systems, 132n, 133n, 134n; vital statistics, 137n, 138n. Education: general supervision, 148n, 149n, 150n, 153n, 155n, 157n, 162n; personnel, 165n, 166n, 170n; curriculum, 176n, 177n, 179n; school buildings, 184n, 185n; medical service, 187n. Dependency and Delinquency: dependency, 191n, 192n, 193n, 195n, 196n, 197n, 198n; police, 201n; jails, 207n, 208n, 209n, 210n. Utilities: municipally owned utilities, 216n, 217n, 218n, 219n, 223n, 224n,

227n, 228n, 229n; specific utilities, 231n, 232n. Incendiarism, 236n, 237n, 238n. Fire hazards, 239n, 240n, 241n, 242n. Odds and ends, 250n

Mandamus, 27

Maryland, Finance: taxation, 65n, 66n, 67n, 68n, 71n, 84n, 86n, 87n, 89n, 90n, 91n; municipal accounts, 91n, 92n, 95n, 96n. Health: general sanitary conditions, 110n, 112n, 113n, 114n; personnel, 116n, 117n; waterworks, 124n, 125n, 126n, 127n, 128n, 129n, 131n; sewage systems, 131n, 132n, 133n, 134n, 135n, 136n; vital statistics, 137n, 138n. Education: general supervision, 148n, 149n, 150n, 152n, 153n, 155n, 157n, 163n; personnel, 165n, 166n, 170n, 174n, 176n; curriculum, 176n, 177n, 179n; school buildings, 184n. Police, 201n. Utilities: municipally owned utilities, 216n, 217n, 218n, 219n, 222n, 223n, 224n, 227n, 228n, 229n. Incendiarism, 236n, 238n. Fire hazards, 240n. Libraries, 246n, 247n

Massachusetts, Finance: taxation, 64n, 66n, 67n, 71n, 83n, 86n, 90n, 91n; municipal accounts, 91n, 94n, 95n; municipal indebtedness, 96n, 98n. Health: general sanitary conditions, 110n, 112n, 113n, 114n; personnel, 117n, 119n; municipal health ordinances, 122n, 123n; waterworks, 124n, 125n, 126n, 128n, 129n, 131n; sewage systems, 132n, 133n, 134n, 136n; vital statistics, 137n; miscellany, 139n, 140n. Education: general supervision, 148n, 149n, 150n, 153n, 155n, 157n, 162n; personnel, 165n, 166n; curriculum, 179n; school buildings, 184n. Dependency and Delinquency: dependency, 191n, 192n, 193n, 194n, 195n, 196n, 198n, 199n; police, 201n; jails, 207n, 208n, 210n. Utilities: specific utilities, 231n, 234n. Incendiarism, 236n, 238n. Fire hazards, 239n, 240n, 241n, 242n, 243n. Civil service, 245n. Libraries, 247n. Ports and harbors, 249n

Maternity, 30
Maternity aid, 30
Mechanisms of control, 39-59; see also each specific mechanism
Michigan, Finance: taxation, 60n, 64n, 65n, 66n, 67n, 68n, 71n, 75n, 76n, 79n, 84n, 86n, 90n, 91n; municipal accounts, 91n, 92n, 95n, 96n; municipal indebtedness, 96n, 98n. Health: general sanitary conditions, 110n, 112n, 113n, 114n; personnel, 117n, 120n; municipal health ordinances, 123n; waterworks, 124n, 125n, 126n, 128n, 129n, 131n; sewage systems, 131n, 132n, 133n, 134n, 135n, 136n; vital statistics, 137n. Education: general supervision, 148n, 149n, 150n, 155n; personnel, 166n, 170n, 174n, 176n; curriculum, 176n, 179n, 181n; textbooks, 182n; school buildings, 184n; finances, 186n. Dependency and Delinquency: dependency, 191n, 192n, 193n, 197n, 198n; jails, 207n, 208n, 210n, 211n. Municipally owned utilities, 216n, 228n, 229n. Incendiarism, 236n, 238n. Fire hazards, 239n, 240n, 241n, 242n, 243n. Libraries, 246n. Odds and ends, 250n, 252n

Minnesota, Finance: taxation, 64n, 65n, 66n, 68n, 71n, 72n, 75n, 76n, 84n, 86n, 89n, 90n, 91n; municipal accounts, 91n, 92n, 93n, 94n, 95n, 96n. Health: general sanitary conditions, 110n, 114n; personnel, 116n, 117n, 121n; waterworks, 125n, 128n, 129n; sewage systems, 134n, 135n; vital statistics, 137n, 138n. Education: general supervision, 148n, 149n, 155n; personnel, 165n, 166n, 170n, 173n, 174n; curriculum, 179n; school libraries, 183n; school buildings, 184n, 185n. Dependency and Delinquency: dependency, 191n, 192n, 193n, 195n, 197n; jails, 207n, 208n, 210n, 211n. Incendiarism, 236n, 237n, 238n. Fire hazards, 240n-242n. Libraries, 246n, 247n. Odds and ends, 250n, 252n

Mississippi, Finance: taxation, 64n, 65n, 66n, 67n, 68n, 71n, 72n, 75n,

76n, 84n, 86n, 90n, 91n; municipal accounts, 91n, 92n, 94n, 95n; municipal indebtedness, 96n, 98n. Health: general sanitary conditions, 110n, 114n; personnel, 117n, 121n; municipal health ordinances, 122n; waterworks, 130n; vital statistics, 137n, 138n. Education: general supervision, 148n, 149n, 150n, 152n, 153n, 155n, 157n, 163n; personnel, 166n, 170n; curriculum, 176n, 177n; textbooks, 182n. Incendiarism, 236, 237n, 238n. Fire hazards, 240n, 241n, 242n. Odds and ends, 250n

Missouri, Finance: taxation, 60n, 64n, 65n, 66n, 67n, 68n, 71n, 72n, 74n, 75n, 84n, 86n, 90n, 91n; municipal accounts, 91n, 92n, 95n; municipal indebtedness, 96n, 97n, 98n. Health: general sanitary conditions, 110n, 113n, 114n; personnel, 116n, 117n, 119n; municipal health ordinances, 122n; waterworks, 124n, 125n, 126n, 128n, 131n; sewage systems, 132n, 133n, 136n; vital statistics, 137n, 138n. Education: general supervision, 148n, 149n, 150n, 152n, 155n, 157n; personnel, 165n, 166n, 170n, 174n; curriculum, 177n, 179n; textbooks, 182n. Dependency and Delinquency: dependency, 191n, 192n, 193n, 195n, 198n; police, 201n; jails, 208n, 210n. Utilities: municipally owned utilities; 216n, 217n, 218n, 219n, 222n, 223n, 224n, 227n, 228n, 229n. Libraries, 247n

Montana, Finance: taxation, 64n, 65n, 66n, 67n, 68n, 70n, 71n; 73n, 75n, 76n, 84n, 86n, 90n, 91n; municipal accounts, 91n, 92n; municipal budgets, 104n. Health: general sanitary conditions, 110n, 112n, 113n, 114n; personnel, 116n, 117n, 118n, 119n, 121n; municipal health ordinances, 122n, 123n; waterworks, 124n, 125n, 126n, 128n, 130n, 131n; sewage systems, 132n, 133n, 134n, 136n; vital statistics, 137n, 138n; miscellany, 140n. Education: general supervision, 148n, 149n, 152n, 153n,

155n, 157n, 163n; personnel, 165n, 166n, 174n; curriculum, 176n, 177n, 179n; textbooks, 182n; school libraries, 183n; school buildings, 184n. Dependency and Delinquency: dependency, 191n, 192n, 193n; jails, 208n. Utilities: municipally owned utilities, 216n, 217n, 218n, 219n, 223n, 224n, 227n, 228n, 229n. Incendiarism, 236n, 238n. Fire hazards, 239n, 240n, 241n, 242n

Municipal health officer, see health

Municipal ordinances, 20, 32

Municipal health ordinances, see health

Municipally owned utilities, 212-234, 269-271; the problem, 212-215; municipally owned utilities generally, 215-230; reports, 215-217; inspection, 217-222; approval of municipal ownership and operation, 222, 223; approval of rates and schedules, 223; review of rates and schedules, 223-227; rules and regulations, 228-230. Supervision over specific utilities, wharves, waterfront developments, dams, waterworks, etc., 231-234; inspection, 231; advice, 231; approval, 231-234

Nebraska, Finance: taxation, 64n, 66n, 67n, 68n, 71n, 75n, 84n, 86n, 89n, 90n, 91n; municipal accounts, 91n, 92n, 95n; municipal indebtedness, 96n, 97n, 98n. Health: general sanitary conditions, 110n, 112n, 114n; personnel, 116n, 117n, 119n; vital statistics, 137n, 138n. Education: general supervision, 148n, 149n, 150n, 155n, 157n, 162n; personnel, 166n, 170n, 174n; curriculum, 177n, 179n. Dependency and Delinquency: dependency, 191n, 192n, 193n, 197n, 198n; jails, 208n, 210n. Incendiarism, 236n, 238n. Fire hazards, 240n, 241n, 242n. Libraries, 247n

Nevada, Finance: taxation, 64n, 65n, 66n, 67n, 68n, 71n, 75n, 84n, 86n, 90n, 91n; municipal accounts, 91n, 92n; municipal indebtedness, 99n; municipal budgets, 104n.

Health: general sanitary conditions, 110n, 112n; municipal health ordinances, 122n; vital statistics, 138n. Education: general supervision, 148n, 149n, 150n, 152n, 155n, 157n; personnel, 165n, 166n, 170n, 174n; curriculum, 176n, 177n, 179n; textbooks, 182n; school libraries, 183n; school buildings, 184n. Municipally owned utilities, 216n, 217n, 218n, 224n, 228n

New Hampshire, Finance: taxation, 64n, 65n, 66n, 67n, 68n, 71n, 73n, 75n, 84n, 86n, 90n, 91n; municipal accounts, 95n. Health: general sanitary conditions, 110n, 112n, 113n, 114n; personnel, 119n, 121n; municipal health ordinances, 122n; waterworks, 125n, 126n, 128n, 130n, 131n; sewage systems, 132n, 133n, 134n, 136n; vital statistics, 137n; miscellany, 140n. Education: general supervision, 148n, 149n, 150n, 153n, 155n, 162n, 163n; personnel, 166n, 170n, 173n, 174n, 176n; curriculum, 176n, 177n, 179n. Dependency and Delinquency: delinquency, 191n, 192n; police, 201n; jails, 208n. Specific utilities, 232n. Incendiarism, 236n. Libraries, 246n, 247n. Ports and harbors, 249n

New Jersey, Finance: taxation, 65n, 66n, 67n, 68n, 71n, 75n, 76n, 79n, 84n, 86n, 90n, 91n; municipal accounts, 91n, 92n; municipal indebtedness, 96n, 97n. Health: general sanitary conditions, 110n, 111n, 112n, 113n, 114n; personnel, 116n, 117n, 119n, 121n; municipal health ordinances, 122n; waterworks, 124n, 125n, 126n, 128n, 131n; sewage systems, 131n, 132n, 133n, 134n, 135n, 136n; vital statistics, 137n, 138n; miscellany, 140n. Education: general supervision, 148n, 149n, 150n, 153n, 162n, 163n; personnel, 166n, 170n, 174n; curriculum, 176n, 177n, 179n; school buildings, 185n; finance, 187n. Dependency and Delinquency: dependency, 191n, 192n, 193n; jails, 208n, 210n.

Utilities: municipally owned utilities, 216n, 217n, 218n, 219n, 223n, 224n, 227n, 228n, 229n; specific utilities, 231n, 232n, 234n. Fire hazards, 239n. Civil Service, 245n. Ports and harbors, 250n

New Mexico, Finance: taxation, 65n, 66n, 67n, 68n, 71n, 75n, 76n, 84n, 86n, 90n, 91n; municipal accounts, 91n, 92n; municipal indebtedness, 96n; municipal budgets, 102n. Health: general sanitary conditions, 110n, 111n, 112n, 113n, 114n; personnel, 116n, 117n, 119n, 121n; municipal health ordinances, 122n; waterworks, 125n, 126n, 128n, 130n, 131n; sewage systems, 132n, 133n, 134n, 135n, 136n; vital statistics, 137n, 138n; miscellany, 140n. Education: general supervision, 148n, 149n, 152n, 153n, 155n, 157n, 163n; personnel, 166n, 170n, 174n, 176n; curriculum, 176n, 177n, 179n; textbooks, 182n. Utilities: municipally owned utilities, 224n, 227n; specific utilities, 232n. Odds and ends, 252n

New York, Finance: taxation, 60n, 61n, 65n, 66n, 67n, 68n, 71n, 73n, 75n, 83n, 84n, 86n, 88n, 90n, 91n; municipal accounts, 91n, 92n, 93n, 95n; municipal indebtedness, 98n. Health: general sanitary conditions, 110n, 111n, 113n, 114n; personnel, 116n, 117n, 119n, municipal health ordinances, 122n, 123n; waterworks, 125n, 126n, 128n, 130n, 131n; sewage systems, 132n, 133n, 134n, 135n, 136n; vital statistics, 137n, 138n; miscellany, 140n. Education: general supervision, 148n, 149n, 150n, 152n, 155n, 157n, 163n; personnel, 165n, 166n, 170n, 173n, 174n, 176n; curriculum, 177n, 179n; school libraries, 183n; school buildings, 184n; medical service, 187n. Dependency and Delinquency: dependency, 190n, 191n, 192n, 193n, 195n, 198n; police, 201n; jails, 208n, 210n, 211n. Utilities: municipally owned utilities, 216n, 217n, 218n, 219n, 222n, 223n, 224n, 227n, 228n, 229n.

Civil Service, 245n. Ports and harbors, 249n. Odds and ends, 252n

North Carolina, Finance: taxation, 65n, 66n, 67n, 68n, 71n, 75n, 76n, 84n, 86n, 90n, 91n; municipal accounts, 94n; municipal indebtedness, 96n, 97n, 98n. Health: general sanitary conditions, 110n, 111n, 112n, 114n; personnel, 116n, 117n; waterworks, 125n, 126n, 128n, 131n; sewage systems, 134n; vital statistics, 137n, 138n. Education: general supervision, 148n, 152n, 153n, 155n, 157n; personnel, 165n, 166n, 170n, 176n· curriculum, 179n; textbooks, 182n; school buildings, 184n; medical service, 187n. Dependency and Delinquency: dependency, 191n, 192n, 193n, 197n; jails, 208n, 210n. Incendiarism, 236n, 238n. Fire hazards, 239n, 240n. 242n. Libraries, 246n, 247n. Ports and harbors, 250n

North Dakota, Finance: taxation, 90n; municipal accounts, 94n; municipal indebtedness, 96n; municipal budgets, 104n. Health: general sanitary conditions, 110n, 111n, 114n; personnel, 116n; municipal health ordinances, 122n; waterworks, 126n, 128n, 130n, 131n; sewage systems, 132n, 133n, 134n, 136n; vital statistics, 137n, 138n; miscellany, 140n. Education: general supervision, 148n, 149n, 150n, 152n, 153n, 155n, 157n; personnel, 165n, 166n, 170n, 174n; curriculum, 176n, 177n, 179n; textbooks, 182n; school buildings, 184n. Incendiarism, 236n, 238n. Fire hazards, 240n, 241n, 242n, 243n, 244n. Libraries, 246n, 247n

Ohio, Finance: taxation, 65n, 66n, 67n, 68n, 71n, 73n, 74n, 75n, 76n, 83n, 84n, 86n, 90n, 91n; municipal accounts, 91n, 92n, 95n. Health: general sanitary conditions, 110n, 111n, 112n, 113n, 114n; personnel, 116n, 117n, 119n, 121n; municipal health ordinances, 122n; waterworks, 125n, 126n, 128n, 130n,

131n; sewage systems, 131n, 132n, 133n, 134n, 135n, 136n; vital statistics, 137n, 138n. Education: general supervision, 148n, 149n, 150n, 152n, 153n, 155n, 157n, 163n; personnel, 165n, 166n, 170n, 174n; curriculum, 176n, 177n, 179n; textbooks, 182n; school buildings, 184n; medical service, 187n. Dependency and Delinquency: dependency, 191n, 192n, 195n, 197n; jails, 208n, 210n. Municipally owned utilities, 218n, 228n, 229n. Incendiarism, 236n, 238n. Fire hazards, 239n, 240n, 241n, 242n. Civil service, 245n. Libraries, 247n. Odds and ends, 252n

Oklahoma, Finance: taxation, 65n, 75n, 90n; municipal indebtedness, 96n, 98n; municipal budgets, 100n. Health: general sanitary conditions, 110n, 111n, 112n, 113n, 114n; personnel, 116n, 117n, 119n; waterworks, 124n, 125n, 126n, 128n, 130n; sewage systems, 131n, 132n, 133n, 134n, 135n, 136n; vital statistics, 137n, 138n. Education: general supervision, 148n, 149n, 152n, 153n, 155n, 157n; personnel, 166n, 170n, 174n; curriculum, 176n, 177n, 179n; textbooks, 182n; school buildings, 184n. Dependency and Delinquency: dependency, 191n, 192n, 198n; jails, 208n, 210n, 211n. Incendiarism, 236n, 238n. Fire hazards, 239n, 240n, 241n, 242n. Libraries, 247n, 248n

Orders, 29, 53, 54, 58, 59; relative to taxation, 83-86; local health personnel, 116; waterworks, 129, 130; sewage systems, 136; conditions in almshouses, 198; conditions in jails, 211; fire hazards, 241

Ordinances, 22, 26, 27, 54, 55, 58, 59; relative to taxation, 86, 87; the set-up of accounts, 95, 96; the set-up of budgets, 104, 105; general sanitary conditions, 114, 115; local health personnel, 115; municipal health ordinances, 124; waterworks, 131; vital statistics, 137; the general supervision of education, 162, 163; the teaching personel, 165-173; the school curriculum, 176-178; the selection of textbooks, 182, 183; school libraries, 183; school buildings, 185, 186; medical service in the schools, 187; almshouses, 198; jails, 210; municipally owned utilities, 228-230; fire hazards, 242, 243

Oregon, Finance: taxation, 60n, 61n, 65n, 66n, 67n, 68n, 71n, 75n, 86n, 90n; municipal budgets, 102n, 104n. Health: general sanitary conditions, 110n, 111n, 114n; personnel, 116n, 117n, 119n, 121n; municipal health ordinances, 122n, 123n; waterworks, 125n, 126n, 128n, 130n, 131n; sewage systems, 132n, 133n, 134n, 136n; vital statistics, 137n, 138n; miscellany, 140n. Education: general supervision, 148n, 149n, 150n, 152n, 153n, 155n, 162n, 163n; personnel, 166n, 170n, 173n, 174n; curriculum, 176n, 177n, 179n; textbooks, 182n. Dependency, 191n, 192n, 198n. Municipally owned utilities, 228n. Incendiarism, 236n, 238n. Fire hazards, 239n, 240n, 241n, 242n. Libraries, 247n. Ports and harbors, 249n. Odds and ends, 253n

Penal institutions, see delinquency

Pennsylvania, Finance: taxation, 90n. Health: general sanitary conditions, 110n, 111n, 114n; personnel, 116n, 117n, 119n; municipal health ordinances, 122n, 123n; waterworks, 124n, 125n, 126n, 128n, 130n; sewage systems, 132n, 133n, 134n; vital statistics, 137n, 138n. Education: general supervision, 148n, 149n, 162n; personnel, 165n, 166n, 170n, 174n, 176n; curriculum, 176n, 177n, 179n; school buildings, 184n, 185n. Dependency and Delinquency: dependency, 191n, 192n, 193n, 197n, 198n; jails, 208n, 210n, 211n. Municipally owned utilities, 216n, 222n, 223n, 228n, 229n. Incendiarism, 236n, 238n. Fire hazards, 239n, 240n, 241n, 242n, 243n.

Libraries, 246n, 247n. Odds and ends, 253n

Places of public assembly, 138

Police, see delinquency

Ports and harbors, 248, 249, 272

Poor relief, see dependency

Provisional orders, 27

Prussia, 15-17, 35-38, 257, 262, 267-269, 271; Prussian district committee, 16; Prussian district president, 16; Prussian provincial council, 16; Prussian provincial president, 15; Prussian Minister of Interior, 15

Publicity, 43; in connection with taxation, 71; in connection with health activity, 11, 112; in connection with education, 157, 158

Public utilities, see municipally owned utilities

Public welfare, see dependency

Quarantine, 122-124

Regionalism, 24, 34; see also centralization vs. decentralization

Registrars of vital statistics, see health

Removal, 16, 20, 27-29, 55, 56, 58, 59; of tax officials, 89; accounting officials, 96; local health officers, 116; waterworks operators, 131; registrars of vital statistics, 138; school teachers, 174-176; police officials, 202, 203; municipal civil service commissioners in New York, 245; municipal civil service commissioners in Massachusetts, 246

Reports, 6, 39, 40, 41, 58, 59; relative to taxation, 64, 65; debts, 97-99; general sanitary conditions, 110, 111; local health personnel, 115; waterworks, 124; sewage systems, 131, 132; vital statistics, 137; general supervision over education, 147-149; education, the teaching personnel, 164; destitution, 191; jails, 208; municipally owned utilities, 215-217; incendiarism, 237; fire hazards, 238; New York civil service commission, 245; Ohio civil service commission, 246; libraries, 246

Review, 29, 30, 51, 52, 58, 59; of tax assessments, 74-82; municipal health ordinances, 122, 123; disputes concerning local boards of education, 163, 164; certain activities of the teaching personnel, 173, 174; rates and schedules of municipally owned utilities, 223-227; local action to eliminate fire hazards, 239

Rhode Island, Finance: taxation, 90n; municipal accounts, 91n, 92n; municipal indebtedness, 96n. Health: general sanitary conditions, 110n, 111n, 112n, 114n; personnel, 117n; sewage systems, 132n, 133n, 136n; vital statistics, 137n, 138n; miscellany, 139n. Education: general supervision, 148n, 149n, 150n, 152n, 153n, 155n, 157n, 162n, 163n; personnel, 166n, 170n, 172n, 174n; curriculum, 179n. Police, 201n. Utilities: municipally owned utilities, 216n, 217n, 218n, 219n, 224n, 227n, 228n, 229n; specific utilities, 231n. Incendiarism, 236n. Ports and harbors, 249n

Sanitary conditions, see health
Sanitary survey, 113
Schedules and rates of service, see municipally owned utilities
School buildings, 184
School curriculum, see education
School finance, 186
School libraries, 183
School medical service, 187
Schools, see education
Services, 46, 47
Sewage systems, see health
Sickness, 106n; also see health
South Carolina, Finance: taxation, 65n, 66n, 67n, 68n, 71n, 73n, 75n, 76n, 84n, 86n, 87n, 89n, 91n. Health: general sanitary conditions, 110n, 111n, 112n, 113n; personnel, 116n, 117n, 119n, 121n; municipal health ordinances, 112n; waterworks, 125n, 126n; sewage systems, 132n, 133n, 136n; vital statistics, 137n, 138n. Education: general supervision, 148n, 149n, 150n, 153n, 157n, 162n, 163n; personnel, 170n, 173n, 174n; cur-

riculum, 176n, 177n, 179n; textbooks, 182n. Incendiarism, 236n, 238n. Fire hazards, 239n, 240n, 241n. Ports and harbors, 249n

South Dakota, Finance: taxation, 65n, 66n, 67n, 68n, 71n, 73n, 75n, 76n, 84n, 86n, 90n, 91n; municipal accounts, 91n, 92n, 95n. Health: general sanitary conditions, 110n, 111n, 112n, 113n, 114n; personnel, 116n, 117n, 119n, 121n; municipal health ordinances, 123n; waterworks, 125n, 126n, 128n, 130n; sewage systems, 132n, 133n, 136n; vital statistics, 137n, 138n. Education: general supervision, 148n, 149n, 150n, 153n, 155n, 162n; personnel, 166n, 170n, 173n; curriculum, 179n; school libraries, 183n; school buildings, 184n; finance, 186n. Dependency and Delinquency: dependency, 191n, 192n; police, 201n; jails, 208n. Municipally owned utilities, 216n, 217n, 218n, 219n, 223n, 224n, 227n, 228n. Incendiarism, 236n, 238n. Fire hazards, 240n, 241n, 242n. Libraries, 246n, 247n. Odds and ends, 252n

State-local relations, see centralization vs. decentralization
State tax commission, see finance
Superintendents of education, 153; see also education
Subsidies, 49, 50; to education, 159, 160
Substitute administration, 57-59; in connection with certain phases of taxation, 90; debts, 97; budgets, 100; local health activity, 117, 118
Swimming pools, see health

Taxation, see finance
Tax conferences, see finance
Teachers' certificates, see education
Teachers' institutes, see education
Teaching personnel, see education
Tennessee, Finance: taxation, 60n, 61n, 70n, 71n, 90n. Health: general sanitary conditions, 110n, 111n, 114n; personnel, 116n, 117n, 119n; vital statistics, 137n, 138n. Education: general supervision, 148n, 149n, 150n, 152n, 155n, 162n; personnel, 165n, 166n, 170n,

174n; curriculum, 177n, 179n; textbooks, 182n; school libraries, 183n. Dependency and Delinquency: dependency, 191n, 192n, 195n, 198n; jails, 208n, 210n. Incendiarism, 236n, 238n. Fire hazards, 239n, 240n, 241n, 242n, 243n. Libraries, 247n. Ports and harbors, 250n. Odds and ends, 253n

Texas, Finance: taxation, 65n, 90n; municipal accounts, 91n, 92n; municipal indebtedness, 96n, 98n. Health: general sanitary conditions, 110n, 111n, 113n, 114n; personnel, 117n, 121n; municipal health ordinances, 122n; waterworks, 125n, 126n, 128n, 130n, 131n; sewage systems, 132n, 133n, 134n, 135n, 136n; vital statistics, 137n, 138n. Education: general supervision, 148n, 149n, 157n, 162n, 163n; personnel, 166n, 170n, 174n; curriculum, 176n, 177n; textbooks, 182n; school buildings, 184n; finance, 186n. Incendiarism, 236n, 238n. Fire hazards, 240n, 241n, 242n. Libraries, 246n, 247n, 248n

Textbooks, 182

Tuberculosis, 30, 139

Tutelle administrative, 19

Ultra vires acts, 13

Utah, Finance: taxation, 65n, 66n, 67n, 68n, 71n, 75n, 76n, 86n, 90n, 91n; municipal accounts, 91n, 92n. Health: general sanitary conditions, 110n, 111n, 113n, 114n; personnel, 116n, 117n; municipal health ordinances, 122n; waterworks, 125n, 126n; sewage systems, 132n, 133n; vital statistics, 137n, 138n; miscellany, 140n. Education: general supervision, 148n, 149n, 150n, 152n, 153n, 155n, 157n, 162n; personnel, 165n, 166n, 170n; curriculum, 176n, 177n, 179n; textbooks, 182n; school buildings, 184n, 185n; finance, 186n. Utilities: municipally owned utilities, 216n, 217n, 218n, 219n, 224n, 227n, 228n, 229n. Libraries, 246n, 247n, 248n

Utilities, 18-21, 33; see also municipally owned utilities

Venereal disease, 30, 140

Vermont, Finance: taxation, 65n, 71n, 73n, 84n, 86n, 89n, 90n, 91n; municipal accounts, 91n, 92n. Health: general sanitary conditions, 110n, 111n, 114n; personnel, 117n, 119n, 120n; waterworks, 125, 126n, 130n, 131n; miscellany, 140n. Education: general supervision, 148n, 149n, 150n, 152n, 153n, 155n, 162n, 163n; personnel, 165n, 166n, 170n, 174n, 176n; curriculum, 176n, 177n, 179n; school buildings, 184n; finance, 186n, 187n. Dependency and Delinquency: dependency, 191n, 192n, 193n, 198n; jails, 208n. Utilities: municipally owned utilities, 216n, 217n, 218n, 219n, 223n, 224n, 228n, 229n. Incendiarism, 236n, 238n. Fire hazards, 240n, 241n. Libraries, 247n. Odds and ends, 253n

Virginia, Finance: taxation, 65n, 66n, 67n, 68n, 71n, 73n, 78n, 86n, 90n, 91n; municipal accounts, 91n, 92n. Health: general sanitary conditions, 110n, 111n, 112n, 114n; personnel, 116n, 117n, 119n, 120n; municipal health ordinances, 122n, 123n; waterworks, 124n, 125n, 126n, 128n, 130n; sewage systems, 132n, 133n, 134n, 136n; vital statistics, 137n, 138n; miscellany, 140n. Education: general supervision, 148n, 150n, 163n; personnel, 166n, 170n, 174n, 176n; curriculum, 176n, 177n, 179n, 181n; textbooks, 182n; school buildings, 184n, 185n; medical service, 187n. Dependency and Delinquency: dependency, 192n, 195n, 196n; jails, 208n, 210n. Municipally owned utilities, 217n. Incendiarism, 236n, 238n. Fire hazards, 240n, 241n, 242n. Ports and harbors, 248n, 249n

Vital Statistics, see health

Washington, Finance: taxation, 65n, 66n, 67n, 68n, 71n, 73n, 75n, 76n, 84n, 86n, 90n, 91n; municipal accounts, 91n, 92n, 95n; municipal indebtedness, 96n. Health: general sanitary conditions, 110n, 114n; personnel, 116n, 117n; municipal health ordinances, 112n, 122n, 123n; waterworks, 124n, 125n, 126n, 128n, 130n, 131n; sewage systems, 132n, 134n, 135n, 136n; vital statistics, 137n, 138n; miscellany, 139n. Education: general supervision, 148n, 149n, 153n, 158n, 162n, 163n; personnel, 166n, 170n, 174n; curriculum, 176n, 177n, 179n; school libraries, 183n. Municipally owned utilities, 217n, 218n. Incendiarism, 236n. Libraries, 247n

Waterworks, see health

Waterworks operators, 119, 129

West Virginia, Finance: taxation, 60n, 65n, 66n, 67n, 68n, 71n, 73n, 78n, 84n, 86n, 87n, 89n, 90n, 91n; municipal indebtedness, 96n, 98n; municipal budgets, 100n. Health: general sanitary conditions, 110n, 111n, 112n, 113n, 114n; personnel, 116n, 117n, 119n, 121n; municipal health ordinances, 122n; waterworks, 125n, 126n, 128n; sewage systems, 132n, 133n, 134n, 136n; vital statistics, 137n, 138n. Education: general supervision, 148n, 149n, 150n, 153n, 155n, 158n, 162n, 163n; personnel, 166n, 170n, 173n, 174n, 176n; curriculum, 176n, 177n, 179n; textbooks, 182n; school libraries, 183n. Utilities: municipally owned utilities, 216n, 217n, 218n, 219n, 223n, 224n, 227n, 228n, 229n. Incendiarism, 236n, 238n. Fire hazards, 239n, 240n, 241n, 242n

Wisconsin, Finance: taxation, 61n, 65n, 66n, 67n, 68n, 71n, 73n, 75n,

84n, 86n, 90n, 91n; municipal accounts, 91n, 92n, 94n; municipal indebtedness, 96n, 98n. Health: general sanitary conditions, 110n, 111n, 112n, 113n, 114n; personnel, 116n, 117n, 121n; municipal health ordinances, 122n; waterworks, 125n, 126n, 128n, 130n, 131n; sewage systems, 132n, 133n, 134n, 135n, 136n; vital statistics, 137n, 138n; miscellany, 140n. Education: general supervision, 148n, 149n, 153n; personnel, 166n, 170n, 174n; curriculum, 177n, 179n; school libraries, 183n; school buildings, 184n, 185n; finance, 187n. Dependency and Delinquency: dependency, 191n-193n, 195n, 196n, 198n; jails, 208n, 210n. Utilities: municipally owned utilities, 216n, 217n, 218n, 219n, 222n, 223n, 224n, 227n, 228n, 229n. Incendiarism, 236n, 238n. Fire hazards, 240n, 241n. Libraries, 247n. Ports and harbors, 250n. Odds and ends, 252n

Wyoming, Finance: taxation, 65n, 66n, 67n, 68n, 71n, 75n, 76n, 90n, 91n; municipal accounts, 91n, 92n, 95n. Health: general sanitary conditions, 110n, 111n, 112n; personnel, 116n, 117n, 119n, 121n; municipal health ordinances, 123n; waterworks, 125n, 126n, 127n, 130n, 131n; sewage systems, 132n, 133n, 134n, 136n; vital statistics, 137n. Education: general supervision, 148n, 149n, 152n, 153n, 155n, 158n; personnel, 166n, 170n, 174n; curriculum, 177n, 179n. Municipally owned utilities, 216n, 217n, 218n, 219n, 222n, 223n, 224n, 227n, 228n, 229n